TOWARD A BETTER WORLD

Memoirs of a Life in International
and Development Economics

Toward a Better World

Memoirs of a Life in International and Development Economics

GERRY HELLEINER

UNIVERSITY OF TORONTO PRESS
Toronto Buffalo London

© University of Toronto Press 2018
Toronto Buffalo London
www.utorontopress.com
Printed in the U.S.A.

ISBN 978-1-4875-0221-8

∞ Printed on acid-free, 100% post-consumer recycled paper with
vegetable-based inks.

Library and Archives Canada Cataloguing in Publication

Helleiner, Gerald K. (Gerald Karl), 1936–, author
Toward a better world : memoirs of a life in international and development
economics / Gerry Helleiner.

Includes bibliographical references and index.
ISBN 978-1-4875-0221-8 (cloth)

1. Helleiner, Gerald K. (Gerald Karl), 1936–. 2. Economists – Canada – Biography.
3. Economic development – Africa. 4. Economic development –
International cooperation. 5. Africa – Economic conditions – 20th century.
6. Autobiographies. I. Title.

HB121.H45A3 2018   330.092   C2017-906626-9

University of Toronto Press acknowledges the financial assistance to its
publishing program of the Canada Council for the Arts and the Ontario
Arts Council, an agency of the Government of Ontario.

Canada Council   Conseil des Arts
for the Arts   du Canada

ONTARIO ARTS COUNCIL
CONSEIL DES ARTS DE L'ONTARIO
an Ontario government agency
un organisme du gouvernement de l'Ontario

Funded by the   Financé par le
Government   gouvernement
of Canada   du Canada   Canada

To Kieran, Tomas, Zoe, Nels, Jannik, and Lotta

Contents

Preface

I have been blessed with a long and active life. A few years after my formal retirement from the Department of Economics at the University of Toronto, when my life calmed down a little, I began to set aside some time to jot down memories and reflections. I did not then and do not now set out to write an autobiography. Neither my memory nor my records are solid enough to permit such an enterprise. What I could do, however, and have enjoyed doing, is to write selectively about elements of my professional life that have been important to me. After a while it seemed to make sense to string a lot of them together. Here they are.

Once one embarks on a venture such as this there are temptations to go on and on. Current events, chance meetings, unexpected emails can all stimulate fresh memories. Sometimes thoughts arise in the middle of the night: How could I have forgotten so and so? What about a fresh chapter on a topic I have neglected? There are so many more stories to tell. But Jean Monnet has advised: "Incompleteness is a part of nature." And he continued on to say, "It needs great art or great wisdom to know when to lay down the brush." I am neither particularly artistic nor especially wise. I am, above all, pragmatic as I lay down my brush. In the pages that follow I tell what seems to me quite a lot – and my editors have set me strict limits.

It is important, however, to be clear at the outset about elements that I have consciously left out. The account that follows does not describe my deepest and closest personal relationships, feelings, or experiences. Family events and experiences, and my love for my wife, Georgia, and my children, grandchildren, and, yes, two great-grandchildren have been the dominant base of my existence throughout my adult life. My youngest child, Peter, seriously challenged in many dimensions, has had a profound impact upon the second half of my life – deepening my appreciation of those who are so challenged and those who love and support them. But I do not try to describe any of these key elements of my life here, except occasionally in passing. This volume is about elements of my own early personal life and my more "professional" activities. I have tried to write about these in a style that will be intelligible to non-specialists, but at times I may have fallen short on this front. The number of acronyms encountered in my professional life may alone be overwhelming; the list of abbreviations may help a little.

For helping me to put this volume together I have a great many to thank. Jennifer DiDomenico and Carolyn Zapf of the University of Toronto Press guided me kindly and graciously through the process of transforming a rough draft into a publishable volume. The Munk School of Global Affairs provided an ongoing university home at the University of Toronto in my post-retirement years and welcome research support for this enterprise. Jose Antonio Ocampo and two other external reviewers of an early draft provided invaluable advice as to its much-needed shortening and sharpening. Eric Helleiner and Jane Helleiner each provided highly detailed commentary and recommendations on next-to-last drafts, for which I am extremely grateful. Bohdan Szuchewycz and Tomas Szuchewycz offered essential technical expertise at various stages of the manuscript's path to completion. My loving and dearly loved life's partner, Georgia, put up with my spending far more hours at my computer on this enterprise than she had been promised; for this and for our fifty-nine years together I owe her the most of all.

I dedicate this volume, as I dedicated my first two published books, to beloved members of my family; but not Georgia (as in my first), and not my children, Jane, Eric, and Peter (as in my second). I dedicate this volume to my dearly loved grandchildren, Kieran, Tomas, Zoe, and Nels, and to my great-grandchildren, Jannik and Lotta, in gratitude for their simply being who they are and in hopes that some day they will most appreciate it.

Abbreviations

AACB	Association of African Central Banks
ABCDE	Annual Bank Conference on Development Economics
ACBF	African Capacity Building Foundation
AERC	African Economic Research Consortium
ANC	African National Congress (South Africa)
C-20	Committee of Twenty
C & F	Commerce and Finance
CAAS	Canadian Association of African Studies
CCF	Co-operative Commonwealth Federation
CCIC	Canadian Council for International Cooperation
CDP	Committee for Development Planning, later renamed as Committee for Development Policy (UN)
CEA	Council of Economic Advisors (United States)
CG	consultative group
CGIAR	Consultative Group on International Agricultural Research
CHOGM	Commonwealth Heads of Government Meeting
CIDA	Canadian International Development Agency
CIIA	Canadian Institute of International Affairs
CJAS	Canadian Journal of African Studies
CLC	Canadian Labour Congress
CPR	Canadian Pacific Railway
CRDE	Centre de recherches sur le développement économique (Centre for Economic Development Research, University of Montreal)

CUSO	Canadian University Service Overseas
DAC	Development Assistance Committee (OECD)
DANIDA	Danish aid agency
DFID	Department for International Development (United Kingdom)
ECOSOC	Economic and Social Council (UN)
EPAG	Economic Policy Advisory Group (South Africa)
ERB	Economic Research Bureau (Tanzania)
ESRF	Economic and Social Research Foundation (Tanzania)
FAO	Food and Agricultural Organization (UN)
FT	Financial Times
G-7	Group of Seven (Industrialized Countries)
G-9	Group of Nine (Developing Country chairs in the IMF/World Bank)
G-10	Group of Ten (Industrialized Countries)
G-15	Group of Fifteen (Summit Level Group of Developing Countries)
G-20	Group of Twenty Finance Ministers
G-24	Group of Twenty-four (Developing Countries)
G-77	Group of Seventy-Seven (Developing Countries)
GATT	General Agreement on Tariffs and Trade
GCA	Global Coalition for Africa
GDP	gross domestic product
GFGI	Global Financial Governance Initiative (IDRC)
GNP	gross national product
HMCS	Her Majesty's Canadian Ship
IDDR	in-depth divisional review (IDRC)
IDRC	International Development Research Centre (Canada)
IDS	Institute of Development Studies at the University of Sussex
IFI	international financial institution (IMF and World Bank)
IFPRI	International Food Policy Research Institute
IIE	Institute for International Economics (Washington), later renamed as Peterson Institute for International Economics
ILEAP	International Lawyers and Economists Against Poverty

ILO	International Labour Organization
IMF	International Monetary Fund
IMG	independent monitoring group (Tanzania)
IPA	Institute for Policy Analysis (University of Toronto)
MDM	Mass Democratic Movement (South Africa)
MERG	Macroeconomic Research Group (South Africa)
MIT	Massachusetts Institute of Technology
NAFTA	North American Free Trade Area
NDP	New Democratic Party (Canada)
NES	Nigerian Economic Society
NGO	non-governmental organization
NIEO	New International Economic Order
NISER	Nigerian Institute of Social and Economic Research
NPSIA	Norman Patterson School of International Affairs (Carleton University)
NSI	North-South Institute (Canada)
OAU	Organisation of African Unity
ODC	Overseas Development Council (United States)
ODI	Overseas Development Institute (United Kingdom)
OECD	Organisation for Economic Co-operation and Development
PACT	Partnership for African Capacity Building
PRSP	Poverty Reduction Strategy Paper
RCMP	Royal Canadian Mounted Police
RDA	Ruvuma Development Association (Tanzania)
SAC	Student Administrative Council (University of Toronto)
SDR	special drawing right (IMF)
SUNS	Southern News Service
TANU	Tanganyika African National Union
UCI	University College Ibadan
UN	United Nations
UNCTAD	UN Conference on Trade and Development
UNDP	UN Development Programme
UNECA	UN Economic Commission for Africa
UNECLA	UN Economic Commission for Latin America
UNECLAC/CEPAL	UN Economic Commission for Latin American and the Caribbean
UNESCO	UN Educational, Scientific and Cultural Organization

UNICEF	UN Children's Fund
UNRISD	UN Research Institute for Social Development
UNTD	University Naval Training Division
UNU	United Nations University
USAID	United States Aid Agency
UWI	University of the West Indies
Vic	Victoria College (University of Toronto)
WBER	World Bank Economic Review
WEP	World Employment Programme (ILO)
WHO	World Health Organisation
WIDER	World Institute for Development Economics Research
WTO	World Trade Organization
YMCA	Young Men's Christian Association

TOWARD A BETTER WORLD

Memoirs of a Life in International
and Development Economics

Introduction and Overview

Economics is not where everyone goes for inspiration or excitement. But I must say that my life as a teaching and practicing economist has been both deeply fulfilling and at times wildly exciting. I think I have probably been extraordinarily lucky. It was my good fortune to enter an academic career in international and development economics during a period of dramatic global political and economic change, and to continue it through five subsequent decades of unique development progress, periodic sharp and disappointing setback, and always intense controversy. Teaching the subjects about which I feel some passion to bright and highly motivated young students would always be pleasurable. To do so in such times and to see some of the best of them enter successful careers in development was a source of much further satisfaction, even absolute delight. It was my further good fortune to have multiple opportunities for direct engagement with economic policymakers at national and international levels, both for purposes of research and in advisory capacities. The continuing effort over fifty years, with valued colleagues in Canada, Africa, and around the world, to address the global scourges of what Julius Nyerere of Tanzania always referred to as "poverty, ignorance and disease" has been both stimulating and deeply rewarding. It has never been dull.

Mine was not a typical academic career. I was privileged, from the outset at Yale, with an unusual degree of freedom – half-time relief from teaching responsibilities – for the purpose of intellectually "frontier" research activity in and on Africa. From 1965 onward I worked from an academic base at the University of Toronto, a large and liberal institution with the capacity to offer its faculty greater freedom for sabbatical and unpaid leaves to pursue special interests than smaller institutions could afford. In the last decade of my teaching career, significant portions of my time were again freed from teaching for the purposes of research and research management. In the years between, I was also engaged to an unusual degree in research, advisory activity, and advocacy in areas of public policy both at home and internationally. My Canadian nationality and base provided both advantage and entry that some of my international colleagues lacked. In Africa, Canadians did not carry as much historical baggage as British, French, and Americans sometimes did; Canada was seen by many as a member of the "like-minded," along with the Scandinavians and the Dutch; and the Commonwealth link at times was very fruitful.

I completed my PhD and took my first academic job, at Yale University's newly established Economic Growth Center, in 1960. It seemed to us then a time of new beginnings. Among many of my generation in North America, there was a sense of fresh possibilities based in a deep idealism, even naivety, about the potential contributions that a new generation of political leaders and a new wave of folk-singing, peace-and-justice oriented supporters could bring to the world. In the United States, a forty-two-year-old John F. Kennedy had just been elected president and, through his youth, early speeches, appointments of favourite Yale professors as advisors, creation of the Peace Corps, and acknowledgment of Keynesian economics, among other indicators, had extended some of the "Camelot" mood of his White House to a new generation of development economists, at least those at Yale. In particular, it seemed to many of us that in the developing world the fresh acquisition of political independence in many countries and sheer provision of knowledge (some of which we believed we could provide) could bring much to human welfare.

To me, Africa seemed to offer particularly exciting – and hopeful – possibilities. Ghana had acquired political independence in 1957. Nigeria followed in 1960, Tanzania in 1961. By the mid-1960s over twenty-five newly independent African nations had joined the United Nations, where other developing countries were also joining in ever-growing numbers. It seemed to me that Africa was that part of the developing world most in need of every kind of assistance – including that of development economists. It is difficult now to convey the enthusiastic and optimistic spirit with which I entered into the serious study of development in Africa, at first living in Nigeria and soon after in Tanzania.

Despite disappointments and disillusions, much of the optimism, idealism, and hope of the 1960s stayed with me. Whatever may have been the contributions of development economists, and that is certainly open to interpretation and argument, there can be no disputing the remarkable record of human progress over the past sixty years in most parts of the developing world. No precedent exists in recorded human history for some of the more positive achievements of this period in Asia, Latin America, and Africa: reductions in infant and child mortality; increases in life expectancy; expansion of rates of literacy, numeracy, and advanced levels of education; and improvements in innumerable social, economic, and political indicators. Of course enormous problems remain – of poverty, inequality, environmental degradation, and oppression. Climate change, political disruption, global economic slow-down, and other uncertainties may cloud future prospects, perhaps especially for Africa. But I believe the record of the past half century, which, in truth, does make some despair, can instead inspire hope for the kind of dramatic positive change that is possible.

My early life and work in immediate post-independence Nigeria and Tanzania may have tempered some of my prior romanticism about the possible contributions of expatriate development economists, and indeed about all of Africa's economic prospects, but it certainly solidified my determination to do whatever I could to be helpful to its peoples, for whom, on the basis of my, albeit limited, exposure, I had developed both great sympathy and deep respect. My family and I had been received warmly by our African hosts wherever we went. Despite the constraints and deprivations of their situations, we were always made to feel welcome. The economic constraints faced by these and other African countries were among the direst in the world. During the time in which we lived in Africa, my outrage at the manifest unfairness of their situation increased. I soon concluded that the greatest contributions that external actors like me could make, particularly if not living and working within these countries, were twofold: (1) to attempt to reduce the many possible negative impacts of external influences upon African economies – whether through deteriorated terms of trade, harmful investment or intellectual property agreements, inappropriate aid, overly onerous debt payment obligations, capital flight, harmful economic policy advice/conditionality, or whatever – and seek to create more positive ones; (2) to help to build national capacities – individual, institutional, governmental – to analyse evidence, make policy decisions Africans feel are best for their countries and peoples, and express their "voice" on international issues that might affect them. These were conclusions that I had no reason to alter over the course of my subsequent career.

This, of course, is not to say that external advice should never be offered – or taken. But it can be extremely difficult, and indeed inappropriate, for foreigners to prescribe major socio-economic remedies for political, social, economic, and cultural contexts of which they know little. External economic policy advice must therefore, I believe, be a matter for considerable caution. International financial institutions and those who control them, however, have interests to protect and do not always exercise due caution. It has always seemed to me potentially useful for other external actors to provide independent second opinions to poor countries (if asked), when powerful financial institutions attempt to press their own policy solutions upon these countries; and I have been among those who have responded to such requests. At the same time, as will become clear in the account that follows, I have not hesitated to join others – within developing countries and internationally – who have advocated conscious efforts to assist the poorest and most vulnerable *within* countries as well as among them.

Living and working in Africa at an early stage in my career significantly moulded many approaches I eventually took in my chosen profession throughout the decades to follow. Above all, I became accustomed to understanding, or at least striving to understand, the perspectives and interests of the weakest national players in the international system. Most of the development literature, and virtually all of that relating to development assistance, was written from the perspective of outsiders from the North. Northern analysts have frequently assessed Southern policy positions with which they disagreed on the basis of presumptions that the Southerners simply did not know any better. The world looks rather different when one is looking northward from a location in the South. If more Northern decision makers in the development sphere, notably in the multilateral financial institutions, had launched their careers from Southern bases, they might have understood more, annoyed less, and had greater success.

The longer I worked in international economic affairs in later years, the more I became bothered by the disparity in knowledge and preparedness for all manner of important international economic negotiations between poor Southern countries and the governments and private firms of rich Northern countries. Quite apart from the deeper power imbalances that this disparity reflects, it alone is bound to affect negotiated agreements and outcomes to the detriment of the poorest and weakest. More generally, both in international and national policy discussion, it seemed increasingly clear to me that distributional issues were no less important than those of aggregate growth and efficiency. Much of my life's teaching, research, advice, and advocacy became directed at increasing the volume and efficacy of the voices of the poorest and most marginalized of the world's nations and, though this is often more problematic, its peoples. Moreover, development outcomes, not least in terms of the distribution of income and power within countries, were by no means a matter purely, or even mainly, of economics. When one was confronting the real problems of particular times and places, the available development economics of the time clearly could not take one far enough. One needed more contextual knowledge, more political understanding, and more specific tools before one could imagine beginning to be helpful. For those like me, with only limited opportunity to live and work within developing countries, there was, it always seemed to me, a special responsibility to work to try to remove, or at least ease, external constraints upon these countries' economic prospects. Ideally one would like to positively assist in their development efforts, but where that was not possible, the medical maxim seemed appropriate: do no harm.

The emphases in the literature on development and development economics, and particularly in the international aid policy community, have been subject to significant shifts over the past fifty years. A complete understanding of economic growth and overall development processes remains a work in progress. Yet there surely has been a great deal of learning through trial and error and the sheer accumulation of experience. Let me try to summarize the main threads of international discussion and debate in development economics as I understood them over the course of my working years in this field. It is important to re-emphasize that the dominant international academic literature and policy debate about economic development over these forty to fifty years, as reflected in the "potted" history to follow, has been overwhelmingly within Northern and multilateral institutions. This comment is neither to deny that there had been a rich prior tradition of development discourse within Southern societies and governments, some of which had influence in the North, not least in the United Nations (UN) in the late 1940s and 1950s (and, later, in its Conference on Trade and Development, UNCTAD, and Economic Commission for Latin America and the Caribbean, UNECLAC/CEPAL branches); nor to doubt that lively local Southern economic policy debate continued. But such significant voices as the Southern News Service (SUNS) and the South Centre came relatively late to the international scene. Among my most important long-term objectives was the building and strengthening of Southern capacities for research and international voice on matters of economic interest to Southern nations and peoples. Until relatively recently, when voices from developing countries were heard in international development discourse, they were more often those of Asia or Latin America rather than of Africa. I therefore took a special interest in capacity building for Africa.

When I first worked in and on Nigeria, in the 1960s, development economists' prime development concern, almost without exception, lay with increasing the rate of economic growth, that is, of the gross domestic product (GDP). This concern obviously placed a high premium upon accurate measurement of GDP and its growth, and many devoted considerable energy to that task. Moreover, at that time, most Northern/ Western economists believed both that increased investment was the prime necessity for increased growth and that foreign capital – private and public – was necessary to reach agreed (increased) growth targets. Economic growth is undeniably a necessary condition for a sustained improvement in economic well-being when one is beginning from very low levels of income. It was certainly the focus of my concern at the time.

By the early 1970s there was growing concern in many quarters that sheer GDP growth might not achieve the development objectives that most had in mind. It was clear that recorded employment was not able to grow as quickly as GDP and, even in circumstances of rapid growth, urban unemployment was also growing. As economists and statisticians looked more closely, they found that the concept of "employment" needed reshaping in the development context, not least so as to incorporate the "informal" sector, and that the real underlying problem was that of income distribution rather than employment. From that perception there emerged a new focus, at least in the North, on bottom-end poverty and the provision of so-called "basic needs." There was lively discussion at that time – the 1970s – of the true meaning of "development": the desirability or possibility of dethroning gross national product (GNP), employing social indicators instead, focusing on absolute poverty, or developing alternative measures of success. Having agonized with Tanzanians in the late 1960s, as Tanzania's leadership sought to build a socialist society there, these critical discussions resonated deeply with many of my own concerns at the time. Friends at the Institute of Development Studies at the University of Sussex were among the leaders of this international debate, and my sabbatical there in 1971–2 greatly enriched my related thinking on it.

It was in the 1970s that my own research turned toward international influences on developing countries' economic prospects. Developing countries themselves had increasingly called attention to the importance of "trade not aid." As early as 1964 they had successfully called forth a new UN body, the United Nations Conference on Trade and Development (UNCTAD), to pursue research and concrete proposals on the international economic front. I took a keen interest in UNCTAD's work from its beginnings and collaborated actively with its secretariat from the 1970s onward. Early research of particular interest to me was the role of multinational corporations in developing countries' exports, at that time a relatively under-researched area. In public advocacy I now began actively to urge much greater attention, in particular, to the non-aid dimensions of Northern countries' relations with developing countries.

The 1970s also brought the first major demonstration of Third World commodity power when in 1973–4 the Organization of Petroleum Exporting Countries (OPEC) succeeded in generating sudden sharp increases in global oil prices. These increases were followed by, and indeed helped to cause, global recession and an end to the postwar "golden age" of rapid global growth. With increased confidence at this time, the developing countries demanded a "New International Economic Order" (NIEO)[1] with new funds to back commodity agreements, new rules for trade and investment, and improved, more development-friendly financial institutions. I did my best to bolster the arguments for such international reforms, most of which had actually been vigorously advocated many years before. Some developing country governments, pressing for international reforms, saw the North's new interest in "basic needs" and domestic reforms (within the South) at this time as an inappropriate and unwelcome diversion from the NIEO agenda; and to a considerable degree, I agreed with their position.

Serious attempts were made at that time to identify and act upon mutual interests between the developing countries and the North, reaching their apogee in the 1980 report of the international Brandt Commission,[2] in which I enjoyed a peripheral role. But the timing of these efforts was off, for by that time another oil price hike and the subsequent Volcker anti-inflation shock policies in the United States had generated another global recession and the roots of a Third World debt crisis. No less important, a new mood and intellectual climate – suspicious of governmental interventions, vigorously pro-market, and unsympathetic to distributional concerns, whether international or domestic – had begun

to permeate Northern governments and the international financial institutions they controlled. The newly elected regimes of Ronald Reagan
and Margaret Thatcher had, to put it very mildly, little interest in the
NIEO. After a great many conferences (and academic papers), the previous Northern stalling and stonewalling of the NIEO were at last successful: NIEO proposals and formulations were forgotten, overtaken by the
new concerns over Third World debt and its implications for Northern
banks.

Development discourse that followed – in the 1980s – was dominated
by discussions of Third World debt problems, particularly, at first, those
of Latin America, which threatened the stability of Northern banks, but
soon also the smaller but more intractable debts of poor African governments to official creditors. Debate centred on the efficacy of the policies
demanded by the major multilateral financial institutions as conditions
for their support: contraction of aggregate spending by the International Monetary Fund (IMF) and structural adjustment by the World
Bank. The developing countries had long argued that there were more
appropriate policy responses. Far from cutting investment in accor-
dance with IMF loan conditions, it was critical to maintain financial
flows sufficient to facilitate required new investment in the exportable
or import-competing activities that would prevent the recurrence of
their payment problems. What was needed was expansion of the right
kind of supply, rather than contraction of demand, and investment
for "structural change" toward greater production of tradeable goods
and services. This was a case that I helped the developing countries to
argue. But unfortunately it was not the kind of structural adjustment
that the IMF and the World Bank were now prescribing. Reflective of
the new market-friendly orthodoxy of the governments of the North,
developing countries were now urged, and often required, to liberalize
and open up their economies, privatize, and downsize their government sectors. Discussion of distributional issues was moved to the back
burner. The mainstream in development discussions of the 1980s now
emphasized the prospect of government failures rather than market
failures, which had previously often been used as intellectual justification for governmental activity. This new emphasis was, of course,
contested, particularly in the adjusting countries, and in Africa, by the
UN Economic Commission for Africa (UNECA). But many critics were
reduced to arguing, along with the UN International Children's Emergency Fund (UNICEF), for "adjustment with a human face" – a softer
version of the mainstream's approach. Only the most ideologically pure

in the new anti-government mainstream seemed to be at all bothered that the IMF and the World Bank, both thoroughly governmental institutions, were now themselves, in effect, intervening in markets to help to bail out private banks. This difficult decade – of slow or negative growth, ideologically driven policy dispute, and financial anxiety – was regarded as a "lost decade" in much of the developing world.

By the 1990s, the pendulum of discussion on development began to shift back toward the centre again. The disappointing performance under orthodox structural adjustment programs – both in terms of growth and distribution – was now plain for all to see. In the former Soviet Union and Eastern Europe, the precipitous shift to the market was uncovering the overwhelming importance of institutions and law. At the same time, the "East Asian miracle" and the phenomenal growth of China suggested that a developmental state might, after all, be possible – and even preferable to a minimalist one. There therefore was now renewed and more balanced debate over the appropriate role of the state in development. Emphasis upon poverty alleviation, health, and educational opportunity, all of which seemed to require a greater degree of state action, returned to development discourse. In 1997 the Asian financial crisis revealed the risks of premature capital account liberalization and generated fierce debate, even within the mainstream, over the efficacy of IMF macroeconomic advice. Malaysia was prominent among those who defied IMF strictures – and prospered. Financial crisis in 2007–8 engendered further doubt about the efficacy of previous Western advice and even some eventual backtracking in the IMF's research department.

This decade also featured the rise of interest in and concern for the environment and sustainability, ideas that had not received the attention they deserved before and remain prominent in current development discourse. The same can be said of gender issues and the potential role of civil society in development.

In the last decades there has been a new focus upon the quality of governance, including the negative roles of corruption, weak institutions, and limited accountability. At the same time there has been increased scepticism as to the efficacy of foreign pressure and aid conditionality. This attitude has contributed to a new emphasis upon national and local ownership of, and participation in, development programs, projects, and policies. The aid donors' Paris Declaration on Aid Effectiveness of 2005,[3] which addressed these issues, is still far from actual implementation. Indeed there has been something of a backlash in some aid circles as budgets tighten and electorates press for early results. But such aid donor rhetoric would have been inconceivable fifty years ago.

What should by now be clear is that economic development truth is hard to find and to agree upon. There are fashions, both in the economics profession and in the development policy community. And shocks throw everything off from time to time. Generalizations across countries and over time can only be offered, if at all, with great care and qualification. This maxim should underline for all the absolutely critical importance, if an economist seeks to be useful, of understanding the historical, geographic, cultural, and political context of development experience and policies. And in turn it makes even clearer the desirability of locally based analytical and decision-making capacity. This checkered history of ideas also underlines the importance of learning from experience, exercising patience, and taking a long-term perspective rather than constantly expecting short-term results from development-oriented initiatives.

How can an individual academic/research economist play a role in public policy? After all, the kind of writing typically required of today's academic economist is unlikely to be read by, and may indeed be largely unintelligible to, the average policymaker. As has been said in another context, 90 per cent of such success resides in just showing up. The truth is, as individuals, unless asked, most academic economists don't show up on the public policy front; or, if they do, they aren't usually very good at it. There are, in any case, few incentives for them to do so, and it is always difficult to prove that a particular analytical or advisory input generated a subsequent effect – the attribution problem. Still, where the issues are socially important and where one has some expertise, the effort must be made; and the relevant political constraints need to be understood and attempts made to address them.

When asked for individual policy input, I have usually responded and have tried not to pull punches. I have also certainly written my share of policy-oriented papers. But, for middle-level, low-profile types like me – no Keynes, Piketty, Sachs, or Stiglitz – it has always seemed to me that collective efforts are what have the greatest prospect of policy impact. In the hope that there is greater strength in numbers and in institutions, many have devoted such effort through think tanks, special commissions, and the like. I count myself among them. Sometimes, in order to gain credibility and weight in the public eye, it has been necessary to include and accommodate those of less progressive views within such efforts; that necessity is reflective of the political reality in which policy is made. I have also learned through painful experience that without determined marketing even the most careful research and the best-crafted arguments will have little impact upon either public opinion or public policy. I cannot prove that the North-South Institute or the Brandt Commission or the numerous UN, Commonwealth, International Development Research Centre (IDRC), and other expert groups in which I participated over the years made the world a better and a fairer place, but I believe that in one way or another they have moved thinking forward.

So, of course, have the cumulative but less organized efforts of like-minded colleagues – scholars, researchers, activists, and policymakers – working tirelessly around the world on a variety of parallel or related anti-poverty fronts. Working relationships among them have often been warm and fruitful, as my own experience can attest. In the chapters that follow, the names of particular friends and colleagues appear repeatedly, reflective of the enormous importance of the epistemic and value-based communities that have added so much to the quality of my international work and life. Exchange of ideas, experiences, contacts, papers – all particularly valuable when among trusted friends – have been critical to my professional existence. The Internet now makes this networking much easier than it was during most of my working life – when communication functioned via mimeographed papers, faxes, and telephone – but its value to me was always beyond price. I hope that this volume may provide further encouragement to those with whom I have had the pleasure of working and to the hosts of others who continue in the struggle.

The volume is divided into five main parts. The first (I) describes my early years and proceeds chronologically, ending with my return from Yale to Toronto, which was to be the base for the rest of my career. The remainder of my account is organized by theme. The next three parts are grouped geographically – Africa (II), international (III), and Canada (IV). The section on Africa (II) is significantly, though by no means exclusively, concerned with efforts to build and strengthen African capacities in economics; sections (III and IV) are primarily concerned with efforts – in international organizations and within Canada – to improve the international economic context within which African and other developing economies must function. The final part (V) offers some summary reflections.

PART I

Beginnings

1 Early Years

Although this volume is to be an account of my life as a professional economist, it may be best to begin at my very beginning and to devote some space to my background and upbringing. They may or may not have been important in the formation of the adult I became, but there are at least some analysts who clearly think they were.[4]

I was born in the town of St Pölten, Austria, on 9 October 1936. Used as a base for touring this part of Austria, St Pölten was and still is, as a guidebook puts it, "a charming baroque town with beautiful old houses and picturesque squares 40 miles west of Vienna." My birth certificate records my name as "Gerhard Karl." In primary school in Canada, I changed my first name – without any legal mandate that I know of – to Gerald, and began to be addressed by friends and teachers as "Gerry."

My father, Karl Helleiner, born in 1902, was a medieval historian who, having encountered political difficulties acquiring academic employment in Vienna, was working at that time as the provincial archivist in St Pölten. His father had been the executive director of the Vienna State Opera. My mother, Grethe Deutsch, was born in 1908. Her father, Julius Deutsch, was a social democratic leader who had been a cabinet minister in the 1920s; commander of the *Schutzbund* (the socialist underground opposition army) during the right-wing Dollfuss regime of the early 1930s, the only leader to escape with his life after the uprising of 1934; and subsequently became a general, in charge of supplies, for the Loyalists in the Spanish Civil War; and then an advisor to the US State Department during the Second World War. (His autobiography, *Ein Weiter Weg*,[5] was published in Austria in 1960.) The fact that Julius Deutsch was Jewish created difficulties for our family after the Nazi *Anschluss* of Austria in 1938. My father was ordered to divorce his wife, who was Jewish under Nazi law, and threatened with induction into the army; he therefore resolved to leave. Early in 1939, my older brothers, Chris and Fred, were sent on a *Kindertransport* train to England, where they lived with volunteer foster parents. By August, my father had acquired a visa to travel to England. My mother and I (just short of three years of age) followed – on the last plane to leave Vienna before the outbreak of war in early September. My mother and father improved their knowledge of the English language while working for a family in Oxford for the next few months. Finally, with the help of an Austrian friend at the Institute for Pontifical Studies at the University of Toronto and the financial assistance of British and Canadian organizations dedicated to assisting scholars to escape from Nazi Europe, we left for Canada in December.[6] We arrived at Union Station in Toronto on Christmas Eve 1939. In a letter of thanks to his sponsors in England, the Society for the Preservation of Science and Learning, on 26 December my father wrote:

> Toronto with its broad streets, the bright winter sky, the countless cars and the elegant residential parts made a great impression upon me. I expect I will like this country. What struck me most were the University buildings, numerous and spacious, in themselves a whole town. What a wealthy country![7]

My father became a quite distinguished professor of economic history in the University of Toronto's Department of Political Economy, and was eventually elected a Fellow of the Royal Society of Canada. Offered an academic post in Vienna after the war, he declined.

My mother has told of my very serious illness in Austria when I was quite small. The frighteningly high fever accompanying my pneumonia led her to promise the nun who was helping to care for me that if I recovered my life would belong to the church. I like to think that, though this promise was not kept, whatever God there might be would not be too displeased with the way I have spent my professional life. I have always felt that the social gospel, which I have done my best to promote, was the most important part of the church's teachings, and I can only hope that He/She agrees.

Early in our years in Toronto, I had my first exposure to organized religion. My father was formally Roman Catholic, and I suspect that it was he who had me attend Sunday school classes at a local Catholic church. The nuns, still dressed in their traditional habits at that time, were mostly quite kind as they introduced us to the catechism, which I remember as a little green book, and eventually to our first communion. I remember very little of the theology they presumably taught us. But I retain a vivid memory of the coloured illustration depicting hell in one of the books they used: it had writhing green serpents and bright red fire, and it was terrifying. I did not stay long with them.

In primary grades, my brothers and I all went to Brown School, the catchment area for which, on the one hand, stretched into the higher-income areas adjoining the prestigious private Upper Canada College and, on the other, reached down into some quite depressed areas near the Canadian Pacific Railway (CPR) mainline track, where we lived, together with other low- and middle-income earners. This economic range made for quite an interesting student mix.

Most of my best primary school friends elected to attend private secondary schools and, with scholarship support and my father's urging, I too could easily have taken that route. But I would have none of it. My brothers had remained within the regular public school system, and it seemed right for me to do so as well.

I began my years at Oakwood Collegiate Institute in a state of high excitement and enthusiasm. My high school grades were always good, but after my first year they were never again quite as high. My lower academic achievement was partly because I was so involved in other activities. But it was also because, in true middle power Canadian style, I was aware that I shouldn't do too well lest I stand out too much and risk losing friends. In my final Ontario-wide exams I did quite well, but not as well as many had wanted and expected me to do. In retrospect, I think that most of our teachers were very good – dedicated, patient, and enthusiastic about their subjects.

It was in high school that I found my first paid employment. By the middle of my grade ten year, I was fortunate to join a couple of friends in the acquisition of a job as an usher at Massey Hall where the Toronto Symphony Orchestra then played. Three or four nights a week for the rest of our high school years, we travelled downtown, donned our scarlet jackets and dark blue trousers, lined up for inspection by the head usher, and told the elite concertgoers of Toronto where they were to sit. It was wonderful experience and, by the standards of possible alternative employment, it paid quite well. We learned gracious manners and met many interesting concertgoers. Not the least of this job's fringe benefits was the opportunity to hear the best orchestras and musicians of the day, mostly classical but also jazz, barbershop, and everything in between. My lifelong appreciation of classical music originated in these experiences as much as from the music in my home. Apart from everything else that this wonderful job did for me, the money it earned provided me with a salutary measure of financial independence, responsibility, and the beginnings of a savings account.

Other short-lived high school jobs and summer income sources included a newspaper delivery route, ushering at a downtown movie theatre, serving as receptionist at the local YMCA, selling socks at Simpson's department store, pulling a cart (and clowning) in the annual Santa Claus parade, paid summer military training at a Canadian army base, and working on a CPR "bridges and building" gang. None of these were anywhere near as appealing as the Massey Hall job.

With growing maturity came greater concern over matters religious and ethical. Our school was roughly 50 per cent Jewish. On Jewish holidays it was not possible to carry on with the regular curriculum. It was difficult not to be aware at Oakwood that I was, in some sense, a Christian – or at least not Jewish. One of my best friends was very active in the Unitarian church and took me along to some Unitarian Youth meetings in which he was heavily involved. But it was another friend's regular attendance at the more conventional United Church of Canada that finally led me to follow him there. I became a regular attendee and developed a strong feeling for what I perceived as the Christian ethic and, with a little more difficulty, faith in the basic New Testament story. The former has remained with me.

I read quite a lot in these years, and was especially fascinated by the history of the Second World War. Among other books, I read all six volumes of Winston Churchill's memoirs of the period, Dwight Eisenhower's memoirs, and Chester Wilmot's classic, *The Struggle for Europe.* I read a lot of Shaw plays, and I was romantic enough to have loved James Hilton's *Lost Horizon,* with its account of the discovery of Shangri-La. By this time I had also become intensely interested in the news of the day, which my group of friends discussed avidly among ourselves on the long streetcar rides to school, and steadily cut back on my previous concentration on the back sections of the newspaper where the sports and comics were to be found. My left-of-centre politics and social conscience continued to evolve.

When my parents announced that they were planning to make a visit to Europe, and particularly Austria, in the summer between my grade twelve and thirteen years, and asked whether I would like to come, I lost no time responding. I was enthralled by everything we did and saw: the ocean crossing (with a good deal of partying every night), London, the Channel crossing, the bicycle culture of Holland, bomb damage along the rail lines we travelled in Germany, the magnificently beautiful Alps. We settled down for several weeks in a little "pension" in Carinthia (in southern Austria), from which we took many excursions to local sites or to the mountains, and to which various relatives came to visit. (Vienna was still in the Russian zone, and my mother chose not to take us there.) Before returning to Canada, we spent some time in the beautiful Austrian Tyrol and a few days in Paris, the magnificence of which "blew me quite away." This early trip back to Europe (I was sixteen) made a deep and lasting impression on me. There was so much in the world to be seen! I acquired a yen for travel that never left me. That there could be social purpose in doing so was still to be discerned.

My Oakwood years ended happily with graduation ceremonies in the fall of 1954. At this event, I was pleased to have been chosen (by the principal, not the students) as the valedictorian. I spoke sincerely – and as eloquently as I could – about the great debt we owed to our teachers. This public speaking occasion taught me the wisdom of carrying backup speaking notes whenever possible. I had gone to some trouble to memorize my speech. But somewhere in the middle of it, my eyes lit upon my mother in the audience who, for some reason, was looking very anxious. She threw me right off. For some awkward silent moments, I couldn't remember a thing. Eventually I did manage to regain my composure and was able to continue. About forty years later, when I was the invited speaker at a student awards event in that same Oakwood auditorium, I recounted this story and, after offering the requisite advice to the graduates, urged the parents in attendance, even if they were worrying, to keep smiling as their student-children made their appearances on stage.

2 Undergraduate Life

In many respects my undergraduate university career – especially its first three years – was little more than a continuation of high school. I drifted onward from Oakwood to Victoria College ("Vic") at the University of Toronto because university study was what was expected of me, and the cost of studying elsewhere would have been prohibitive. At the University of Toronto, as the son of a faculty member, my tuition was free; and I could save other costs by living at home. Even the daily streetcar fare was now gone because I could walk to the campus in about twenty minutes. Of the university's constituent undergraduate colleges, I chose Victoria because that was where my best friend was going and, I suppose, in part, because of its United Church association. It was a good choice. Vic's mainly middle-class and fairly liberal student body was one in which I felt comfortable. And that is where – in my very first week – I met my lifelong partner, a beautiful and outgoing eighteen-year-old girl from Sarnia, Ontario: Georgia Stirrett.

Like many others entering university both then and now, I had very little idea of what I eventually wanted to do and knew probably even less about what courses might prove most useful or interesting. I didn't have the great yen for the sciences that is necessary for success in those areas or in medicine. I had done very well in mathematics (algebra, geometry, and trigonometry), but didn't have confidence that I could weather the notoriously difficult "math and physics" program at the university level. An aptitude test in high school had suggested I might be suited for accountancy, and my father had encouraged me to think about taking economics. I therefore enrolled in the four-year honours program in Commerce and Finance (generally known as C & F), run by the Department of Political Economy (my father's department). Its title was a bit of a misnomer: it was not so much a business course as a concentrated program in economics. The C & F courses were known to be rather demanding, with a high proportion of dropouts in the first year. The program offered a bit of a challenge, which appealed to me. But it was not a wise choice.

I did not find C & F difficult, but parts of it were, at least to me, mind-numbingly boring. The very worst was the course in accounting (so much for the aptitude test). The introductory economics course was somewhat better. It seemed to have little analytical content and would not today be recognizable as economics at all. Its text was basically a study in economic geography. The course in actuarial science was so boring to me that I stopped attending – and subsequently nearly failed the final exam. The only courses I enjoyed were those in political science and calculus (in which I eventually earned a grade of 100 per cent). For a university student, purportedly in a demanding program, I spent remarkably little time in the library. But I was enjoying life hugely, making many new friends and learning a great deal through a variety of new non-academic experiences.

By year-end I had decided to leave C & F and register instead in the less prestigious and considerably smaller honours program in political science and economics. No more accounting or other business-oriented studies for me. Instead I now had more political science (initially with the renowned Marxist scholar, C.B. McPherson), history, and religious knowledge (essentially comparative religion), all of which were stimulating and interesting. The compulsory course in economic theory, although given by a well-known professor, was not up to modern standards; but it was much better than the previous year's economics course, and included some challenging reading. I finally began to benefit from the library and from university-level instruction more generally.

I did not escape, however, from one potentially unpleasant second-year requirement: a compulsory course in European economic history. I had nothing against Europe or economic history. The problem was that the professor in that course was my very own father. I found it more than a little troubling to be sitting in his classroom, and so did he. About twenty-five years later, when my son Eric also studied at the University of Toronto, I thought he could have enjoyed and benefited from my undergraduate course in international economics, but there can be no doubt that I was relieved when he elected not to take it.

My main interests and fondest memories of my undergraduate university years, however, were not academic. From the very first days – a weekend spent in residence at Vic in early September before classes began – it seemed a whirl of activity. There were many new and interesting friends. Above all, there was a budding romance, with frequent meetings – both "chance" and planned – around the campus and, of course, a variety of evenings "out." I had originally met Georgia at a mixer in her residence during the introductory frosh weekend. We talked a lot. We shared values. Her father had even run for Parliament under the correct (Co-operative Commonwealth Federation, CCF) political banner. One thing led to another. We became very good friends. Over the next few years our dates included just about everything on the campus and Toronto scenes: dances, football games, movies, concerts, plays, opera, dinners, and a variety of churches.

Much time – in retrospect, certainly much too much – was spent, both in first year and over the next four years, having lunch and coffees at the Vic student union. There my student friends and I argued religion, politics, and all manner of other topics, often much more interesting – it seemed to us – than our lecture material. Yes, a lot of time was wasted. But it was primarily in these discussions and debates, rather than in classrooms, that I was forced to clarify and hone views on many issues that I was to carry for years to come. Did morality or spirituality require belief in God or church membership? Were biblical accounts believable? Did our democratic political system actually work toward a more just society? In order to promote a better world, was it better for us to work across-the-board in political parties, churches, and the like, or to specialize in one important area in which our expertise could make a difference? Was economics likely to be a useful subject in which to specialize? My strengthening sense of social justice and my searching, though profoundly agnostic, spirituality owed a lot to these undergraduate discussions.

In search again of summer employment (and some adventure), I signed up in my first fall with the University Naval Training Division (UNTD). This division was designed to train supposedly intelligent young Canadians for positions as officers in Canada's reserve navy. The prospect of more summers in an army camp did not much appeal to me, but the navy offered the prospect of something completely different – and of travel. Once a week all winter long I donned my handsome naval officer's uniform and rode the streetcar down to HMCS York on the Toronto waterfront. There we took classes in navigation and meteorology, and did a certain amount of marching around, for all of which we received a modest stipend. But the main event for us "Untidies," as we were known within the force, was in the summer.

My first naval summer was spent at HMCS Stadacona in foggy Halifax harbour. The second was on the beautiful west coast at HMCS Esquimalt, just outside Victoria, BC. Again we took a variety of naval courses, complete with examinations. We learned how to use navigational aids, tidal tables, and military equipment. It was there that I learned the traditional rules of the navy: "If it moves, salute it. If it doesn't move, move it. If it won't move, paint it." The real highlight was a marvellous three-week cruise to the Caribbean on one of the Canadian navy's two cruisers, HMCS Quebec. Again it was the non-academic side of these experiences that really seemed to matter to most of us. There was great camaraderie and a lot of fun amid the more serious business of the navy. We lived and slept in fairly close quarters: bunk beds, about twenty to a room, when on shore; hammocks, re-slung every night, when at sea. There were lots of silly songs, practical jokes, and fun-filled evenings and weekends off. There were many new friends from other branches of the University of Toronto, notably pre-med students, and from other universities.

Unfortunately, one of the prime forms of entertainment for young men – whether naval or not, whether at university or not – was, and still is, drinking. On grounds of principle I never touched alcohol. (In fact, it wasn't until many years later that I would even accept a glass of wine with dinner.) My naval friends had few such scruples. The result was that I did a great deal of good-humoured "cleaning up" after others, helping to get them home in reasonably good shape and covering for them as necessary. I learned a lot about hangovers and, to my disgust, morning-after "beer breath." My strong sea legs and stomach unfortunately forced me into a similar role in rough weather at sea. While others reeled and retched, I was among the very few who were always able to clean up the floors as required.

At the end of my third winter in the navy – as soon as was permitted – I retired with a commission as a sub-lieutenant in the Royal Canadian Navy (Reserve). I am grateful that I was never subsequently called up from the reserve into active service. Probably just as well for the defence of the country too. I cannot honestly say that I ever much liked, or excelled at, the serious parts of my exposure to the Canadian military. But, truth to tell, I have often wished that I could remember more of what I was taught about astronomy, weather, navigation, and many other interesting subjects during my brief naval career.

In my third year, after a year as president of the sophomore year, I was elected as Victoria College's male representative on the university's Student Administrative Council (SAC). Serving in student government at the university level was a thoroughly broadening experience. Previously most of my non-academic university experience had been within the cosy confines of Vic. I knew many students in the other arts and science colleges since we were in classes together, but I didn't have much social contact with them. I now interacted quite deeply and vigorously with students from all over the university: medicine, engineering, forestry, nursing, law, as well as the other federated colleges (Trinity, University, and St Michael's).There was also now much greater involvement with the student newspaper, *The Varsity*, which reported on our activities and whose editor at the time was an always rumpled-looking and chain-smoking Peter Gzowski, later an icon in Canadian media circles. The SAC met frequently, both for business and socially, and its members became quite close. We debated issues large and small: whether to make a statement about the Hungarian Revolution, how to support student refugees at the University of Toronto, and how much funding to provide for various campus activities.

I had never seriously thought of postgraduate study until the summer after my third undergraduate year (1957). Having abandoned the part-time naval officers' UNTD career that had occupied my two previous summers, I took a summer job as a junior economist with the Economics and Research Branch of the Federal Department of Labour in Ottawa. My immediate boss, the director of the branch, was a relaxed and friendly recent PhD in economics from Duke University, Douglas Hartle. I shared an office with another, more senior, summer employee, an economics PhD student at Yale University, Ian Drummond. Doug Hartle and Ian Drummond, both later to be my departmental colleagues at the University of Toronto, had a profound impact upon me that summer and upon my whole future.

Doug assigned me a research task – to discover all that was known about the differential employment impact of different kinds of governmental construction expenditure – and left me simply to get on with it in whatever way I could. Ian had the task of analysing the income and employment implications of immigration, and was also left more or less on his own. I was quite excited about my task and my title, and worked hard at it. I recall filling out, with great pride, my occupation – "economist" – on my application to use the services of the Ottawa public library system. (I could have said "student," but I didn't.) The report I eventually wrote, though fat, was certainly forgettable. (Although I was proud of it at the time, I no longer have a copy. Perhaps it is in a file somewhere in Ottawa.) The summer's significance and impact came from the conversations over coffee and lunch, not the work. Doug convinced me to think very seriously about postgraduate study in economics; and his open, lighthearted, and sceptical, while still serious, approach to his work in economics made an impression on me. (Among other bits of wisdom he imparted was to work hard at what you are doing while you are in the mood for it, but to take time off from it and do something else – like go for a walk – when you are not. I have often acted on this advice.) Ian influenced me to think more specifically about studying at Yale University, whose economics department, he told me, was already one of the very best and likely to continue to strengthen.

Many years later, when Doug Hartle was my colleague in the University of Toronto department, and after he had already, among other accomplishments, directed Ottawa's Treasury Board, served as research director for the (Carter) Royal Commission on Taxation, and helped to establish the University of Toronto's Institute for Policy Analysis, he approached me about the possibility of his doing something "more useful" in, say, Africa. When the managers of the Ford Foundation–financed Williams College advisory program in Botswana next came to me, as they regularly did, to seek my services or the names of other suitable candidates, I was happy to give them Doug's name together with a strong recommendation. He spent what was by all accounts a very happy and productive four years there, advising the Ministry of Finance and Planning, and eventually took over the Botswana advisory program's management, moving it to Toronto. I was very pleased to have been able, at last, to reciprocate his early advice and assistance in this way.

All in all, that summer in Ottawa was quite a magical and memorable one for me. I had my first "real" job, making serious money. In my spare time, I read a great deal, walked quite a lot, and spent plenty of quality time with some student friends from Toronto, also with Ottawa summer jobs, who had jointly rented an apartment nearby. It was with them that I acquired my great love of Beethoven's sixth (pastoral) symphony, which was one of their few records and was often played as background against our bridge games and conversations.

In my final (fourth) year, newly engaged to be married (to Georgia of course) and now serious about heading toward graduate school, I resolved to cut back sharply on my extracurricular activities. When, early in the academic year, my father was hospitalized with a suspected heart attack (but in the end it wasn't), I anticipated much heavier claims upon me at home and hospital, and cut back still further.

In preparation for postgraduate study, I also tried to be much more serious about my study of economics. I attempted to read a nearly incomprehensible new book, *Three Essays on the State of Economic Science*, by Tjalling Koopmans[8] of the pioneering Cowles Foundation, formerly at the University of Chicago but recently relocated to Yale. I enrolled in a very small (only three students) class to study econometrics, which, I had been led by Doug Hartle to believe, was an important new area of economics and the focus of the Yale-based Cowles Foundation's activities. The instructor was William (Bill) Hood, who would later work at the Bank of Canada and, still later, become the chief economist at the

2.1. Graduation, Political Science and Economics, University of Toronto, 1958

IMF. We met in his office where he wrote equations and formulae copiously on his blackboard, and we dutifully copied them down, none of
us understanding enough ever to ask a question. He was not a talented
teacher, but I'm sure we were even worse students. Fortunately for us,
he must have realized that there was a problem, and he set an easy exam.

In the fall of that final undergraduate year, I applied for a Woodrow
Wilson fellowship and, when asked on the application form for my top
three preferred universities, I listed Yale as number one. A few months later
the fateful letter arrived: I had won a $2,000 fellowship (plus tuition) for
postgraduate studies in economics at my first-choice university. Georgia
and I now made plans to marry in the summer and move together to Yale.

3 The Yale Years

Graduate Study in Economics

Yale University is an urban institution located in the middle of a Connecticut industrial town that has seen better days. Though surrounded by the downtown, the university occupies several contiguous city blocks of space and, even though cars buzz along many of its streets, has managed to create a separate world of its own. Many of its constituent colleges have internal courtyards, Oxbridge-style, which during our time were still accessible to the public. Spacious lawns and yards, together with the adjacent city "green" and a large cemetery, and the presence of some architecturally interesting buildings provided further buffers against the more dispiriting atmosphere of the city of New Haven. The Department of Economics at Yale, newly energized by its likeable and ambitious (Canadian-born) chairman Lloyd Reynolds, worked out of a collection of wonderful old houses on spacious Hillhouse Avenue on the edge of the main campus. The Cowles Foundation offices and its very useful library, with the latest issue of every imaginable journal very easily accessible to students, were located in a stuccoed heritage house across the lawns and street from an even older house in which many of the other senior faculty had their offices. More faculty offices were located in a more traditional university structure a few blocks closer to the centre of the campus and the city. The magnificent main Sterling Library, at the centre of the campus, had two large study rooms, walls lined with periodical collections, for the exclusive use of postgraduate economics students. It was within these various spaces that I was to spend the better part of my next seven years.

The Yale department was collegial in its atmosphere and small enough for everyone to know one another. The incoming crop of PhD students numbered only about twenty-five. We were warmly received with introductory gatherings and social occasions; the faculty members were friendly and courteous; and there was little of the aggressively competitive atmosphere that characterized some other American institutions of postgraduate education. Plenty of hard work was expected of students, but we all pretty much supported and liked one another. This environment suited me. I had always been rather diffident in university classrooms and seminars, very rarely asking questions or volunteering comments. I doubt whether I could have survived the reputed rough-and-tumble, dog-eat-dog atmosphere in the seminars of, say, the University of Chicago's Economics Department. At the same time, the professors were varied, open, and fairly eclectic in their approaches to economics, rather than wedded to any particular ideology. Again, this spirit suited me admirably. Though I still rarely said much in classes unless required to do so, I did very well in all of my course assignments, essays, and exams.

Although I was particularly interested in international economics, I don't think I received a very strong base in my chosen field of specialization. Certainly it was nothing as useful as that which students of Charles Kindleberger, of whom I later knew quite a few, were getting at that time at the Massachusetts Institute of Technology (MIT). Robert Triffin, who became my thesis supervisor, was a nice man; he had lots of international experience and was at that time directly involved in current policy discussion. (Once, in October 1959, he was called out of our class to take a call from Senator John F. Kennedy, who wanted him to explain the implications of that day's spike in the price of gold.) But his heart didn't really seem to lie in teaching. Interestingly, he never spoke of the major role he had played in advisory missions on monetary affairs in Latin America during the Roosevelt administration; I learned of this only in recent years. Such major excitement as I got from my courses was primarily concentrated in the field of macroeconomics, where Art Okun offered a course with his uniquely enthusiastic and riveting delivery. Also in macroeconomics, Nobel Prize–winning James Tobin offered a challenging, largely theoretical, course on money that I greatly enjoyed.

For the longer term, it was probably Lloyd Reynolds's seminar on national economic organization that had the most impact on me, though I wasn't aware of it at the time. Reynolds was best known at that point for his textbook on labour economics (and for his leadership, as chairman, in the rebuilding of a first-rate Yale economics department), but he also had a sharp eye for new frontiers of economic research. A wag at the time had it that if anyone wanted to know what would next excite the economics profession, all they had to do was to check out what Reynolds was up to. He admitted to us at the outset of his course that the reason he was offering the seminar was that he wanted to learn more about different economic systems; and I do not recall his ever having himself given us a lecture. But his reading list and our seminar presentations covered a fascinating range of material, including Communist economic systems, the economics of developing areas, and the functioning of different kinds of capitalist market economies. Because he was travelling with John Kenneth Galbraith on an exchange to the Soviet Union in the coming summer months of 1959, one of his (optional) final examination questions requested a list of queries that should be directed at Soviet industrial plant managers to uncover how their incentive system actually worked. He so liked my answer (the only one he got for this question, he later told me) that he carried it with him for use in his interviews there. For his course I did a research paper on the economics of education and health expenditures in developing countries, and argued, some years before Theodore (Ted) Schultz's well-known writing on human capital,[9] that education should be regarded as investment rather than consumption. (I also argued that health and other social expenditures were more in the nature of luxury goods and would have to be constrained in poor countries in order to further productive investment. I was much later, at UNICEF and elsewhere, to alter my ill-informed early views on this issue.) That essay was my first formal foray into development economics. I did not take the course in economic development at Yale since its reputation at that time was weak. Nor had I done an undergraduate course in it. In retrospect, the reading and thinking I did for Reynolds's course, and my connection to him, had started significantly to move my career in economics "Southward."

Postgraduate students at that time, as now, were poor and overworked (though I have to say that Georgia seemed to work just as hard on the lesson plans for the private school in which she taught as I did on my studies). We saved our pennies and daily made sandwich lunches. Our social life at first consisted of Saturday evenings with graduate student friends, movies at the local artsy cinema, and a fair number of visiting relatives and friends from home. We enjoyed drives and hikes in the lovely New England countryside, and loved the spectacular fall colours and the brilliant pink and white dogwoods in the spring. After a few years, we lucked into informal membership in a folk-singing group of graduate students, junior faculty, and spouses who gathered, with guitars and babies in carrycots, in one another's living quarters on quite a regular basis. The group included some good musicians and people who knew all the verses. It was in that company and at that time that we developed our deep appreciation for the contributions of Pete Seeger, Woody Guthrie, Joan Baez, Odetta, and all the rest. One memorable weekend was spent with friends at a friend's parents' summer home on Cape Cod. Another highlight of that period was the afternoon lecture series at the Yale Art Gallery, given by Vincent Scully, still not as famous as he later became, on his interpretations of the history of art. On most Sunday mornings we attended the interdenominational service in the Yale chapel, presided over by an inspiring William Sloane Coffin, long before he became a national figure as a civil rights and anti-Vietnam campaigner.

It was an exciting time to be in the United States. We attended both the Nixon and Kennedy rallies on the town green in the fateful presidential contest of the fall of 1960. We exulted in JFK's victory and were moved as we watched his famous inaugural address on a neighbour's television. Constructing his first administration, so the Yale story went at the time, JFK called up our professor James Tobin and invited him to chair his Council of Economic Advisors (CEA). Tobin at first demurred. "But I'm rather an ivory tower kind of economist," he said. "That's all right," Kennedy was said to have replied, "I'm rather an ivory tower kind of president." Whether the story was accurate or not, we Tobin students loved it. And it seemed to epitomize the atmosphere of intelligent and exciting "new beginnings" in the United States at the time. Soon, Art Okun, our popular macroeconomics professor, also joined the Washington team. Of course, this excitement only lasted a few years before the war in Vietnam, desultory progress with Washington reforms, assassinations, and civil rights riots, among other events, brought us all back from "Camelot" to often unpleasant realities.

Comprehensive PhD exams at Yale, both written and oral, were conducted in the fall, typically after students had completed two years of course work. In the spring of 1960, the year of my "comps," we received an invitation from college friends doing a study year at St Andrews in Scotland to join them for a tour of Scotland and then Europe in their Volkswagen bug. Using their friends, my relatives, and youth hostels, they calculated that it would actually be cheaper for us to tour Europe with them than it would be to stay in steamy New Haven for the summer. It was an opportunity, however ill-timed, too good to be able to resist. Included in our sparse luggage, as we took off, were some of my key course notebooks, from which I hoped to be able to cram at some point in our travels. We had an absolutely marvellous time.

My written comprehensives – done in the next few days after our return – went reasonably well. The orals, however, at least as I perceived them, were something of a disaster. All might have been satisfactory, I thought, had it not been that one of my examiners in international economics had been on our charter flight to and from Europe only a few days previously. This professor, Bela Balassa, a refugee from the 1956 Hungarian uprising, recently himself graduated from Yale and not yet as well known as he was later to become, had just published a paper on purchasing power parity. Unfortunately I hadn't read it. I had no idea what he was after as he pressed and pressed in his effort to get me to provide the "correct" interpretation to which his paper should lead its reader. I panicked. Instead of trying to reason my way through the issues, all I could think of was – I still remember it as vividly as if it were yesterday – "My God. I don't know the answers, and I have no idea what he wants from me. Isn't this awful!" That mindset was not a helpful approach to thinking through a response. I thought at the time that he might have been "out to get me" because he had seen me on the plane and knew that I had been swanning around Europe all summer instead of preparing for his exam. But, to be fair, he probably would have nailed me in the same way anyway. When I got home I broke down in tears, certain that I had failed. That night I slept very badly. The next day I went in to see the director of graduate studies to ask what on earth I should now do. I guess I looked a little distraught. He calmed me down, told me that they were not going to fail me, and urged me to go home and get some sleep. At the welcome meeting for incoming graduate students shortly after, I cringed as he sternly advised the newcomers against travelling to Europe in the summer before their comprehensive exams.

Then there was the thesis. Still primarily oriented toward interests in macro and international economics, and with a pragmatic bent that emphasized statistics rather than theory, I chose to explore Canadian-US financial and exchange rate connections. This topic was one that involved the assembly of fresh data from Ottawa and Toronto as well as from the United States, providing an opportunity to return home a little more frequently. It involved the econometric testing of some fairly straightforward propositions, and was therefore unlikely to drag on forever as some thesis research unfortunately tends to do. By this time I was getting quite weary of being a student and wanted to get the degree requirements over with. My desire for speed was given fresh impetus when we learned that we were to become parents in June 1961. I would need to earn more money. My thesis research, I was told, thereupon set a new Yale economics speed record: completed in less than a year.

Although my thesis had nothing to do with developing countries, my interest in development issues had been growing. Fellow students came from those countries or had worked in them or were planning doctoral theses on their economic challenges. I had begun to read more about them myself. At one point during that year, a group of graduate students interested in developing countries began a series of evening discussions on development issues to complement our more formal studies. One such meeting was conducted in our crowded third floor flat. It was a very distinguished group, including (now Sir) Richard Jolly, T.N. Srinivasan from India (later a Yale professor), Dharam Ghai from Kenya (later director of the UN Research Institute for Social Development), and Donald Mead (later, after many years in a variety of developing countries, a pillar at Michigan State), among others. But with the pressures of other work, this effort was not sustainable, and we met only a few times.

When, early in 1961, Lloyd Reynolds offered me an assistant professorship, cross-appointed between the new Yale Economic Growth Center, which he was now to direct (with Gus Ranis as his deputy), and the Yale Department of Economics, I was eager and quick to accept. I was told that if my thesis was submitted in its final form by the start of the fall term, my salary in my new assistant professorship would be increased by $1,000 (from $5,000 to $6,000); this offer provided further incentive for early completion. I had one heart-stopping moment that summer – this time mainly spent in New Haven with new baby Jane – when I went to see my formal thesis supervisor, Robert Triffin, for advice. I had submitted a complete draft of the thesis for him to read and was anxiously awaiting his feedback since he had not seen anything much from me after the initial approval of my proposed topic. "I have bad news for you, Gerry," he said, as I sat down for our meeting. My spirits sank. He went on: "I can't think of any comments to make on the draft of your thesis." The other committee members were equally satisfied. But I nonetheless nearly missed my extra $1,000. After approval from my committee, I was required to get the thesis formally bound and submitted to the School of Graduate Studies by a prescribed date. A couple of days before the deadline I eagerly took my work to a recommended cheap bindery, an informal business operating out of the basement of a somewhat rundown private home near the campus. The elderly woman who ran it promised to get it back to me in time. But when, the evening before the deadline, I returned to pick it up, she told me that she had not been able to complete the job. There had been unsettled weather all that afternoon, and it was continuing; she was terrified of thunder and lightning, she told me, and she never went down to the basement at such times. I pleaded with her, explained the $1,000 situation, and offered to do it myself if she told me what to do. Finally she relented and, carefully holding my hand as we descended the stairs, she finished the job, flinching at each thunder clap. I offered her a share of the reward, but she graciously declined.

Beginning a Career in Academic Economics

The newly established and well-funded Yale University Economic Growth Center, with its burgeoning library, was to represent the academic "frontier" in its subject area. Brainchild of Simon Kuznets, a subsequent Nobel Laureate in economics, the Economic Growth Center represented a grand new scholarly enterprise to improve understanding of economic growth processes, standardize relevant data sets, and assist governmental efforts to address the problem of global poverty. Its planned series of country studies was to be an early and important element in its program.

With my Yale faculty appointment, I was to be mandated and supported, along with other forthcoming Growth Center appointees, to undertake a data-based country study of a developing country of my choice. My choice of Nigeria is discussed in chapter four. I became literally the Yale Economic Growth Center's first junior faculty member. Our country studies were intended to be the definitive works, based on all the available existing data, on the chosen countries' experiences of economic growth and development. It was a time of great excitement, unbridled enthusiasm, high ideals, and almost boundless optimism.

Some of my country-studying colleagues were already good friends, particularly Carlos Diaz-Alejandro, Donald Mead, and Donald Snodgrass. Carlos and I stayed closely in touch in later years, working in parallel on a variety of development issues and at one point writing a policy paper together. My files contain scores of hilarious messages in Carlos's unique curly script, often on postcards sent from exotic places. I was very sorry to have been unable to get to his funeral when he died unexpectedly and prematurely, at the age of forty-eight, of complications related to AIDS in the summer of 1985. At a Festschrift conference in my honour in Ottawa in 1994, I was moved and honoured by Gus Ranis's friendly reference to Carlos and me as the "Gang of Two." Don Mead has remained a lifelong friend.

In addition to the initial six of us who had embarked upon country studies, another young development economist, Reginald Green, soon joined us fresh from his award-winning thesis at Harvard. He was later to pursue a remarkable career in African economics.

In our first year, some of the visiting professors at the Growth Center (Dudley Seers, Alexandre Lamfalussy, later to head the Bank for International Settlements, and Joseph Grunwald) joined interested Yale faculty in organizing lively evening discussion meetings on development issues in their homes. Dudley Seers, with his fresh and often iconoclastic approaches, had a particularly profound impact upon me. At that time he was already writing and speaking controversially on "the limitations of the special case" (rich country economies), "why visiting economists fail," and "the meaning of development." A few years later, he tried to entice me to join his staff in the new British Ministry of Overseas Development in Harold Wilson's Labour government. I eventually did work with him in the early 1970s at the Institute of Development Studies at the University of Sussex, where he had become the founding director, and later in a Commonwealth mission to Uganda after the ouster of Idi Amin (see chapters six and twenty-one).

Among the visitors who put in periodic appearances was Simon Kuznets, whose work on the statistics of growth and development was soon to earn him a Nobel Prize and who was the Economic Growth Center's intellectual father. On one (later) occasion he came to the Growth Center to hear presentations from some of us on the progress of our country studies. When he heard of the difficulties I was having constructing accurate and up-to-date estimates of Nigerian national income and my hopes of concentrating my work instead on data that were more reliable, he reacted with vigour. He very much wanted me to keep trying to do the impossible. "Better a glorious failure," he declaimed, "than an inglorious success." I'm not sure whether this is the right way to approach research – or life. It is certainly no way to acquire tenure in today's universities. But I often recall these words when I have come to critical decision points. I have not always followed his advice (and didn't, in fact, even follow it then).

After its first year, the Growth Center took on a whole new cohort of assistant professors, more than doubling the previous number. Included as country studiers were Stephen Hymer, Howard Pack, Albert Berry, and Brian Van Arkadie, among others. Together with our original group of six, all of whom returned to Yale after a research year abroad, and other visiting faculty (including Brazilian Celso Furtado), it was a very bright and lively collection of young economists. Most went on to make a name in the development field. Surprisingly, though, very few of the second cohort ever completed the country studies for which the Growth Center had primarily hired them. Al Berry eventually became my close colleague at the University of Toronto.

In those days we all usually took the time for morning and afternoon coffee breaks, where the conversation was invariably stimulating. Some of us, almost invariably Carlos and I, also went to lunch together, walking down Prospect Street to the cafeteria in the university commons, where the conversation with other faculty members was always rich and usually topical. It was on one of these occasions in April 1965 that the esteem in which we had held Jim Tobin, now back from the Washington policy scene, fell several notches. The United States, on what seemed rather questionable grounds, had invaded the Dominican Republic on the previous day; Carlos and I and many others had been genuinely shocked. Discussion about the invasion was animated. To our surprise and dismay, Tobin took the side of the US government, arguing, among other things, that the government almost certainly knew much more about the real situation than we did. What kind of an intellectual argument was that! Shades of the Vietnam mess, which was also building at that time.

I very much enjoyed my first Yale teaching experiences. My first class was the economics portion of an interdisciplinary political economy course offered, together with political scientist Fred Greenstein, in an intensive and accelerated smaller class for exceptional Yale students. I felt honoured to be entrusted with them and found it quite exhilarating.

I was also able to tolerate and even learn from my first academic administrative duties. Upon returning in 1963 from my Yale Growth Center–supported research year in Nigeria (see chapter four), I found myself appointed the director of undergraduate studies in economics, an assignment which I retained for my remaining two years at Yale and for which I received some teaching credit. It provided me with another office and obliged me to be there to meet students for a variety of purposes at specified hours. I handled admissions, course assignments, grade submission, and the like, and met with each and every undergraduate economics major to advise on and approve individual course programs. From time to time I wrote reports on one aspect of the program or another and reported at departmental meetings. It was in this job that I learned, from a systematic study we undertook, that the sons (there were still no women at Yale at the time) of Yale alumni were not only more likely to be admitted to Yale, other things equal, than others, but also, once admitted, earned grades that were statistically significantly lower. In recent years there have been bestselling exposes of these Ivy League practices, but everyone on the inside already knew.

At that time I also taught an undergraduate course in economic development, which I didn't think went down very well, filled as the class largely was with quite conservative and unsympathetic students. For one term, I offered a postgraduate course in international trade theory for students in Yale's special economics program for economists and administrators from foreign countries. In the latter course, I had some distinguished students, including Guillermo Calvo from Argentina, later prominent at Columbia University and the IMF, and Edmar Bacha from Brazil, also later to become quite well known in the profession. Calvo, a very bright student, wrote a theoretical paper for my course that was a challenge for me to understand. For one semester, to earn a little extra cash and to gain further experience, I drove the half hour up to Wesleyan University in Middletown, Connecticut, where I gave another introductory economics course to a very enthusiastic class of undergraduates.

At home, daughter Jane was soon joined, in December 1963, by our first son, Eric, and our family was nearly complete.

* * *

I enjoyed my assistant professorship at Yale enormously and would happily have stayed longer if that had been a serious option; but it became clear that it probably wasn't and that the most I could hope for was a non-tenured associate professorship for a limited term. In 1964–5 I therefore began to explore the job market. We drove up to Dartmouth University at their invitation, where I gave a not-very-exciting seminar on Nigeria, and evidently failed to impress; there was no follow-up from them. I travelled to Princeton for interviews with Arthur Lewis and Fred Harbison, who "did" the development courses there at the time, and the chairman; I heard nothing further from them either. At the same time Dudley Seers, now in charge of economic research at the new British Ministry of Overseas Development, tried actively to attract me to his staff; and for a time we considered it seriously. In Canada, however, the University of Toronto had made it known that they would be happy to have me whenever I was ready. In those days, hiring at Toronto (and most other places) was pretty much at the discretion of department chairs and job seminars were not required. They knew me in Toronto as a former good student and at that time that was enough. It probably did not hurt that Vincent Bladen, the dean of the faculty at the time, had been one of my professors. That my father was to be my colleague was of concern to me, but evidently not to them. The only other exploration I undertook in Canada was a trip to Peterborough for discussion with the principal of the newly created Trent University, Tom Symons. From his viewpoint, as he sought to build a university oriented toward Canadian studies, I think I said all the wrong things, emphasizing the need, as I saw it, for Canadian students to spend less time on Canadian matters and much more on international ones. I never heard from him again either.

Tom Easterbrook, the chairman of the Toronto Department of Political Economy, an economic historian of considerable note under whom I had once studied, made me a firm offer early in January 1965: a tenured associate professorship with very attractive teaching opportunities, lecturing to fourth year (honours) students in international economics and graduate students in development, at what seemed at that time like a princely salary of $11,000 and a generous moving allowance (although we did not have much to move). Despite some continuing doubts about the wisdom of accepting membership in a department that still included my father, we decided to accept. With only a few breaks, I remained there for the rest of my academic career.

The department I joined was unusual for its time in that it still encompassed the study of both political science and economics within its rubric of political economy. Indeed the Department of Political Economy handled courses in commerce as well and had only relatively recently hived off its responsibility for those in sociology. This breadth of approach had been characteristic of earlier social scientific enquiry in the realm of economics and had to appeal to anyone studying economic history or development. By the 1980s, however, this departmental structure proved unsustainable, and I found myself in an orthodox Department of Economics.

The University of Toronto was very good to me. Its size and diversity made it possible for me to engage in a wide variety of extracurricular activities and to take periodic full and partial leaves (without pay) without ever endangering its overall programs, something that a smaller university probably could not have done for me. It provided plenty of stimulating academic company and a great many excellent students. Its physical surroundings were pleasant. The city of Toronto, as it continued to attract more immigrants, grew more exciting every year. And there, we were able to remain much closer to our parents in their final years than we had been before. I took all of my university responsibilities seriously and did what I believe was a fair share of teaching, committee, and administrative duties, and eventually far more than my share of PhD supervision. All things considered, it would be difficult to imagine having had a better base, over the next thirty years or so, for my various research, advisory, and advocacy activities, or for key elements of family life.

We had no regrets over our move to the University of Toronto. But after less than a year there, we responded to what seemed a unique opportunity and took what proved to be a two-year (unpaid) leave to work in newly independent Tanzania (see chapter five), our second stay in Africa.

In the later years of my tenure in the Department of Economics, tensions arose between those who, like development economists, saw the need for continuing breadth in its teaching programs and those who promoted deeper theoretical and technical expertise. My take and role in these important debates can best be understood only after an account of my professional work in economics. I therefore save a fuller account of these issues and my subsequent academic life in Toronto for a later chapter (see chapter twenty).

PART II

An International and Development Economist in Africa

4 Nigeria

When appointed to my first academic post – involving, as already noted, a commitment to a serious country study for the Economic Growth Center at Yale – I chose to undertake research in Nigeria. Why Nigeria?

I had long wanted to work in, and somehow to help, Africa on problems of economic development. Newly independent countries seemed in the early 1960s to offer particularly exciting possibilities. Nigeria was an English-speaking country (my French has never been very good); and it was, apart from South Africa, far and away, the biggest and potentially most powerful country on the African continent. It seemed to me the obvious choice. I never had any cause for regret.

During the first year of my faculty appointment at Yale, I read everything there was to read about Nigeria and Africa (not nearly as much at that time as is available today), and I immersed myself in the available data. I also benefited enormously from exchanges with the rest of the Growth Center faculty, now including Gustav (Gus) Ranis, Richard Ruggles, Raymond Goldsmith, and Dudley Seers, recently arrived from a stint in the UN Economic Commission for Latin America (UNECLA), among others. The rest of the first wave of the country study contingent (Carlos Diaz-Alejandro on Argentina, Werner Baer on Brazil, Donald Mead on the United Arab Republic, Donald Snodgrass on Sri Lanka, and Jan Tumlir on Greece) soon arrived. Together, we tried to bring ourselves up to date on the state of the art of what was still the young field of development economics, and to put together an overall program that could make our total product exceed the sum of our separate studies. Our seniors, particularly Ruggles, supported by Kuznets, worked on a standard set of national accounts and other statistics, which we all would attempt to collect or to estimate to facilitate international comparisons, whatever else we might succeed in doing. By the time of our departure for Nigeria, I had a fairly detailed prospectus of my study plans, which I could share with anyone who asked. Of course, it went through a lot of changes during our stay in Nigeria and thereafter. But I think it fair to say that I was well prepared for my work in Nigeria – much better prepared than a good many other Western scholars I was subsequently to meet in Africa.

Our first African experience began in the evening of 6 August 1962, when our little family of three landed, full of excitement and more than a little nervous, at a steaming Lagos airport on an Alitalia flight from Rome. Our daughter, Jane, was a little more than one year old; we were in our mid-twenties. First impressions are important. And Nigeria had an enormous impact on us, right from day one.

The first few hours in Africa left an indelible impression. As the plane taxied toward the terminal – by now darkness had fallen – the windows of our air-conditioned cabin steamed up, and an attendant came through spraying insecticide. When the doors finally opened and we stepped outside onto the stairs, the tropical heat hit us like a blast furnace. A rickety bus with wooden seats carried us from the plane to what seemed to us extremely serious customs and immigration officers. Once outside the terminal, we were besieged by, in our minds, quite an unruly crowd of shouting taxi drivers, all seeking our business. A customs officer delivered us into the hands of what appeared to us as a particularly malicious-looking (at least unsmiling) driver, who shouted a single message repeatedly at me, which I finally realized was an asking price: "One pound. One pound." Not yet accustomed to Nigerian pricing systems, I failed to make a counter-offer, thereby undoubtedly losing respect all around, and accepted his price. We piled our possessions into his old car and set off toward the airport hotel, where we were to spend the night before driving up to our new home in inland Ibadan the next day. The night was pitch black, the road was bumpy, and the car seemed to be travelling at breakneck speed. Robed figures and goats loomed on both sides of the road, and all were greeted with toots of our car horn. The trip through the tropical darkness seemed to take much longer than it should have. How far, after all, can an airport hotel be from an airport? I had an awful thought: "We are entirely in this mad driver's control. What have I done, bringing Georgia and Jane to this terrible end?" But we got there, had a good night's sleep, and everything looked much brighter in the morning. We were enthralled by all of the sights and sounds on our morning two-hour drive to the

University of Ibadan, which was to be our home for the following year. Tropical vegetation, mud-walled tin- or thatch-roofed villages, colour-fully dressed people thronging the roadside with the women artfully balancing all manner of loads upon their heads, ubiquitous Nigeria-specific billboard advertising, speeding "mammy wagons" with their hopeful painted slogans ("Depart, yee unbelievers"; "Truth shall make you free"; "Why worry. God is love"), hump-backed long-horned cattle on the road – one new sight after another.

I later came to know the Lagos–Ibadan road quite well as I travelled it frequently. It was always a fascinating and colourful trip in terms of people, scenery, and sheer experience. But at that time it was also a winding and dangerous journey. One would invariably come across recent wrecks on the side of the road. Once I came around a bend and over a hill to encounter the remains of a severe accident involving a mammy wagon and a lorry, which must have occurred only a couple of minutes before. The last time I travelled this road, several years later, I nearly lost my life. A university-supplied driver was taking me back to the airport after a conference in Ibadan, and it was only after a couple of very near misses with oncoming lorries that I realized he was utterly stoned, probably on kola nut. I ordered him out of the driver's seat and drove the rest of the way myself, while he went to sleep on the back seat.

As an introduction to Africa, it would be hard to do better than Ibadan, a huge quasi-traditional city, then with a population of about one million. The great bulk of its buildings were traditional in material (mud with tin roof) and structure (simple and flat), with a commer-cial centre of more modern two-story buildings, out of which rose one "skyscraper" of about eight floors. Roads made their way through the dwellings in an unpredictable and winding fashion, except for one sec-tion of straight road built some years back by a determined Welshman, who simply demolished everything in his planned path (the "Taffy highway"). It was a city where, as one North American colleague at the university put it, "Every time I drive in, I see something that I have never before seen in my entire life." Its open markets, open people, and open sewers combined colours, smells, noise, and sheer exuberance in ways we had never experienced before. We were fortunate to be able to share in local celebrations, festivals, and political events. One of my highlights was an unforgettable evening funeral celebration in back-street Ibadan, with much traditional music and dance, in which I was privileged to participate (and dance) as an honoured guest.

Nigerian culture – music, drama, art, history – is fascinating and rich; and we revelled in learning more of it. Its people – at least those with whom we interacted – were friendly, frequently boisterous, and received us, everywhere we went, with extraordinary warmth. Our blonde-haired one-year-old Jane assured us of an extra warm welcome whenever she came with us. We were extremely fortunate in our contacts, benefiting from introductions to local chiefs, museum directors, Peace Corps personnel, and all manner of other interesting and informed people. When we travelled, we had expert advance guidance as to special places to see or people to meet. Although our time in Nigeria was not without some health and other difficulties, including my own serious bout with viral encephalitis, which eventually cut short our stay after a year, it certainly hooked us on Africa.

As a research associate, I worked from an office in the Nigerian Institute of Social and Economic Research (NISER), located in the University of Ibadan (in those days it had just graduated from being known as University College Ibadan, or UCI). The university was located outside the city proper in beautiful grounds with carefully maintained lawns and gardens. Its buildings were architecturally modern, combining white stucco with wooden doors and windows – very pleasing to the eye. Our flat was on the ground floor of an attractive three-story building, about a five-minute drive from my office. It had attractively tiled wooden floors and simple wooden furniture, all locally made. The comfort and beauty of our accommodations and my office vastly exceeded our expectations. We had been quite prepared to live a lot more simply.

Shortages and disorganization in the Department of Economics led me to offer to take responsibility for the compulsory first-year course in economics (sixty-odd students, only one woman). Although this was very time-consuming, I was very glad to be able to offer something (who knew at that time whether my work would ever generate anything useful?) in return for all of the assistance I was receiving. My diary records my own frequent dissatisfaction with my lectures. Trying to drive through Samuelson's *Economics* (everyone's textbook at the time)[10] in an African context may not have been the greatest idea even for an African lecturer, let alone an expatriate. Although I knew the straight statistical facts about the Nigerian economy about as well as anyone and I made strenuous efforts to incorporate Nigerian content wherever I could (for example, demand and supply of cocoa beans, some of the methodology behind the estimation of Nigerian national income, an analysis of the new Nigerian development plan, and so forth), should I really have undertaken to offer this course only two months after arrival in Africa? In any case, I eventually found it richly rewarding, and some of the students seemed to be "turned on" at least some of the time. Certainly my lectures on the new Nigerian development plan were met with rapt attention. One student, whom I hired as a research assistant after the end of the school year, eventually became an eminent academic economist.

In 1962–3 almost all the faculty in the university were expatriate, principally white and British. Many, especially those in senior positions, were thoroughly colonial in their attitudes to Nigeria and Nigerians. The director of NISER, who doubled as the professor of economics, regularly departed the country on the last day of term, returning only on the day before classes resumed. We attended some perfectly awful social events with the old guard. Fortunately, there were many enthusiastic and idealistic younger scholars – in anthropology, political science, sociology, ethnomusicology, medicine, and economics – from whom we learned enormously. In the end, we spent most of our spare time with younger Brits, North Americans (black and white), most of whom were engaged in research or other activities rather than teaching, and with Nigerians.

Georgia did some volunteer teaching both in an Ibadan school and in a nearby bush school, in both of which her work was greatly appreciated. When we left, they threw a big party in her honour. Unfortunately I was very ill at the time, and she did not know how serious the party was to be. She didn't go, and when we heard what had been planned for her, we, of course, felt terrible.

There were only two Nigerian economists in the university at that time (two others had recently left for jobs in Lagos), and both had only returned home relatively recently: Ojetunji (Tunji) Aboyade, with a Cambridge PhD, and HMA (Bola) Onitiri, with a London PhD. Both were very able, and both received me warmly. When I arrived, Tunji was acting head – for six months – of the planning unit in the federal Ministry of Economic Development, following Wolfgang Stolper who had taken responsibility for the creation of the first post-independence Nigerian development plan (and subsequently wrote a book on his experience, *Planning without Facts*[11]). Tunji became a firm friend, and was enormously helpful to me in all manner of ways. For a twenty-five-year-old neophyte economist (me), it was exhilarating to be directly involved in discussions, with Tunji and other Nigerians at the highest possible professional levels, of a huge newly independent African country's needs and policy issues. Whenever I was in Lagos, I had a direct line to the professional economics and statistical "top." Among those who were helpful to me was the permanent secretary of the Treasury in the Western Region, and secretary of the Nigerian Economic Society (NES) at that time, Adebayo Adedeji, later the energetic (and controversial) head of the UN Economic Commission for Africa (UNECA). Unfortunately for Nigeria, it appeared to me that its politicians were nowhere near as able or as highly motivated as the economists and statisticians with whom I had the privilege of interacting. Corruption was already emerging as a major problem for the newly independent nation.

We developed particularly close relations in Ibadan with Sayre and Letta Schatz. Sayre was an American economist, with comfortably radical leanings, working in NISER on problems of entrepreneurship and small business in Nigeria. Letta was writing English-language children's books based on Nigerian stories. Another good colleague was Douglas Anglin, a political scientist on leave from Carleton University, later to become the first vice chancellor of the University of Zambia. The two of us drove around northern Nigeria in a Volkswagen for eight days in November, during which we conducted interviews on our respective research projects and shared many adventures, including an unfortunate road encounter with a wandering goat that, apart from the animal's demise, covered our car with its excrement. Stimulating colleagues and an exciting environment made for lively discussions and an active social and cultural life.

Georgia and Jane joined me on innumerable weekend excursions in our Volkswagen bug to Oyo, Oshogbo, Ife, Abeokuta, and other parts of our surrounding environs of Yorubaland. In March 1963 we went on a memorable two-and-a-half week trip around the entire country, during which we combined essential data gathering and interviews for my research with further learning about the geography, culture, and politics of Nigeria. We travelled eastward to Benin, then on to Enugu, capital of the Eastern Region, as it was then called, crossing the Niger River at Asaba on a dilapidated ferry that turned around a couple of times in mid-river before managing to struggle to the other side. (The bridge across the river was not yet built.) From there we drove south to Port Harcourt, where the oil industry was just beginning to get underway, visiting centres of weaving and crafts en route. Returning to Enugu, we then travelled eastward again, all the way, very much out of the way, to the Cameroun border. We stayed for a couple of days in the wonderfully temperate climate of a simple cattle ranch rest house in the highlands at Obudu, enjoying fresh strawberries, great steaks, and cool, fresh air. From there we drove – a very long and dusty trip – northward to Makurdi, Jos, Bauchi, and finally Kano. Kano was, as promised, magnificently "Northern" and different – solid Islamic and Arabic influences, horses and camels, men wearing white. From there we travelled south to Ibadan again via Zaria, Kaduna, Bida, and the one-track bridge (for both road and rail) across the Niger at Jebba. A marvellous trip.

Georgia and Jane also flew to join me in Accra when I attended, with two carloads of Ibadan colleagues, the First International Congress of Africanists[12] there in December 1962. The list of attendees in my diary reads like a who's who of the best-known Africanist scholars of the period. But most of the papers were extremely general, and many, especially the Russians' presentations, weren't very good; perhaps I had become spoiled at Ibadan, but I found the sessions tedious. It was interesting, however, to experience Kwame Nkrumah's Ghana firsthand, with its Black Star Square and its monuments, and to see Osagyefo (the title of Redeemer that the new president had been granted) and his praise singers and drummers in the flesh at the opening of the congress. I also met lots of interesting people and renewed friendship with Reginald Green, already working in Ghana, with whom I was to have much more contact over the years. Our little family drove home together along the beautiful Togo coastline and through Dahomey (now Benin). We had planned to stay longer in Ghana and along the coast, but Jane came down with German measles so we thought it best to head directly home – and her facial spots seemed to speed us through the customs posts en route. Virtually everywhere we went, we were warmly received; and we learned and learned and learned.

In June 1963, after a year of recurrent fevers, successfully treated with antimalarials, I suddenly acquired an even higher fever and a splitting headache that didn't even begin to go away with aspirins. The headache got worse and worse. For several days I lay moaning with pain, waiting for the next shot of morphine, which the university doctors were still able to supply although the country was said to be getting low in its supplies. At one point they moved me into the hospital for further testing. Needless to say, I don't remember very much about any of this. Georgia tells me that at one point I asked for a gun. The attack eventually cleared. The doctors said it appeared to have been viral encephalomeningitis, and I still possess their letter stating that there didn't seem to be any permanent damage to my brain. The neurologist treating my dystonia in later years was very interested in this medical history and implied that, since there were no obvious genetic links, this episode might be responsible for the neurological problems that came on in my sixties. That drastic experience resulted in my loss of about twenty pounds in the space of a couple of weeks, and we decided to head for home a little earlier than originally planned.

I returned to Nigeria in the summer of 1965, immediately following our move back to Toronto. This trip permitted me to bring my research material fully up to date and to gather some feedback on the first draft of my book. By this time I was already regarded in some circles as "the authority" on the Nigerian economy, and my manuscript was circulating widely. Out of all this experience eventually came my first book, *Peasant Agriculture, Government and Economic Growth in Nigeria*.[13] It has become something of a classic for Nigerian students of economics and economic history, detailing Nigeria's pre-oil experience with particular attention to its system of agricultural export marketing boards. Bits and pieces of the manuscript had appeared in various journals and conference proceedings before the book itself, but it was the book that attracted the greatest attention – and good reviews. One of my great regrets, at the time, was that a draft section on the economics of Nigeria's potential disintegration was removed on the advice of a reader who thought it too pessimistic. Biafra's secession and the Nigerian Civil War followed shortly thereafter!

In the following years I went to Nigeria from time to time for conferences on postwar reconstruction, the marketing board system, and social science research in Africa. I also once travelled to Ibadan, as a favour to Tunji Aboyade, in the capacity of external examiner in the economics department. Surprisingly, I did not return to Nigeria for the next thirty years. My only direct contacts with the country took the form of exchange with the large number of Nigerians who participated in the activities of the African Economic Research Consortium (AERC), which are discussed later in chapter eight. I was, of course, kept fully aware of the extreme political and economic difficulties suffered by the peoples of Nigeria during these years, and my heart went out to them.

In 2001 I was informed that I had been elected a fellow of the Nigerian Economic Society (NES), the first and so far the only non-Nigerian to be so honoured. I was unable to attend my scheduled formal induction in August 2002 and did not know whether I nonetheless had acquired this status or not. Early in 2007, however, I was contacted again, told that in order to be a fellow I had to be physically present for the induction, and invited to the fiftieth anniversary conference of the NES later in the year

4.1. Helping to celebrate the fiftieth anniversary of the Nigerian Economic Society, Abuja, 2007

in the new federal capital, Abuja (which did not exist when I was last in the country). At first I demurred, citing uncertainty about my health, difficulty in writing a paper, and related conditions. But the Nigerian organizers seemed to take my highly conditioned response as a "yes" and set about finding funds for my travel. I was very glad I went. From the very moment I entered the country, I was treated like royalty. The immigration officer at the Abuja airport studied my passport and my face, and sent me quickly on my way with a "Welcome home." Had he been briefed to watch for me? Was he a former economics student? At the hotel, the first person I saw was my former best student and research assistant, Femi Kayode, now semi-retired from his senior academic position and a former president of the NES and important figure in the AERC; he greeted me most warmly. The induction ceremony for all seven of us (five former NES presidents, the governor of the Central Bank, Charles/Chukwuma Soludo, and me) was formal and flowery, in good Nigerian style, and the citations were long. We were each presented with a plaque and the gowns and hats we wore for the occasion, and the photographs were extensive. The 200 to 300 participants, including friends and acquaintances from many years past, were all extremely welcoming, friendly, and solicitous of my needs. And so it went. The conference presentations were interesting and, together with the lively local press, allowed me to get myself somewhat more up to date on Nigerian economic and political issues about which I had lost touch. In my address at the celebratory anniversary dinner, I reflected on the past fifty years of development economics and issues for the future of the economics profession in Nigeria, concluding with a Keynesian toast to the Nigerian Economic Society, all of which seemed to go down quite well. For me the most intriguing part of the evening was the praise singing for "Prof Gerry" done by the high-life band that played throughout the evening. Before returning to the airport for the trip home, I did a quick taxi-tour of the impressive new city with its throughways, shining new buildings, huge national mosque and ecumenical church, and its great variety of peoples. It certainly did not look like the Nigeria I had known. In fact, it "fair blew me away." But could Abuja's inhabitants relate to the rest of the country and all of their problems? I couldn't help wondering.

5 Tanzania

Although Tanzania was not our family's first place of residence and work in Africa, it holds a special place in our hearts and our memories. Between 1966 and 1968 I was supported by the Rockefeller Foundation to be the first director of the Economic Research Bureau (ERB), a newly established independent research institution located within the University of Dar es Salaam, designed to produce policy-relevant studies in support of the newly independent government. The invitation came during our first year back in Toronto, and might have been stimulated by the Foundation's knowledge that I was communicating with Donald Mead in Uganda about spending some of the summer of 1966 with him. The opportunity of developing a new research institution in a very poor newly independent country with a progressive young president appealed to all my idealistic instincts. How could I possibly resist? We found renters for our newly purchased and much-loved house, and left Toronto in May, the end of our first academic year back home.

Originally contracted for only one year, I found the work so satisfying and the environment so exciting that we decided to stay on longer. Those years in Tanzania may well have been the best years of our lives. Jane and Eric were five and three years old, respectively, when we arrived there, perfect for the casual outdoor living of a tropical environment. My professional life was very busy but, quite unlike other times, I was home a lot; typically, I was even home for lunch. My work at the university involved close and collegial relationships with professionals from a variety of other disciplines, as it had done in Ibadan, something I have missed in later years. We had good friends and a lively social life. Daughter Jane began school at the local international school, and son Eric attended a nursery school that Georgia, with some friends, began on our front lawn before it moved to a Danish-financed purpose-built permanent facility. Our special son, Peter, was born in the Ocean Road Hospital in Dar es Salaam in April 1968.

The initiator of the ERB, the new research body that had brought us to Tanzania, was the Danish professor of economics, Knud Erik Svendsen, a remarkable Marxist economist and former secretary of the Communist Party of Denmark, with whom I developed a very strong and mutually respectful friendship and professional relationship. My job was not only to begin immediately to generate policy research and papers that might be useful for the formulation of governmental policies but also to find resources and staff to expand and improve the quality of the effort. My own principal research was on matters of agricultural marketing and pricing policies, and on trade policies. I was able to attract further support for the ERB from the governments of Canada, Denmark, and Germany, among others. By the time I left Tanzania the ERB's full-time professional staff numbered eight. I believe that the ERB had already become an established part of the policy landscape in Tanzania, and indeed its policy-oriented focus was seen by many, elsewhere in East Africa, as a useful potential model for others.

These post-independence times were exciting and unforgettable in Africa, particularly so in Tanzania where a young and idealistic president, Julius Nyerere, provided inspiring leadership to his desperately poor country. It seemed then as if all things might now be possible, or at least worth trying. To be involved in high-level policy discussion and debate in these circumstances (for there were few other trained economists for policymakers to consult) was a rare privilege, and was quite exhilarating. Less than a year after our arrival in Tanzania, dramatic policy change (in which I was not involved) suddenly added further excitement and drew worldwide attention. In February 1967 the president and governing party issued the Arusha Declaration,[14] announcing their intention to turn the country's economy in a markedly socialist direction. Quickly thereafter, as if to demonstrate its seriousness, the government nationalized the banks and most of the country's productive enterprises. On behalf of the ERB, I offered immediate assistance, if it should be required, in the management of the nationalized banks, and for a brief time our relatively junior, and certainly inexperienced, economists did indeed preside over some of them.

Nyerere's emphasis on the need for equity in the struggle for development, and his personal honesty and insistence upon equivalent standards within his party and government, won widespread international respect. One of the results was that Dar es Salaam at that time attracted many of the "best and brightest" in the international social science and policy communities and, of course, many from the international left. I was greatly honoured to be included, despite my relative inexperience and at the ripe old age of thirty, within the Tanzanian policy community: appointed to the boards of the central bank (the Bank of Tanzania) and the nationalized sisal industry (the Tanzania Sisal Corporation), the National Economic Council, innumerable planning committees, and the like. I did my best to develop the tradition of independent policy-relevant economic and related research, to build a staff to conduct it, and to write quality papers of my own. I was particularly pleased to learn that my public lecture on "Trade, Aid and Nation Building in Tanzania,"[15] which by chance happened to have been scheduled in the weeks immediately following the Arusha Declaration, was so appreciated by the president that he ordered all of his cabinet members to read it. Word of this apparently got out and was somewhat misconstrued: there followed an article in the *Washington Post* attributing Tanzania's turn to the left to the influence of a young Canadian economist who had the ear of the president.

The superficial impression that I carried significant influence within the government – my influence was, in fact, extremely slim, probably close to non-existent – generated some annoyance on the part of the local academic left, particularly within the political science department at the university, which considered me to be not nearly left enough .The Hungarian professor of economics who succeeded my friend Erik Svendsen was a Marxist theoretician of development. To my intense frustration, he took minimal interest in the real-world complexities of day-to-day policy formation in Tanzania, rarely even attending the regular seminars in economics, usually on policy issues of the day, held under ERB auspices. In a subsequent conference, which I had been instrumental in setting up and for which I returned to Dar es Salaam about a year after my departure, he and I squared off in a debate as to the role of ideology – or lack thereof – in the teaching of economics to Tanzanian students. He emphasized Marxist ideology and the importance of interdisciplinary approaches within a Marxist framework. I emphasized the traditional tools of my discipline. I recall one of my better rhetorical flourishes: "What exactly is the ideological content of the elasticity of demand, or the measurement of the balance of payments?" These concepts, to his mind, were of minor relevance, relative to his larger questions. No doubt he was as exasperated with me as I was with him. And I suspect that neither of us made any converts. Each side was quite deeply dug in. I considered myself fortunate to have left the university in mid-1968, before the ideological struggles there turned uglier.

But these struggles had certainly begun. Since I had always considered myself to be somewhere on the left, both within the overall political spectrum and in my chosen profession, I found this all more than a little distressing. I was genuinely shocked, for instance, when my radical friend and neighbour, historian Walter Rodney from Guyana (widely known for his bestselling revisionist history, *How Europe Underdeveloped Africa*[16]), with whom I had played friendly games of monopoly, rose in a university meeting to denounce the "bourgeois economics" that was still being taught and practiced in an ostensibly socialist country. (Sadly, Rodney was later assassinated when he attempted to develop a radical political opposition to the government upon his return to his home country.) A vigorous debate developed as to the appropriate role of academics and the university within the emerging Tanzanian polity, economy, and society.

A major conference was organized on the role of the university in a socialist society. It was held downtown rather than "on the (university) hill" in order to attract more participants and, I suspect, to appear more immersed in local society. Many embassies sent representatives who took copious notes. Some participants came from abroad. (I recall Gray Cowan, an eminent African analyst from the United States, sadly shaking his head and volunteering that he had seen all this before.) One of the best publicly expressed lines of the conference, I thought, was that of a relatively moderate (by the standards of the place and time) American teaching economist, Idrian Resnick: "Socialism is an idea. It is a good idea. But it is not the only idea." It was an extremely stimulating event, but, again, few minds were changed. Many of the more traditional academics found it quite frightening. I attended but said next to nothing, believing it not my place and uncomfortable with the leadership being taken by more radical expatriate lecturers. I knew that, in any case, the key decisions would not be made at a conference of this character.

Heavy pressure was applied thereafter in some academic quarters, notably in the social sciences, toward Marxist conformity, pressure that intensified in the years to come. It was in Tanzania, and in my struggles with the academic "far left" there, that I was first forced to come seriously to terms with what sort of a socialist I really was, or if indeed I was one at all. What certainly became much clearer to me at this time was my deep antipathy to Marxist (or any other) certainties. I was quite astonished at many Marxist colleagues' ideological rigidity, particularly those in political science, and their apparent lack of interest in "traditional" economic analysis, quantitative evidence, or the details of immediate policy. My socialist sympathies were evidently to be constrained forever after by my professional insistence on the need for evidence-based analysis and pragmatism in the search for effective paths to more equitable development.

Interestingly, the only halfway serious discord on matters of political economy that I recall having had with my Marxist colleague in economics, Erik Svendsen, and it was minor, related to my Nigerian economist friend Ojetunji Aboyade. I had recommended him as an external examiner for the Dar es Salaam students in economics, and Erik, keen to have an African in this role, readily invited him. I never did see the reports Tunji wrote on the Dar es Salaam economics program or those on the performance of its students on their examinations, but I gathered that the reports were vigorous and critical. As he was by now the head of the economics department at the University of Ibadan, he would have had pretty clear ideas as to what was appropriate in the teaching of economics in an African university. Although he subsequently wrote a quite "fresh" and original textbook, I can guess that his views at that time were fairly orthodox. I very much doubt that they would have included any positive references to Marxist thought, and they probably would not have included much political content of any kind. Erik did not seem to hold this misstep against me.

I gathered that the visit I had arranged on that occasion between my Nigerian friend Tunji and President Nyerere (arranged through our indefatigable friend, Joan Wicken, who worked as the president's staff assistant and principal speechwriter) did not go totally smoothly either – no doubt for the same reasons. I had thought that Africa's foremost political leader would have an entirely constructive meeting with the person I considered Africa's foremost economist, and perhaps it was so. But economists can frequently be seen, particularly by politicians and political scientists, as conservative and/or lacking in vision or political understanding. I was given to understand that both Nyerere and Svendsen had some serious disagreements with my Nigerian friend, whom I nonetheless continued to consider the top African economist of his time. (Sadly, he died a few years later, much too early.)

While Tanzanians with postgraduate degrees were still few and far between, there were already some faculty appointees in history, law, education, and, of course, in the university's administration. Wilbert Chagula had already been the Tanzanian vice chancellor of the university for a couple of years when I arrived. But there were not yet any Tanzanian economists either in the teaching department or in the nascent Economic Research Bureau. The first to be appointed to the university was in the ERB, Simon Mbilinyi, much later to become a high-level government official. His wife, Marjorie, an American, also soon joined the education faculty and became an important analyst and activist in the Tanzanian and African women's movement. In my first year in Dar es Salaam, I received a visit from Kighoma Malima, later one of the first Tanzanian lecturers in economics but then still a graduate student at Princeton, when he returned for a home visit. As I recall, I urged him not to plan on an academic career but to work in government where the need for his skills, I thought, was greatest. The following year he ignored my advice and joined the Department of Economics. But he ended up doing what I had recommended, before his premature death, and became the country's minister of planning. The only other Tanzanian university economist during my time, and a very able one, was Justinian Rweyemamu, who joined the teaching department in my last year there. He was later to become a staff member of the international Brandt Commission (see chapter eleven). Unfortunately he too died at a relatively early age, the victim of a car accident. Within less than ten years, however, the entire economics staff – both teaching and research – was Tanzanian.

It is striking, in recollection, how much input to Tanzania was made at that time by the Department of Political Economy of the University of Toronto. My friend Cranford Pratt had been the first vice chancellor of the University of Dar es Salaam, spending four years there before returning to Toronto in 1965. Shortly after we moved from Toronto to Dar es Salaam, we were followed by the chairman of our department, Tom Easterbrook, who worked in the Ministry of Economic Development and Planning (Devplan, as it was colloquially known) for a year, financed by the Ford Foundation. Soon after, David Nowlan, an economist of about my own vintage, joined him there as head of a several-year support program for the ministry that was run by him from our department, financed by the Canadian International Development Agency (CIDA); he also stayed for a year. Another recent Toronto graduate, David Beatty, later to become chief economist for the newly independent government of Papua New Guinea and later still a prominent Canadian businessman and (most recently) a faculty member of the Rotman School of Management at the University of Toronto, came to Devplan from postgraduate studies in England while we were there. Another Toronto graduate, who worked in Devplan after our return home, was W. Edmund (Ed) Clark, who wrote his Harvard PhD thesis on Tanzanian issues; he went on to a distinguished career in the federal civil service and in Canadian banking. Subsequently, Jonathan Barker and Richard Stren, both political scientists from my home department in Toronto, also worked in Dar es Salaam. So did Donald Forster, another economist, who by that time was serving as provost of the University of Toronto; he worked for a summer in Devplan under the auspices of the Ford Foundation–financed training program for which I was by then responsible. It may also be relevant to mention George Davies, a student in one of my early undergraduate courses in Toronto, who went from there directly to a Canadian University Service Overseas (CUSO)–supported post as a regional economist in rural Tanzania (in Bukoba, on the shores of Lake Victoria); he was later prominent in public service in both Ontario and Manitoba, and in international consultancy, and still later was chair of the North-South Institute board.

As I felt was appropriate, I left virtually all of the records of my work in Tanzania – files, minutes, drafts, memos, correspondence, and the like – in the Economic Research Bureau at the university. I have no regrets about having done that. But I now wish that I had made a few copies of some of the contents of my files, because I find that my memory is not good enough to permit me fully or accurately to recall some of the details of what I did there.

Of course, I wrote papers on policy and measurement issues, quite a lot of them. I also hosted an East African conference on agricultural policy and edited its proceedings for publication.[17] But my position required much more than such academic pursuits: fundraising and staff hiring, expatriate staff orientation and handholding, faculty meetings, governmental meetings, and hosting innumerable visitors.

Some activities do stand out in my memory. They include a wonderful tour of the southern and southwestern parts of the country, as part of a three-person team sent by Devplan to assess planning and financial needs at the regional level. We discovered extremely frustrated local leaders who were unable to fix the most obvious and pressing problems – such as repairing washed-out roads – without applying through the relevant central ministry for funding, a process that was extremely slow and uncertain in its results. Our recommendations resulted in the creation of regional development funds, made available to regional authorities to permit them to undertake urgently needed activities without going through the central bureaucracy. This tour included an unforgettable visit to the Ruvuma Development Association (RDA) in a relatively remote part of southwestern Tanzania. The RDA was a remarkable and independent (that is, non-governmental) commu- nal farm, supported by Oxfam and others, which soon thereafter so impressed President Nyerere that he appeared to model his policy of rural socialism upon it. Perhaps they staged it on our behalf (I don't really think they did), but the ox-carts we saw, full of laughing villagers returning from their fields in the late afternoon, certainly did make for rather an idyllic scene. Some years later, party officials – jealous of its success and determined to impose party discipline – closed it all down, a disastrous harbinger of the further major problems associated with the government's attempts to impose socialist villages upon a dubious peasantry.

I also vividly recall a trip to Brussels, in the role of economic advi- sor to the East African team that was attempting to negotiate a prefer- ential trade agreement with the European Economic Community, an agreement on which I was not very keen but which was nevertheless eventually (after my time) achieved. It was in Brussels that I had my first taste of real-world negotiations between unequal parties. The East African delegation was led by Mwai Kibaki (later to be elected Kenya's president), who was intelligent and eloquent, but it was very weakly prepared. Sheikh Mohamed Babu, the radical Zanzibari Tanzanian minister on the team, spoke with vigour about European faults and the need for independence of the French-controlled Comoros Islands in the Indian Ocean, but, as far as I could tell, had little interest in or knowledge of the negotiation details. Although only having arrived in East Africa five months earlier and with much else to do, I was brought along as a technical advisor. Unfortunately, I had little grasp of many of the issues myself. I wrote a simple paper attempting to quantify the potential trade gains to Tanzania from improved access to the European market and gave a seminar at the university on it (for which I was sub- sequently rebuked within government for disclosing confidential infor- mation, which wasn't actually confidential at all). But when the subject of "rights of establishment" emerged, in conversation with European delegates in Brussels, as a major objective of the Europeans, I hardly even knew what the phrase meant. Perhaps there were other better East African strategy meetings somewhere, but the ones I attended in our hotel were equally lacking in background knowledge. I also came to suspect that our rooms were bugged by the Europeans. I hadn't learned about such real-world realities in graduate school.

Off-work life in Dar was busy. We led quite an active social life, entertaining lots of other faculty and a never-ending stream of visitors. Among our better friends were Ole and Bente Moelgaard Andersen and their young family. In subsequent years Ole, by then working for DAN-IDA, the Danish foreign aid agency, was to involve me in all manner of worthwhile ventures in Tanzania, Uganda, and elsewhere in Africa.

We had very little interaction with the diplomatic community. Invited once for dinner by the Canadian chargé d'affaires, we found the multi-courses, several wines, and servants quite off-putting. Once an officer came to visit me at the university to see whether I, with my governmental contacts, could serve as a source of information for him. I believed my position in Tanzania to be one of significant local trust, which I did not want to risk abusing in any way, and I declined as politely as I could. It was subsequently reported to me by another (non-diplomatic) Canadian that my name had arisen in connection with some expatriate debate about Tanzanian events. "Helleiner?" the officer was reported to have said, "Oh, you'll never get anything out of that bastard." I took some (no doubt bizarre) pride in that.

I returned to Tanzania repeatedly after our return to Toronto. When I went back, I found that my department had arranged with the Ford Foundation to begin a modest training program for African civil servants, a program that I was to direct. That program provided an excuse for me to return to East Africa several times during the three years of its duration. There followed a Ford Foundation evaluation of its technical assistance to East Africa in which, together with Benjamin Lewis, an experienced and amiable senior American economist, I participated.

In 1978, much against my better judgment, I was persuaded to lead a World Bank mission to advise on incentives for the promotion of Tanzanian processed agricultural and other products for export. Its work is quite properly long forgotten. I agreed to lead this effort on the basis of my understanding, from Steve O'Brien, then chief economist for Africa within the World Bank, that the Tanzanians had asked for such advice and had specifically asked for me. My antennae should have been alerted when the Bank chose the other members of the (small) team from its own staff, and none had ever worked on Tanzania before. One was Sudanese; the other two were Asians. In the end, none contributed very much to the final report. I have never forgotten some elements of the reception we received upon our arrival. It took several days before our Tanzanian "demanders" were able to find the time to receive us for-mally, days during which I certainly had reason to wonder whether the Tanzanians' purported request for our services had been very urgent or indeed existed at all. The World Bank had long been known to push its missions upon weak borrowing countries that are unable to object.

When we were finally formally welcomed to the country by an appro-priate authority, the welcome consisted of the usual friendly exchange of greetings, inquiry as to the comfort of our lodgings, hope for our enjoyment of our visit to the country, and only the vaguest of refer-ences to the ostensible purpose of our mission. I got a better feeling for my position when I visited, alone, the then principal secretary of the Ministry of Commerce and Industries, Fulgence Kazaura. "So," he said, looking up sceptically from his cluttered desk as I entered his office, "You're the World Bank expert." In my more sceptical mood of the time, it was the wrong thing to say to me. And I reacted with vigour. "I am not from the World Bank. I am not much of an expert. I came because I was told that you wanted my advisory services in your efforts to promote processed exports, and I'm happy to try to provide them. If you do not really want them, I do not want to be here, and I'll head back home as quickly as I can." Or words to that general effect. Kazaura responded well, calmed me down, allowed that, whatever the mission's origins, he thought Tanzania could benefit from our presence, and we subsequently developed a good working relationship on these and, much later, other matters. The quiet young Tanzanian who was assigned as my assistant, Fadhil Mbaga, later was to become Tanzanian high commissioner in Ottawa where, after several years' service there, his seniority led him to become the dean of the Ottawa diplomatic corps. The mission report was delayed for months after our return as I waited for my team mem-bers to submit their promised material to me; they continually pleaded the pressure of other World Bank work and responsibilities. Finally, having received nothing further, I put something together on my own; Steve O'Brien did some serious editing, and a report was submitted to the Tanzanians. It wasn't very good. The whole episode is not some-thing of which I am very proud. I never heard anything further about the report or any response to its recommendations from its recipients. I have long since learned that a good many other such missions have been equally dubious in their origins and equally useless.

In the early 1980s I became a member of what became known locally, no doubt sardonically, as "the three wise men" (together with my colleague Cranford Pratt and Ernst Michanek, former head of the

Swedish aid agency).We were funded by the World Bank to try to find an accommodation between the government of Tanzania and the IMF, relations between which had more or less collapsed. Robert McNamara, then president of the World Bank, was an admirer of the idealistic Tanzanian president, Nyerere, and like many others, was unhappy about the collapse of these relationships, which carried implications for the continuation of the Bank's and other aid donor programs. A senior member of his staff who had previously worked in the planning ministry in Tanzania, Bevan Waide, called me early in 1981 and asked whether I might participate in a World Bank–financed mediation effort in Tanzania that would involve the provision of independent advice on adjustment policies. I told him that, because of other commitments, I could not possibly spend extensive amounts of time in Tanzania but would be happy to support any such efforts. We discussed possible approaches, and one of the ideas that emerged was the creation of a two-tier mechanism: a senior group carrying overall responsibility for the effort, together with a more permanent staff working with the government in Tanzania on the nuts and bolts "on the ground." This idea was subsequently implemented. Michanek, Pratt, and I were to constitute the senior group, with Michanek as our chair. Although the task was overwhelmingly about the development of economic policy, neither Michanek nor Pratt was an economist. I therefore felt that a disproportionate share of the burden of responsibility rested upon me. For the permanent staff, to work in Tanzania for what proved to be about a year, we were fortunately able to recruit Brian Van Arkadie, who had been the principal draftsman of the Second Tanzanian Plan (following the Arusha Declaration), as its head and John Loxley, who also had considerable Tanzanian experience, as his principal support, together with a number of Tanzanian economists seconded from the government for this task.

When our senior group of three (the "wise men") journeyed to Tanzania to initiate the enterprise in the summer of 1981, we were invited to see the president at his beach house. We were greeted most warmly and welcomed back to his country. He wished us well in our efforts. But: "You know," he told us," I asked for money, not advice." In characteristic Nyerere style, he had told us exactly where he and we both stood. A more succinct account of the conditionality issue has probably never been stated. Our efforts were directed toward the development of an alternative adjustment program – one that involved less "shock" and more "gradualism," greater attention to the equity of the burden of its inevitable costs, and the retention of a greater, though still diminished, role for the state in development processes.

In the end, the efforts of our group failed. Neither the government of Tanzania nor the IMF found our suggested adjustment program acceptable. Our failure to persuade the Tanzanians that a significant degree of currency devaluation was required was especially disappointing. I came to the conclusion that, while there may have been pressing political pressures for maintaining a seriously overvalued currency, neither the president nor anyone in his office truly understood exchange rate issues. This incomprehension was perhaps not surprising since they can be complex. What was surprising – and disappointing – was the failure of the planning minister, Kighoma Malima, a respected former professional colleague at the university, to acknowledge the need for devaluation. On more than one occasion, when he was feeling particularly pressed on this issue, he invited a Cambridge University economist, Ajit Singh, to write in the party newspaper and explain to all and sundry the reasons why (apparently) the exchange rate should never be altered. The most charitable interpretation of his position was that the Tanzanians should never undertake policies in which they did not themselves believe in response to pressures from the IMF. With that much I could certainly agree. I recall one long evening in Kighoma's home, at the conclusion of one of our visits to Dar es Salaam, when we debated the merits of alternative possible means of redirecting substantial resources to the agricultural/rural sector. At its conclusion, I agreed to write a memo for Kighoma explaining the reasons why devaluation seemed the best available instrument for the (agreed) purpose. Upon my return to the hotel, I stayed up very late to do so. I later learned that my memo had made him angry. Presumably my attempts to phrase the arguments in terms that could be understood by all, including if necessary those in the president's office, made it appear as if I did not sufficiently recognize his professional expertise. Perhaps I should have tried to make the argument in more political terms. But our evening's discussion had not been concerned with political constraints or concerns. Eventually, of course, devaluation became inevitable; and it was undertaken, of necessity, to a much greater degree than we had originally recommended

Because there has been so much subsequent controversy over Julius Nyerere's attempt to build socialism in one very poor country, it may be worth summarizing my own take on it. (A fuller account can be found in my paper, "An Economist's Reflections on the Legacies of Julius Nyerere."[18]):

> It is now conventional wisdom in Washington ... and in donor capitals, that poverty needs to be addressed as a matter of highest priority; that political stability and good governance (notably reduced corruption) are prerequisites for development; and that national ownership of programmes is critical to their success. It has taken them a long time to reach these positions. But Julius Nyerere was espousing them and trying to build practice upon them 30 years ago. His slogan of "socialism and self-reliance," if transmitted today as "equity, honesty and ownership" would win universal assent. He was decades ahead of his time in these matters.
>
> Yes, Julius Nyerere made some economic policy mistakes. In this he was certainly not alone. He also left a country capable of learning from its experience with a minimum of political ruckus, a country now moving forward economically on a firm political and value base. That is a significant legacy.[19]

Among the most satisfying of my subsequent activities in Tanzania were those undertaken, with the principal support of the government of Denmark, to improve aid relationships in the 1990s. Previously the darling of the aid community, post-Nyerere Tanzania had by 1994 run into serious difficulties with its traditional sources of external finance. Relations became particularly strained in 1993–4 after the finance minister, Kighoma Malima, publicly blamed broken aid promises for problems that the aid community attributed to his own mismanagement. My old colleague and friend from the University of Dar es Salaam in the 1960s, Ole Moelgaard Andersen, now the chief economist for DANIDA, the Danish aid agency, came up with the idea of establishing an independent group to assess the state of aid relationships in Tanzania and to make recommendations for their improvement. He soon won the support, although it was sometimes grudging, of other members of the Nordic group and from the Tanzanians for his proposed initiative. Membership of the group, agreed upon with the government of Tanzania, consisted of two Tanzanians, Benno Ndulu, then at AERC in Nairobi, and Nguyuru Lipumba of the University of Dar es Salaam; Knud Erik Svendsen, now director of the Centre for Development Research, Copenhagen; Tony Killick of the Overseas Development Institute (ODI), London; and me. I was chosen as chairman. We received excellent cooperation from all and got along very well as a group. We were thus able to produce a unanimous report by mid-1995.[20]

By happy chance of timing, the report proved quite influential. We had consciously written it in such a way as to be potentially useful to a newly elected government later that year. When Benjamin Mkapa assumed the Tanzanian presidency in late 1995, he quickly moved to restore good relations with the IMF and thereafter began to draw upon our recommendations. By September 1996 the government of Tanzania had arranged a very fruitful meeting with the Nordic group of aid donors at which the recommendations in our report were discussed and a significant degree of agreement was reached. The most critical further step in the emerging Tanzanian relationship with the aid donors was a meeting between the government of Tanzania and the entire aid donor community in Dar es Salaam in January 1997, a meeting in which Benno Ndulu and I were active. Against all odds, and with noticeable foot dragging in some quarters, this meeting was able to construct "agreed notes" (it would have been impossible to achieve an agreement or probably even to agree on minutes), which were to serve as the basis for a "radical change of rules and roles between the partners in development." Tanzanian "ownership," one of our report's prime points of emphasis, was now to be consciously furthered, according to the agreed notes, both by Tanzanians and by aid donors. Sixteen specific points on which progress could be objectively monitored were agreed. These points included desirable changes in the behaviour of aid donors. It was considered a major triumph – one greatly assisted by the Nordics and the World Bank resident representative, Jim Adams – that donor successes and failures were henceforth to be monitored, as well as those of recipients. To my knowledge, this type of aid relationship had never been set up before. Perhaps most important of all, there was agreement that progress toward the agreed objectives in the new aid relationship would be independently monitored. This change too constituted a major breakthrough.[21]

I was subsequently chosen, with the agreement of the government of Tanzania, to undertake this monitoring function; and I reported to the next few meetings of the consultative group (CG), the annual meeting between the donors and the government to review resource requirements and development progress. In March 1999, at the request of the government of Tanzania, and again with Danish support, I conducted an across-the-board evaluation of progress toward the agreed new form of aid relationship in Tanzania; my report was presented to the

5.1. With President Benjamin Mkapa, United Republic of Tanzania, 1999

CG meeting in Paris a few months later. (President Mkapa very much wanted this meeting to be held in Dar es Salaam, as did I, and my report said so.) I reported that significant progress toward increased Tanzanian ownership of its own development programs, and to improved aid relationships more generally, was, in fact, achieved. The Tanzanian model in this respect later attracted international attention. It undoubtedly played a role in the lead-up to the Organisation for Economic Cooperation and Development (OECD)'s 2005 Paris Declaration on Aid Effectiveness, with its stress on the need for local ownership, recognition of local priorities, and improved donor coordination.[22] As a Danish journalist put it many years later (in a friend's translation):

It would be an exaggeration to claim that this report completely revolutionized global aid and paved the way for the Paris Declaration, which leaders from all over the world adopted in 2005 and which was recently reviewed in Busan in Korea. But it is not wrong, either.[23]

One of the recommendations in my 1999 progress report was that the independent monitoring process should be institutionalized, and this recommendation was readily accepted in principle. I returned to Tanzania for the next (and my last) CG meeting in 2000, where I received a very warm welcome (not least from President Mkapa) and tried to help in the working out of details. I particularly insisted, over some donor objections but eventually successfully, upon the proposed new Tanzania Assistance Strategy being kept separate from (though parallel to) the IMF/World Bank–dominated Poverty Reduction Strategy Paper (PRSP). After some sparring over its terms of reference, the donors and the government of Tanzania agreed on an independent monitoring group (IMG), consisting of two Tanzanians, a Swede, a German, a Brit (Tony Killick again) and a Ugandan – six people to do the job of one! Responsibility for organizing the task rested with an independent Tanzanian research institution, the Economic and Social Research Foundation (ESRF), the director of which was to chair the group. The IMG submitted its (excellent) report to the Tanzania CG meeting in Dar es Salaam in December 2002. This model of independent monitoring of the aid relationship also garnered widespread international attention. (An account of the entire Tanzanian experience with the development of local ownership and the monitoring of aid relationships can be found in my article "Local Ownership and Donor Performance Monitoring," published in 2002.[24]) Subsequent IMG reports were done by similar independent groups, the next chaired again by the same Tanzanian (Sam Wangwe).

Some years later, at a conference in Ottawa, I attempted to summarize what I thought had been learned from this experience:

– Better processes and increased coordination at the recipient country level are possible.
– There are no panaceas in SWAPs [sector-wide approaches], basket funds, or budget support or any other "cure," per se, particularly if they are still subject to stop-go funding (with the IMF as the inappropriate gatekeeper and the risk of other politically motivated rug-pulling), without longer-term commitments.
– Some donors want to move. Some are reluctant. It is best to go forward with those who are willing rather than wait for those who are not.

- Systematic and independent monitoring, by informed and respected personnel, with broad terms of reference is helpful. And supportive local donor(s) may be needed to push the idea since local government cannot.
- Do not expect short-term miracles. Change takes time. Slow and steady is better than crash programmes (and flops).
- There is a risk of "process" overloading and higher transactions costs. Addition of new (programme-based) processes may be a problem if old ones also continue.
- There is likely to be varying success even within the same partner country; for example, in Tanzania, genuinely improved partnership in the health sector seems to work, in some others progress has bogged down.
- Mutual trust and respect are critical. Accountability, transparency, and commitment to learning are essential.
- It is helpful to have considerable devolution of donor authority, with adequate capacity to act and, of course, headquarters support for overall objectives (in this case, WB, now UNDP and UK, and always Scandinavians were key).
- Personalities matter (on both sides). Tanzania was lucky. There were remarkable Tanzanian(s) and donor representatives (including World Bank).
- Technical assistance is especially sensitive – because it is often unwanted by partners, has a poor benefit/cost record, and is usually tied.

Conclusion: The Tanzanian model isn't for everyone, but it is replicable and deserves attention.[25]

Parts of this entire experience with country-level aid relationships were enormously pleasurable and satisfying to me. I renewed many old friendships, made many new friends, saw some of the details of aid relationships "up close" in a way that few outsiders are privileged to see, learned a lot, and, I hope, contributed something. Particularly memorable was the time I spent (only a few days but, in retrospect, it seems as if it was much longer) in a comfortable seaside hotel on the outskirts of Dar es Salaam, recommended by Benno Ndulu as a perfect place to do my required writing without interruption, when I was competing my report in March 1999. My room had a view over the Indian Ocean. I was indeed able to write without interruption, and, wonderfully, to look up from my work from time to time to watch the dhows and the hovercraft to Zanzibar go by. I was blessed with the secretarial and editing assistance of John Zutt (my former student Kate Fleming's husband), who worked for me in the evenings on a purely voluntary basis in addition to his full-time job at the United Nations Development Programme (UNDP) office. Kate, who was a UNICEF program manager for Tanzania, brought their three little children over to the hotel for a swim and a meal one day, and I shared my last dinner at the hotel with John and Kate. A month later John emailed the devastating news that Katie had left us. (Shortly after, Georgia and I flew to her home town, Thunder Bay, with her other good friends, Stephen Lewis and Michele Landsberg, for her heart-wrenching funeral.)

The generally pleasurable experience of this extended effort to improve aid relationships in Tanzania, however, also had its costs. Shortly after my return to Toronto from the fateful Dar es Salaam meeting of January 1997, I developed a high fever. Initially assuming I had contracted malaria (again), I went down to the emergency clinic at the Toronto General Hospital, where I thought they would be better able to handle it than in any nearby facility. The malaria tests turned out negative, however, and I set about my return home on the subway. But I had not realized how sick by that time I had become. It was all I could do, with several long periods of rest on the way, to drag myself from the subway stop to our house. It turned out that I had hepatitis A, no doubt picked up from food or water about which I had not been careful enough while in Dar es Salaam; and I spent the next few months in bed, with periodic more difficult intervals, when things turned sharply down for me, in the hospital. My good friend and colleague Albert Berry took over my remaining teaching obligations. I guess I also need to add that my return from Dar es Salaam (and Sri Lanka, where I had run a Technical Group meeting of the G-24 in Colombo before going to Tanzania) in late March 1999 had also left me pretty well exhausted, with my right arm and shoulder twitching and painful. As I said above, I am proud of it all – but there were some costs.

What I thought was to be my last visit to Tanzania, in 2000, seemed to be charmed. As we flew in across Kenya and Tanzania, snow-topped Mount Kilimanjaro, which was more often hidden by cloud, stood out magnificently against a clear sky, even more magnificently than I had remembered it – one last hurrah, it seemed, just for my benefit. (Experts on global warming say that there will quite soon be no more snows on Kilimanjaro.) There followed another happy "last hurrah" – in the newly built Dar es Salaam airport, upon my departure. I was putting in time waiting for my flight home in a little gift shop in the airport when I spotted a pile of watercolours, done by local painters, of Tanzanian scenes. Flipping quickly through them I noticed one which seemed to be very familiar – it looked very much like a picture of the Ocean Road Hospital where our son Peter was born. I asked the attendant if she knew what it was. She didn't. I flipped through some more and, to my delight, found another of the same scene, this time clearly marked by the artist, "Ocean Road Hospital, Dar es Salaam." This one was tattered and dirty; but, of course, I had to have it. It cost me all of five dollars. Clean, spruced up, and framed, it now hangs proudly on the living room wall of our condo in Toronto. This story goes on. Shortly after my return, I recounted this experience to my friends, Cranford and Renate Pratt. To my astonishment they told me that their daughter, Anna, had also been born there. "Could I possibly get another?" Of course, I knew there was another. I emailed Benno Ndulu, still working in Dar es Salaam, described the picture and where it was, and asked if he could get it for me. It arrived – by courier – a week later, in time to serve as a university graduation present for Anna. I gather it has hung on the walls of her offices at Brock and York Universities where she has been teaching. Let me complete the story. When he heard of it, Benno bought still another copy of the picture for himself – he too had a child born in the same hospital.

My very last visit to Tanzania came in connection with a conference in Arusha in September 2007. The conference, organized by International Lawyers and Economists Against Poverty (ILEAP), a non-governmental organization (NGO) with which I was associated (see chapter seventeen), was to focus on trade-related capacity building issues, and it attracted excellent international and African representation. I had foolishly offered to serve as backup in case those invited to be keynote speakers were unable to come; and in the end none of the first-choice invitees were able to make it. I had no difficulty stepping into the breach since the subject was fairly close to my heart. It was a good meeting. Our conference chair, Ali Mchumo, a Tanzanian, was able to get us quite high-level attention and television coverage. I was quite moved when Benjamin Mkapa, the former president of the country, at his formal conference-opening address, departed from his text to say some kind words about me.

The great beauty of this last trip was that I was able to persuade daughter Jane to accompany me (to look after her fragile dad). She had not been back to Tanzania since we left when she was only seven years

5.2. With Jim Adams, World Bank, and Benno Ndulu at Tanzania Aid Donors'
Consultative Group meeting, Dar es Salaam, 2000

old. After the conference we flew down to Dar es Salaam where Ibrahim Nguyuru Lipumba, now leader of a major opposition party, met
us at the airport and took us ably in hand. His generous loan of his
party car and driver made it easy for us to visit many of our old haunts:
State House, Ocean Road Hospital (where Peter was born), Oyster Bay,
Kariakoo market, the beaches, the university. Heavy traffic, commercial billboards, and a greatly expanded city gave it quite a different air
from the old days; but, in many respects, it had not greatly changed. We
stayed very comfortably in the old Kilimanjaro Hotel, now Kempinski-
owned luxury accommodation, overlooking the harbour. The harbour
scene and its people were just as interesting – beautiful in their own
way – as ever. On the other hand, the depleted stock in what used to be
quite a decent bookshop off Independence (now Samora Machel) Avenue and the chugging, smelly generators in front of most of the shops in

the area – protection against the frequent power outages – were rather depressing. On the university grounds we were able to find our old house on Koroshoni Road, now looking altogether different with much shrubbery and grown trees that were not there forty years previously. We had a relaxed lunch at a lovely and almost deserted beach resort (Kunduchi Beach), enjoyed watching the Swahili fishermen bringing their boats back to next-door Kunduchi village, as they long have done, and wondered what tourism was doing to their way of life. On our last afternoon we boarded a ten-seater plane for a quick trip to Zanzibar, where we explored the ancient UN Educational, Scientific and Cultural Organization (UNESCO)–heritage Stone Town (now with an unfortunate plethora of tourist curio shops in the central area). The view of the blues and greens of the Indian Ocean and its offshore reefs from a small plane was, as always, quite breathtaking. Quite a wonderful way to say a truly final goodbye to Tanzania.

Sadly, by 2016, Tanzanian aid relationships, on which such apparent progress had earlier been achieved, had soured again. Although Tanzania's overall economic performance was quite respectable, aid donors were fed up with what they saw as Tanzanian government malfeasance, the government of Tanzania saw donor behaviour as unduly intrusive and unreliable, and mutual trust had broken down once more. Efforts were being made to reopen genuine dialogue, building upon the "Helleiner model" of the 1990s. But the political and economic context and the personalities were now quite different, and so inevitably would have to be workable solutions.

6 Uganda

I have had a long-standing relationship with Uganda. It began with my good graduate school friend Donald Mead, whose PhD thesis addressed some of its problems, and it continued when Don, who had previously accepted a Rockefeller Foundation–financed appointment in Makerere University's economics department in Kampala, invited me as a visiting professor for the summer of 1966 (one year after our move from Yale to Toronto). That visiting appointment never materialized since we went to Dar es Salaam, Tanzania, instead. But from my Tanzanian base I had many opportunities to visit Uganda in connection with my ERB responsibilities and my participation in Tanzania governmental committees.

I subsequently participated in three quite exciting "missions" in Uganda. The first, led by Dudley Seers, at that time the director of the Institute of Development Studies at the University of Sussex, was sent by the Commonwealth Secretariat to assess the economic situation following the Tanzanian invasion that overthrew the brutal Ugandan president, Idi Amin, in the spring of 1979. At the behest of the then Commonwealth secretary-general, Sir Shridath (Sonny) Ramphal, I had travelled to Sussex from Oxford, where I was on sabbatical at the time, to persuade Dudley – not without some difficulty – that he absolutely had to undertake this assignment. He eventually agreed, and we set about putting together a multi-skilled team. Sir Egerton Richardson, an eminent Jamaican ex-diplomat, agreed to be Dudley's deputy. My colleague in the economics department at Toronto, David Nowlan, who had worked in the planning ministry in Tanzania at the same time that I had been there, agreed to join the team, taking responsibility for analysis of the transport sector. Deryke Belshaw, an agricultural economist who had worked for many years in the Faculty of Agriculture at Makerere, also agreed to join, and proved to be a critically important element of the team. Others with African experience included Michael Bentil from Ghana and Sam Montsi from Lesotho. Further skills were provided by two Australians and an Indian, who offered the extra bonus of the requisite Commonwealth balance. In retrospect, it is striking that the group contained not a single Ugandan. The two-volume report – *The Rehabilitation of the Economy of Uganda*[26] – was really very good; it is unfortunate that it is such a museum piece, not found in very many libraries. From start to finish this mission proved to be an extremely exciting enterprise, about which more in the "Commonwealth Post–Idi Amin Mission" section later in this chapter.

The next of my Uganda missions followed the victory in 1986 by the young troops of the rebel former cabinet minister, former University of Dar es Salaam student, Yoweri Museveni, over those of the corrupt and brutal government of Milton Obote. Obote had returned from Tanzanian exile, to the hopes of many, following the ouster of Idi Amin, but led his country disastrously downward again. Suleiman Kiggundu, a young Ugandan economist whom I had come to know while he had been working in the Nairobi office of Canada's International Development Research Centre (IDRC) with my ex-student Jeffrey Fine and who was close to Museveni, invited me to lead a mission, to be financed by the IDRC, to offer macroeconomic advice to the new revolutionary government. I was unable to undertake this job at the time, but recommended my former colleague in Tanzania, now in Manitoba, John Loxley. It was eventually agreed that John and Suleiman would be joint leaders of the "IDRC group." I agreed to put in a few days in Uganda working for the group, and subsequently did so, writing short papers on currency reform and the necessary degree of exchange rate action, neither of which ever saw the light of day. The joint leadership generated great difficulty when Kiggundu, who should have known much better, followed his "political" instincts and held out for the presentation of a (lunatic) currency *revaluation* option in the final report as well as the certainly required massive currency devaluation. Although the report accurately predicted the disastrous results that would follow from the revaluation option, that was the policy that the government at first chose to pursue, before being driven by experience to a more sane course. This mission too proved to be an exciting, if somewhat depressing, experience, about which more in the "Missions with Museveni" section later in this chapter.

In 1993 I chaired another independent working group in Uganda, this time sponsored by the government of Denmark. Sven Riskaer, the head of the Danish Industrialization Fund for Developing Countries, had heard me speak at a seminar in Copenhagen on African adjustment programs in the previous year and had evidently been impressed with some of my critique of World Bank approaches and analyses in Africa. He had been asked by President Museveni for fresh advice on elements of Uganda's efforts at stabilization, adjustment, and development. This group included two prominent Ugandans, Ezra Suruma, the managing director of the National Bank of Commerce, the state-owned commercial bank, and William Kalema, a businessman who was also treasurer in the court of the traditional monarch, the Kabaka of Buganda; Riskaer himself; and two other Danes, Per Pinstrup-Andersen, director-general of the International Food Policy Research Institute (IFPRI), for which I was then the chairman of the board, and my old friend from Tanzania days, Ole Moelgaard Andersen. It was clearly intended, in the context of Uganda's austere IMF and World Bank–supported adjustment programs, to offer the government a second opinion regarding Uganda's needs; and it did so sufficiently effectively that, when our report was published by the government, it began with a statement by the president that Ugandans should "leave no stone unturned in the effort to implement its recommendations." Not everyone within Museveni's government, however, thought so highly of our effort. This story too requires, and will receive, a more complete account in the "Missions with Museveni" section later in the chapter.

The Commonwealth Post–Idi Amin Mission

The Commonwealth (Seers) mission to Uganda, following the Tanzanian overthrow of the Idi Amin government, which itself followed the Ugandan invasion of northwest Tanzania (the "Kagera Salient"), provided adventures from start to finish. The "advance guard" of the mission – Seers, Richardson, and me – had to travel to Entebbe, the capital, by somewhat unorthodox means since the airport there was closed. Our route was via Dar es Salaam, Tanzania, to which we travelled by very comfortable British Airways. The transition from the first leg of our travel to the second was therefore something of a shock. The second leg consisted of cramped back seats on a small plane belonging to the Tanzanian Air Force; the plane landed for refueling in Mwanza on the shores of Lake Victoria before heading off across the lake to the closed airport at Entebbe. Dramatic thunderhead clouds reflected the sun of a beautiful East African afternoon. Our planeload was somewhat apprehensive about what might lie before us in the chaotic situation of postwar Uganda, but the sheer beauty of our surroundings overcame some of our anxieties – at least for a while. Our situation, however, soon became quite alarming as we approached the airport. Our Tanzanian pilot radioed the control tower in the Entebbe airport about our impending arrival, seeking clearance for landing. There was no reply. He radioed again. No reply. Again and again he sought to make contact with the airport. By now we were overhead and could see the landing strip, which had several bomb craters in it, and the main airport building's shattered windows – evidently the product of the fighting of previous days. Still more alarming was the string of anti-aircraft batteries surrounding the runway. It was obvious to us all that in the chaos of the situation there was, in fact, no one in the airport's control tower, and the guns surrounding the runway were mandated to discourage unfriendly landings and were pointed more or less in our direction. Praying that the Tanzanian gunners would recognize the aircraft as one of their own we went in for our landing – and I guess they did. A small group of Tanzanian officers came to meet us and escorted us through the broken glass and gloom of the half-destroyed airport building. There were no immigration or customs formalities! Our departure about three weeks later was to be no less unusual.

The thirty-mile drive from Entebbe to Kampala, where we were to work, was just as beautiful as I had remembered it. Uganda has often been described as "the pearl of Africa."[27] Its green and fertile soils, rolling tree-covered hills and mountains, bounteous banana plantations, and the animation and colourful dress of its diverse peoples have long combined to create an overwhelming impression upon European travellers. All was as it had always been for me, except scattered along either side of the road was now the detritus of war: blown-out military vehicles, half-destroyed buildings, shattered glass. What a mess humanity makes, I remember reflecting, of the basic beauty of the earth. Will we never learn?

The food distribution system of Uganda had broken down during the war and the chaotic period thereafter. Whereas there was plenty of food in the rural areas and villages – as we saw most dramatically when we were invited one Sunday afternoon to a sumptuous celebration in a village not more than twenty miles outside Kampala – there was very little food available in the markets and shops of the main cities. Our hotel had just as much difficulty acquiring food as anyone else. The principal food available everywhere was the staple: bananas. So we ate bananas. We had bananas for breakfast and, at lunchtime, we sent someone out to get more bananas. Only at dinner in the hotel was there modest variety – I still don't know how they managed it – as we sat at table every evening, with the electricity flickering on and off, and sporadic gunfire in the background. Some years later I read of a banana diet that was said to be very effective for weight reduction. I can vouch for the truth of this promise: I lost about twenty pounds in three weeks. Exercise may also, however, have had something to do with it. My room was on the twelfth floor of a hotel in which the elevator functioned only sporadically. In truth, none of us was too confident about the elevator (we could not imagine when it might last have been inspected), and we usually walked up and down even when it appeared to be functioning.

One of those with whom I walked up and down the stairs, chatting about the local situation, was a Ugandan businessman and former minister in an Obote cabinet, who had been in exile in the United States and was considering moving back, he told me, following the demise of Amin. He thought there could be a real business opportunity in chicken farming. His room was on the same floor as mine. His name was Godfrey Binaisa.

My hotel room was interesting. The sheets were, for obvious reasons, never changed. The towels looked as if, in the words of one of my colleagues, "they had first been used by the entire Tanzanian army." The (cold) water was of dubious quality. I was pleased to discover that in the drawer of the bedside table, where there is frequently a Bible, there now was an English-language copy of the Koran, no doubt part of Idi Amin's effort to build a different Uganda. Never having read this important religious text, I was quite looking forward to the furtherance of my (inadequate) religious education in my spare time in the evenings (if the power was on). But on the third or fourth day there, when I opened the drawer, what should I discover but that the Koran had gone, replaced by a Gideon Bible. Uganda was reverting to previous form. On our first Sunday there, at the Anglican cathedral, I saw further evidence of the degree of changeover. Fervent prayers were offered thanking the Almighty (and Julius Nyerere) for having "delivered" Uganda from its oppressive leadership, and, it seemed to me, the traditional hymns were sung with even greater gusto than usual. In the early days, the newspapers were full of advertisements in which various business people expressed their thanks to Julius Nyerere and the Tanzanian army for their efforts on behalf of the Ugandan people. Inevitably, as the occupying Tanzanians stayed on, Ugandans' enthusiasm began to wane. Even the best of occupying armies behave inappropriately from time to time; and this one was certainly no exception. I had more than one stressful encounter with Tanzanian soldiers myself.

One took place outside the central bank, the Bank of Uganda, where then governor, Charles Kikonyogo, had received me and explained some of the difficulties of working under the Amin regime. For some time the government had been printing money without appropriate authorization through the device of "ways and means advances." The protests of monetary authorities went unheeded. Indeed the corridors of the central bank were filled with stacks of its old annual reports, which contained objective analyses of the emerging monetary (and inflationary) situation; the reports had been printed but the government had refused to authorize their distribution. As I left the bank, I failed to notice that an armed Tanzanian soldier was trying to get my attention, indeed, as I was to discover, was ordering me to stop for questioning. "Sssst," I heard; but I failed to take it in. Again, "Sssst," and then again. Only then did I notice that a number of Ugandans were waving at me and pointing to the soldier. Needless to say I stopped. The soldier came over, and he did not look friendly. His machine gun was pointed at me. A crowd quickly gathered about us presumably to watch the entertainment. Fortunately for me, the entertainment did not last long. Someone had raced up to the governor's office to tell him of what was transpiring for his recent guest on the street below. He quickly came down and calmed the situation, explaining who I was and why I was there. But this incident made me far more careful from then on to keep my eyes and ears on my surroundings and their possible unfriendly surprises.

Late one afternoon, when our main work for the day had been done, Sir Egerton and I took one of our cars, with its Ugandan driver, to go and see the war damage done in the nearby town of Mbarara. We had been told that the damage to the town during the fighting had been extensive, and we wanted to try to make an estimate of what the costs of rebuilding it might be. As we neared the town we were stopped at a Tanzanian military checkpoint. Sir Egerton and I were sitting in the backseat, and he was carrying his briefcase on his lap. The Tanzanian military person looked in on us and launched into an angry and energetic exposition in Swahili, which was directed at us but which neither of us understood. Since he was carrying a submachine gun, which he brandished and periodically pointed at us, this situation was more than a little disconcerting. There followed an extensive inter-change between the Tanzanian soldier and our driver. At first the sol-dier seemed to be showing expressions of disbelief such as persons in authority frequently display when excuses are offered. Gradually, however, his mood began to change, he eventually even smiled, and finally he nodded and with evident good humour waved us on our way. "What on earth was that all about?" we asked our driver. The Tanzanian soldier, he told us, had delivered a passionate lecture in which he told us that in his country they no longer allowed Africans to be beholden to wazungu (white men) and that they would not allow it in Uganda either. Apparently he had assumed that the very black-skinned, silver-haired, and distinguished senior diplomat – about thirty years my senior – sitting beside me, briefcase in hand, was my assistant. Unfortunately, in the African context of the time, this assumption was not so unreasonable. When it was patiently explained to the soldier that the reverse was, in fact, the case – that Sir Egerton was my boss – what had initially appeared to be a difficult situation turned quickly into a minor celebration.

Nearly three weeks into our Ugandan assignment there were dra-matic and unexpected political developments that put an early end to our work in Kampala. I woke up late at night to the sound of loud chant-ing and cheering in the distance. I went to my window and saw crowds and commotion in the vicinity of the other major hotel, Nile Mansions. Soon a large crowd began coming in our direction. As it got nearer, it was possible to make out some of what they were chanting: "Lule, Lule, Lule," the name of the acting head of the government, who had invited us to Uganda and with whom we met shortly after our arrival. The marching and cheering came right past our hotel. Suddenly, seemingly from above us (probably from the roof of our hotel), there was a burst of machine-gun fire. The crowd scattered. More machine-gun fire. Shouts of alarm. Panic. Then, a little further away, the resumption of the chant: "Lule, Lule, Lule." Periodic further bursts of machine-gun fire and crowd noises did not offer much opportunity for sleep for the rest of the night. I wrote in the small diary that I kept at the time, "All things con-sidered, I would rather be in Philadelphia," the sardonic inscription on a New England tombstone of which I had read. Michael Bentil later told me I had been crazy to go to the window that night; he had himself gone under the bed. Assembling early the next morning around a radio, we listened to the BBC news. President Lule had been replaced overnight in a coup in Uganda, we heard, according to a press statement from the new government. The new acting president was Godfrey Binaisa, my chicken farming acquaintance at the hotel.

We learned as well, from the BBC, which seemed to be much better informed about what was going on around us than any of us were, that the airport at Entebbe, only recently reopened, was once again closed to international traffic. Needless to say we worried. Further machine-gun fire in the vicinity of the hotel and some further demonstrations added to our unease. Eventually word came from the Commonwealth Secretariat: they had permission to send in a small aircraft to "lift" us out. We travelled to the airport with a military escort. Dudley Seers and I shared a car in which soldiers with rifles sat on either side of us, and military vehicles led and backed our convoy. When our little aircraft – the only one that left Entebbe that day – landed in Nairobi, Michael Bentil leaned to the Kenyan ground and kissed it. I went to a telephone as quickly as I could and called Georgia in Oxford to tell her that we were out and we were safe. "What do you mean, safe?" she asked. Happily, she had heard nothing of what was going on – and was certainly foremost in our minds – in Uganda.

Missions with Museveni: 1986 and 1993

In the June/July1986 mission in support of the new Museveni government, led by John Loxley, I arrived late and left early. Some vivid memories nevertheless remain.

I have never forgotten the amazingly young soldiers who came to inspect our rooms at our hotel – looking for hidden weapons, they said. (I was sharing quarters with Just Faaland, a prominent Norwegian development economist whom I had known for some years and with whom I would subsequently work again at IFPRI.) As we stood somewhat nervously aside, three or four boys with rifles, their voices not yet changed, very politely and very earnestly poked about our bedclothes and our bathroom until satisfied that we constituted no threat to anyone. They were very disciplined, very polite, and very efficient. They could not have been more than thirteen years old. Some of our experiences at the many checkpoints within the city of Kampala at the time were similar. It was an army the like of which I had never previously imagined. Sadly, child soldiers have since become a more common phenomenon.

Also memorable were the bags of bank notes that we carried with us to undertake even the most minor of transactions. The largest denominations available did not purchase very much. At that time the cost of printing a bank note (at De La Rue in the United Kingdom), I learned from the central bank, was about US 8 cents, whereas its domestic purchasing power was much less than that. I had read about this phenomenon in textbooks, but I had never before seen such hyperinflation up close.

In the 1993 mission I was to be in charge. President Museveni had asked, or perhaps had been persuaded to ask, for a mission of economists to offer a second opinion on the advice he was receiving from the IMF and the World Bank. Since Uganda was at that time among the most-cited models of successful IMF/World Bank activity in Africa, and by now the recipient of enormous new aid flows from the very impressed donor community, this mission seemed too golden an opportunity to miss. Uganda was at last fairly stable (except in its North) both in political and economic terms. Whether short-term stabilization could lead to renewed and sustained development, however, was still an open question.

On the way to Uganda this time I was seated beside a slightly older, distinguished-looking African. Over a late high-altitude dinner we got to chatting. I discovered that he was Ugandan, and he seemed very knowledgeable about the local scene. We chatted some more, and I discovered that he was, in fact, the husband of Germina Ssemogerere, an economist at Makerere University who had long been active in the AERC network and whom I knew quite well. (She had come to my hotel during our 1986 mission, as a friend, to tell us of the plight of ordinary Ugandans and to plead with us for a report that would be both sympathetic and technically useful. Later, I was to be an external referee for her academic promotion.) Perhaps more important, he was at that time the leader of the political opposition and a vigorous opponent of Museveni's one-party rule, a matter about which I then heard a great deal more. He was, for obvious reasons, very interested in my "mission," about which he had not heard. As it turned out, neither had anyone else. In the immigration area at Entebbe airport, I met Paul Collier who had been on the same flight. He and some UK colleagues were prominent in the provision of policy advice to the government at the time, and he knew nothing of us either. Later, I learned that he had been highly critical of such "second opinion" missions at a public conference in Europe, although when I subsequently asked him about it he denied that he had any problem with our report.

I have a very fond memory of our group's initial meeting with President Museveni at his State House. We all assembled on chairs under a large shade tree on the lawn of the grounds, where we discussed his expectations of our work. I had the impression that he was at first a little vague about why we were there, but he eventually warmed to the subject, offered all possible assistance, and wished us well. Several photographers recorded our meeting under the tree, and I would have dearly loved to have had a record of it; but unfortunately I never received one.

During this first visit, some tensions arose as to the nature of the enterprise and, in particular, the role of its sponsor, the Danish government. The Danish embassy in Kampala, while organizing some of our visits, had announced us, I discovered, as the "Danish mission" rather than the presidential mission that I had been led to believe it was. Moreover, Sven Riskaer, its prime organizer, brought a young acolyte along for our initial interviews, making for a very large crowd indeed. When I expressed my discomfort, in confidence, to my old friend Ole Moelgaard Andersen, who had persuaded me to head this mission, he supported me completely and urged me to act on my views as I saw fit. I did so at the next full meeting of the group, held at the Danish embassy with the ambassador and, to my even further discomfort, several more Danish staff in attendance. I insisted that the mission be described in all subsequent communications as a presidential mission rather than a Danish one, and that only mission members should attend mission meetings, thereby excluding not only Mr Riskaer's assistant but also the ambassador and his staff. The ambassador was very angry. I stood my ground. He eventually calmed down and, by the time our work was complete, we were on cordial terms again. I suspect that Ole played an important role in smoothing these waters.

Our second (three-week) period in Uganda included an unforgettable trip around the southwest of the country from which both Ezra Suruma and the president had come. We spoke with many local leaders, businessmen, and representatives of other groups, and we visited farms, cooperatives, and small factories. We travelled in three cars, and everywhere we drove we were accompanied, to ensure our safety, by armed guards. For me the highlight of the trip was a meeting with a women's group in Ezra's beautiful home area. The meeting took place in a small building in a village on top of a hill to which about a hundred women came from all directions. I asked them, through a translator (Ezra), what they would like us to tell the president, and they spoke eloquently of their problems, which included the difficulty of acquiring credit and the

6.1. Presidential Advisory Mission – with Ezra Suruma, Kate Fleming, Ole
Moelgaard Andersen, Per Pinstrup-Andersen, Sven Riskaer, and William
Kalema, rural Uganda, 1993

laziness of their men. I promised them that we would pass their words
on to him, and I like to think that, in our report, we eventually did.
Kate Fleming, our rapporteur and secretary, about whom more shortly,
interacted wonderfully with them and their children, holding some of
the children for photographs.

Our return to the capital offered another remarkable experience. To
save us time, an army helicopter was sent to pick us up at a small air-
field not far from the western border, and, after treating us to a wonderful low-level aerial tour across the country – low enough for us to see
the villagers looking up at us and waving as we passed overhead – it
dropped us on the front lawn of the Entebbe hotel where we were to
finish the drafting of our report.

I spoke of Kate (Katie as we called her) Fleming. I had known Kate
ever since meeting her when I was a visitor lecturing at St Francis Xavier

University in Antigonish, Nova Scotia, many years before. She later was a Rhodes scholar at Oxford and worked with Stephen Lewis, then Canadian ambassador at the United Nations. Still later she became a student in one of my postgraduate courses and a very good friend. At this time she was working for UNICEF in its Nairobi office, and she had her husband, John Zutt, and a young daughter with her. I had been able to think of no one better suited to provide secretarial and other backup for an enterprise of this kind, and she was already in the general area. Her intelligence, commitment, knowledge, and sheer energy seemed to me to be exactly what we needed. I was able to persuade UNICEF, through Richard Jolly, to lend her to us, and DANIDA to finance her. When we had our first mission meetings in Uganda she brought her family with her, and my colleagues were as delighted as I was to meet them. Her contributions to the success of the mission – as organizer, secretary, and all-round support person, apart from her wonderful company – were enormous. Sadly, as I have recounted earlier, a few years later, while serving as program director in the UNICEF office in Dar es Salaam, her scintillating and productive life came to a premature end. The receipt of the news was devastating for family and friends, and for me.

Our report addressed many policy issues, but the most important message was that it was time for both the government and peoples of Uganda to think beyond short-term stabilization and begin planning, both politically and in terms of policy, for longer-term development.[28] Strict repression of demand on macroeconomic grounds was throttling all prospect of voluntary investment. After our report was completed and printed – a few weeks later – we returned for a meeting with President Museveni and senior members of his cabinet and civil service. Sitting beside him, I was very impressed to see that he had scribbled comments and questions beside several paragraphs. He asked unusually technical questions for a head of state: How were we able to estimate the savings rate? What exactly would privatization do for the development effort? At one point when one of his people – Emmanuel Tumusiime-Mutebile, then permanent secretary of the Ministry of Finance – tried to voice his views, Museveni told him, "No. No. I want to hear the Professor." How many leaders, I wondered, take this much trouble to read technical materials and listen to outside views on them? Since parts of what we said were implicitly critical, his own government was not as keen on our report as he, at least at first, seemed to be. After a public meeting to discuss it a few months later, which I was unable to get to but which, I was told by Per Pinstrup-Andersen who did attend, had featured considerable criticism of us, the report was quietly shelved.

My admiration for Yoweri Museveni was subsequently considerably tempered as his administration fell prey to many of the manifestations of governments that have been in office too long. Increasing corruption, continuing persecution of opponents, and a constitutional amendment to enable Museveni to continue in office beyond the originally stipulated terms were all disturbing. So were his support for rebel military activities in the Republic of the Congo, scorched-earth tactics in response to the (Lord's Day) rebellion in his own North, and his very odd support for the US war in Iraq. Nor was I impressed with his wife's overwhelming and unhelpful emphasis upon sexual abstinence, rather than condoms, in Uganda's battle against HIV/AIDS. (The previously quite successful Uganda anti-AIDS campaign had featured an "ABC" slogan: Abstinence, Be Faithful, Condoms.) Later, through friendship with a fellow African Capacity Building Foundation (ACBF) board member, I learned more details of the emerging political situation in Uganda. Before her flight into exile, Winnie Byanyima had been a highly popular and critical MP representing the Mbarara constituency; she had previously been an ally of Museveni but was now married to his principal opponent, and his former doctor, in the renewed Ugandan presidential elections, Kizza Besigye. She is now the head of Oxfam International. Her stories of her husband's and her own personal persecution and her flight were not reassuring.

7 South Africa

During the years of apartheid government in South Africa I was moderately active, though obviously not in the (overseas) front lines, in the struggle against it. I participated in the founding meetings and some of the activities of the Committee for a Just Canadian Policy Towards Africa in the 1970s. This group, organized in the first instance by my friend and political science colleague Cranford Pratt, was best known for its Black Paper,[29] which argued forcefully for a tougher stance on the part of Canada and other countries in their policies toward the South African government. I had a role in such economic analysis as it contained. I also co-authored, in 1971, a committee paper with Robert Matthews and Linda Freeman on "The Commonwealth at Stake,"[30] arguing in advance of a Commonwealth heads of government meeting (CHOGM) that Canada should side with the developing country members in opposition to Mrs Thatcher's government's plans to sell arms to the South Africans. More than once I journeyed to Ottawa to lobby politicians, notably Trade Minister Jean-Luc Pepin, on the need for Canada to distance itself more effectively and reduce encouragements, at that time even including tariff preferences, for trade with South Africa. Periodically I supplied questions on these issues for friendly members of Canadian Parliament, such as Andrew Brewin, to ask the Canadian government during parliamentary question period. I once gained some press and thereby immediate partial success in June 1971 as a result of my testimony before a House of Commons committee. It followed an unsatisfactory exchange of letters with External Affairs Minister Mitchell Sharp in which I had urged the cessation of all sales cooperation between Air Canada and South African Airways, both of them at that time Crown corporations, and he had argued against doing so. I then testified to the effect that Air Canada, through an agreement with South African Airways on a package tour, was in formal breach of UN-approved international sanctions against Rhodesia. The press reported my testimony, and the following day Air Canada announced that it would stop distributing the relevant brochures (although unfortunately it did not stop selling the tours). Perhaps ultimately more satisfying for an academic was the request, made by the committee chairman on that occasion, that I supply them with more complete information on the welfare of black South Africans, relative to other South Africans and Africans in other countries; I was happy to do so.

On one unforgettable occasion in May 1970, a group of academics and activists held a conference at Carleton University on these issues, stimulated by the failure of the Department of External Affairs to hold a "policy review conference" on Africa, although it did so for every other major area; Minister of External Affairs Mitchell Sharp, presumably as a sign of his openness to all points of view, held an official luncheon for us. Wine was served, and the waiters, as they often do, had wrapped the bottles in white towelling. One of the guests asked a waiter to unwrap a bottle so that we could see what we were drinking. Unbelievably, the wine was South African – this after we had spent half the morning discussing how to reduce or eliminate governmental encouragements to Canadian trade with South Africa. The word was quickly spread, and all of the luncheon guests quickly turned their glasses upside down. One of his aides informed Mr Sharp. There followed a somewhat flustered apology, and a new wine was ordered.

My primary involvement with South Africa had to await the release of Nelson Mandela from prison in early 1990 and the subsequent transition to a democratically elected African National Congress (ANC) government. In June 1990 Mandela came to Canada and requested of Brian Mulroney, then prime minister, among other things (notably, support in the area of constitutional reform), assistance in the development of a capacity for economic analysis and policy formulation on the part of the members of the Mass Democratic Movement (MDM, as anti-apartheid groups were collectively known at that time). Responsibility for the response to this request was assigned to the IDRC (of which at that time I was a governor) and it, together with the Department of Economic Policy of the ANC, soon asked me to lead a mission to assess the immediate needs for economic policy analysis, and the existing capacity of the MDM within South Africa to conduct it, and to suggest next steps to address identified gaps. The mission was to be composed of

South Africans nominated by the ANC and a small number of "external members," jointly selected; it was to be serviced by the then IDRC representative (although he wasn't yet called that) in South Africa, Marc van Ameringen. I made it a condition of my participation that Benno Ndulu, a Tanzanian, then research coordinator of AERC in Nairobi, be one of the limited number of external members. The other was an old friend from Tanzania days, whom I had helped to bring to Canada, John Loxley; in this case, I did not select him myself, but I certainly supported his name when it was offered.

Our group travelled to Johannesburg in July 1991. Although Benno had much more direct means of travelling from Nairobi to Johannesburg, the situation in South Africa was still sufficiently uncertain at that time, so we readily agreed to his suggestion that he enter the country by travelling together with us from London. At the Johannesburg airport, we carefully positioned ourselves in the immigration line so that, in case of any possible harassment of Benno, he was between John and me. But there was no trouble.

There were four full-time South African members, headed by Max Sisulu, head of the Department of Economic Policy of the ANC (recently returned from exile, and son of the storied senior ANC leader, Walter Sisulu, whom I was eventually to meet in Ottawa later that year at an IDRC-organized event marking the public release of our report). Like so many other ANC members in exile, Sisulu had studied political science and was much better schooled in the history of struggle and revolution than in the more mundane issues of economic analysis and policy. Two other young staff members of the same ANC department, Jaya Jose and Vivien McMenamin, and David Lewis (periodically substituted for by his colleague, David Kaplan) from the University of Cape Town completed the team. Over the course of the next three weeks we visited a wide range of groups in Johannesburg, Pretoria, Cape Town, Durban, and their environs; and, under intense pressure and with a great deal of hard work, we finished a draft of the report before leaving. It was published in August 1991 – *Economic Analysis and Policy Formulation for Post-Apartheid South Africa*.[31] The report contained detailed recommendations both for the ANC and for those external actors who wanted to help. It identified what we saw as the top-priority areas for research, analysis, and preparation of policy positions on the part of the MDM/ANC and their supporters. Above all, it provided evidence that there already existed considerable capacity for economic analysis within the "MDM-sympathetic" South African community, although its members

had for some years been starved – by sanctions – of international contact. We argued that this capacity could and should be quickly mobi-
lized, while at the same time longer-term black South African capacity
was to be built and/or strengthened. Less necessary than the external
technical assistance, which was being offered from all sides, was the
"freeing up" of this existing domestic capacity for use by the "shadow"
ANC government as it prepared to assume power. For this purpose, we
recommended the immediate creation of a Macroeconomic Research
Group (MERG) to stimulate and coordinate policy research and capacity building in the identified areas of policy priority. The MERG was formally launched on 23 November 1991. I was not able to be there myself
(John Loxley represented us), but Nelson Mandela described the launch
event, so John reported, as "one of the most fascinating and stimulating
in his life." "It filled him," Mandela said, "with strength and hope."
Even allowing for a degree of hyperbole at a highly political and cere-
monial event, these words were very nice to hear. Never before or since
have policy recommendations in which I have been involved so quickly
been adopted. My involvement in South Africa continued through the
MERG and MERG-related activities, notably through a small group of
economists called the Economic Policy Advisory Group (EPAG), for
some years thereafter. Out of these activities came quite a lot of useful
research; opportunities for those who were later to enter government at
the highest level to undertake research and consultations in preparation
for their new tasks; the first ANC-supported macroeconomic model of
South Africa; and a book-length analysis of the country's future economic problems, complete with detailed recommendations (many of
which, unfortunately, still await action).

My experiences in South Africa included some of the most moving
and memorable of my life.

It was sobering to meet not only long-oppressed black and coloured
activists but also white people who had struggled courageously against
apartheid within South Africa for so many years. From outside, we had
often tended automatically to distance ourselves, with some obvious
exceptions, from anyone with a white skin and a South African accent.
Yet here were those who had chosen to stay, under extremely difficult
and dangerous circumstances, rather than flee. I quickly developed an
enormous respect for them and resolved to be more careful about my
assumptions in the future. On the other hand, it was upsetting to see
some local whites, particularly within the business community, who
now attempted to persuade us that they had been against apartheid

all along – although there was no evidence that they had ever done anything but profit from it – and who now sought an early "foot in the door" with the emerging new political dispensation. It was striking, though it should certainly not have been surprising, that very few of those the ANC deemed both friendly and possessing capacity to contribute to economic analysis and policy formulation from within South Africa were blacks; those who were coloured or black had typically returned only recently from exile, and had not lived through the apartheid years within their own country. When I later spoke about South Africa to a group of activists and interested academics back in Canada, I was asked, because there were a lot of church people in the group, whether our team had met with anti-apartheid activists in the South African churches. I had to admit that we had not; the ANC had evidently not considered the churches as a likely source of expertise in economics.

It may be difficult to convey the horrendous quality of strict apartheid, and the behaviour accompanying it, to a generation that has never experienced it. We encountered it everywhere, both in the large and in the small. The living arrangements surrounding Johannesburg and Cape Town – rich white enclaves, surrounded by poverty-stricken black townships from which pass-carrying workers had to travel long distances daily by overcrowded trains – seemed to epitomize the "banal evil" of apartheid's grand design. The specifics of urban planning in the apartheid regime were explicitly designed to support racial discrimination and exploitation. The small encounters of our racially mixed group's day-to-day living also frequently showed what apartheid really meant.

On one of our first evenings in South Africa, the Canadian ambassador, Chris Westdal, invited our entire group for dinner. Instead of receiving us in his home, he made a point of taking us out to a restaurant in Pretoria, the erstwhile capital of apartheid. The stares and glares we received from the white diners in the full restaurant as our mixed-race group paraded in were impossible not to notice. In Cape Town, we were pretty certain that Benno was the first black ever to have been accommodated in our hotel; and he was sufficiently nervous about it to request that we all stay together as much as possible while we were there. When we visited the Reserve Bank of South Africa, the central bank, in Pretoria (an unforgettable visit about which more later), we joked that the elaborate security machinery as we entered – involving a see-through cubicle and sliding doors – was undoubtedly programmed to reject dark skin.

One afternoon, during our stay in Johannesburg, the external members of the group (the South Africans thought it best not to accompany us) were invited to visit one of the black townships nearby, one in which there had recently been some violence and resistance. We were cordially received and shown around by two leaders of one of the local civic organizations in the township. The township of Alexandra was a scene from hell. Dominating the entire area and the sky were very high light towers/stanchions in the oppressive concentration camp style, erected at about 200 yard intervals by the security services (police and army) so that they could keep a better eye on movements after dark. On the ground, garbage was piled high everywhere, reflecting the fact that the government did not provide much in the way of garbage collection (or any other) services. The unemployment rate, we were told, was over 50 per cent. Many of those who were employed came from elsewhere and lived in barracks from which they only rarely emerged because relations with the locals were tense. The situation, as explained to us by our hosts, was extremely fragile and ultimately unsustainable. After our small group had walked around the unpaved roads of the area for a while, talking to people, seeing the different standards of housing, and getting a feel of the place, our hosts called our attention to an armoured military vehicle, a "hippo" in local parlance, parked a few blocks away on a hill. "They are watching us – trying to figure out who you are," one of the counsellors told us; and indeed we could make out a small figure on top of the vehicle and the glint of reflected sunlight on binoculars. "They will soon be over." And so they were. A few minutes later the hippo came to life and roared up to us at high speed, coming to a sudden halt in a cloud of dust directly in front of us. A young blond soldier in combat dress addressed us in English with an Afrikaans accent, "Everything all right? Getting some water, were you?" We assured him we were fine. They looked us over, no doubt trying to think of what they should say about us in their report, and off they went. In Alexandra, the "new South Africa" still seemed, sadly, a very long way off.

We experienced similar depression when we visited the "Cape Flats," the squatter settlements outside Cape Town, the scene (in Khayelitsha) of a well-known governmental attempt to bulldoze dwellings and relocate the inhabitants. In one place we visited there, the government had some time previously erected row upon row of stand-alone toilet shacks – nothing else – in the hope that this "site and service" scheme would be sufficient to attract future squatters to the area and satisfy their prime needs. But the squatters, for reasons of their own, had chosen to settle elsewhere. Evidently their views had not been canvassed in advance. The rows of toilet shacks remained – looking a little like a war cemetery – another monument to planners' ignorance of people's true needs and wishes.

In a rural area near Durban, we visited an area where there had recently been intense clashes between ANC and Inkatha supporters. It was very moving to see the plaque in what had been the home of Mahatma Gandhi, the apostle of non-violence in the later struggle for India's independence (whose memorial in New Delhi I had also once visited), honouring his life and work, including that earlier in his career in South Africa. The house had been burned out. Powerful symbolism.

Our meeting with senior management at the Reserve Bank of South Africa – notably in the person of an Afrikaner vice president by the name of van der Merwe – was a highlight, or more accurately a low-light, of the mission. As far as we were able to ascertain, there were virtually no blacks in professional positions anywhere within the bank. We were therefore concerned to emphasize the need for black training, internships, fellowships, and the like, and an early, orderly, and effective Africanization of the staff. During the course of an hour and a half, Van der Merwe delivered himself of one faux pas after another. At one point he actually said, "I have a dream," a totally bizarre echo, for us, of Martin Luther King. He went on: "I dream that all of these black chaps who spend so much time talking politics all get some training and become good plumbers." I had never before seen Benno, a very gentle man, beginning to turn angry. Shortly thereafter, Benno was happily able to engender absolutely jaw-dropping surprise for Van der Merwe when he delivered a concise and brilliant summary of South Africa's current and prospective macroeconomic constraints, much superior to the rather unimaginative account of the issues that had previously been offered us by Van der Merwe himself. (On the day our mission left the country, its ANC members presented to Benno – along with the ANC ties and lapel pins that we all received – an enormous plumber's wrench as a memento of his South African experiences.) At another point, this same bank vice president, warming to his subject (I have forgotten what it was), told us, "We must stick to our guns." Both black members of our mission and white ones blanched. It was so dreadful an interview that it was actually funny. Not the least of our concerns at the time, however, was our knowledge that this still powerful man was completely insensitive to how dreadful it had been.

A genuine highlight was our meeting with Nelson Mandela. We were all thrilled to be able to meet and interact with a living icon of the global struggle for justice and peace. I still treasure the photographs that were taken on that occasion. Oddly, Mr Mandela, who seemed to have been badly briefed, spent a good deal of his time with us defending the need for an active state and the ANC's long-standing alliance with the South African Communist Party. We already shared his view that hasty privatization of state assets in advance of the transfer of government to the black majority was unlikely to be in the broader national interest. And we didn't really need to be reminded that the Soviet Union and its allies had supported the anti-apartheid struggle for years while the West continued to argue for "constructive engagement" with the apartheid regime; or that the West had found it expedient to ally with the Communists in struggle against Nazi Germany. I trust that by the time the meeting ended he was persuaded that we had all been very much "on the same page" as him from the beginning on all of these matters and others that arose during our discussion.

Perhaps the most memorable of all the events in which I participated in South Africa was the funeral of Chris Hani in April 1993, nearly two years after my initial visit, and still some time before the first democratic elections and the subsequent change of government in April/May1994. Chris Hani was a hugely popular senior ANC leader, particularly popular among ANC youth. He had earlier been the chief of staff of *Umkhonto we Sizwe* (the Spear of the Nation), the ANC military wing. At the time of his unfortunate assassination in front of his home in Johannesburg by a right-wing Polish immigrant, he was secretary-general of the South African Communist Party. News of the tragedy reached us as we (John Loxley and I) were preparing to travel to Johannesburg for an EPAG conference and meeting of the MERG advisory committee. Many feared it would trigger violent and unpredictable reactions throughout South Africa. We followed the news as best we could during our day stopover in Zurich (it happened to be Easter Sunday), and finally decided to travel on. The conference went ahead, but paused for the ANC-declared national day of mourning on the day of the Hani funeral. As guests of the ANC, the foreign participants in the conference were particularly invited as honoured guests not only to the funeral itself but also to the "lying in state" the night before. Both were conducted in the enormous outdoor stadium in Soweto, the

7.1. With Nelson Mandela, IDRC/ANC Advisory Group on Macroeconomic
Management for Post-Apartheid South Africa, Johannesburg, July 1991

black township on the southwest (hence its name) side of the city. We
felt honoured to be able to accept both invitations. We first travelled
out to the stadium in the evening where we found large crowds, many
clearly intending to stay the entire night within the stadium. It was
amazing – and moving – to discover that among the ANC people who
were skillfully maintaining order were the secretaries who had already
been working all day for us at our conference. They didn't seem tired;
and they went about their job in a most matter-of-fact manner, as if it
were all part of a normal day's work. They were at it again in the stadium the next day. Perhaps they spent the entire night there. We never
did find out. One by one, we each approached the coffin where Chris
Hani lay in the open air in the dusk of the Soweto stadium, bowed our
heads, thought our individual thoughts, and returned to the group. I
was pleasantly surprised to meet an old friend from Tanzania days,

Paul Puritt, now representing the Canadian Labour Congress (CLC), among the mourners in the stadium awaiting their turn to offer their respects; he had been visiting local unions on CLC business. It was all very moving. But it didn't begin to compare with the emotions of the funeral in the stadium the following day.

One of the young local ANC participants in the conference, Maria Ramos, still completing her thesis on financial development in South Africa in London but soon to become the top civil servant in the South African finance ministry and subsequently head of the largest para- statal, picked up a small group of us (Mats Lundahl, a Swedish econo- mist, John Loxley, and me) in the late morning in an ANC van. As we approached the stadium in Soweto, the crowds grew larger and larger. There were many flags, raised fists, and a lot of noise. In a car full of whites, in the midst of what could reasonably be assumed to be an angry black crowd, we were very happy to have the ANC flag flying from the hood of our vehicle. While still some distance away, we were able to see a somewhat worrying plume of dense black smoke rising from the vicinity of the stadium. We decided nevertheless to continue. It proved to be a raging fire, set by demonstrators, only a few yards away from the entrance. No one seemed to be trying to put it out; no doubt there were too many other pressing matters to which to attend. Around the stadium there were a good many armoured cars and what seemed like whole platoons of fully armed (white) soldiers. ANC organizers, iden- tifiable by their armbands, sought to maintain some order, and cleared a path for our vehicle. We were ushered by more ANC organizers into a section of the stadium, already full to bursting, reserved for the dip- lomatic community and other luminaries. The (obviously unarmed) ushers were polite, efficient, and calm. It was striking to see that what seemed to be the entire diplomatic community was in attendance. The one government most evidently unrepresented was that of the Republic of South Africa!

We were fortunate to be seated sufficiently high that we could see and hear some of the events transpiring outside the stadium, nota- bly the crowds assembling from all directions. From one side, in the middle distance, came a column singing and doing the toyi-toyi, the exuberant mixture of marching and dance that had symbolized black defiance during the darkest days of apartheid. On the other side, the fire continued to rage. The next few hours of the extended funeral ser- vice proved unforgettable. Consisting of prayers, hymn singing, and speeches – interrupted periodically by staccato bursts of gunfire from outside or the deafening buzz of low-flying helicopters, and accompanied throughout by clouds of black smoke drifting across the stadium from the external fires – the funeral service proceeded before its huge crowd of worshippers, as if it were in any local church. Hani may well have been an atheist (I don't know what he was), but he would surely have appreciated such a powerful public demonstration of respect and love. The singing, mainly traditional Christian hymns, managed without any apparent direction from anywhere to collect strong voices from throughout the stadium to create outstandingly beautiful multipart harmony. As the bier was carried, to the accompaniment of full-throated traditional hymns, to its place of honour in the centre of the stadium, two South African military helicopters swooped provocatively over the event and briefly actually drowned out the music. The symbolism was staggering. Indeed the contrast, throughout the afternoon, between the quiet, respectful, and orderly ANC-managed event inside the stadium and the chaotic gunfire and belligerent military behaviour outside it could scarcely have been more striking. At one point, an organizer interrupted the funeral service to inform us that unruly events outside the stadium made it unwise for anyone to leave until further notice. Archbishop Desmond Tutu delivered a powerful eulogy, in which he contrasted the life and the principles of his Communist friend, Chris Hani, with the behaviour of the so-called "Christians," who had for so long delivered only brutality and oppression to the people of his country. Nelson Mandela also spoke of his late friend at some length. So did Joe Slovo of the Communist Party, whose wife had been assassinated by South African agents some years previously; he received a thunderous ovation, much larger than that for Nelson Mandela. Needless to say, we were frequently in tears that afternoon, not least when the entire crowd – numbering probably 60,000 or more – rose to sing, lustily and beautifully, "Nkosi sikalele Afrika" (God bless Africa), the ANC anthem.

After our return to the hotel, we all watched the news and the remainder of the funeral events on a television that had been set up in a common area on the ground floor. Responding to appeals from ANC leaders, the African population, to the amazement of most newscasters and to our enormous relief, had remained calm in most parts of the country. There had been some violence and some rioting, but, by and large, the political explosion that many had feared did not take place (although the next morning, one of our ANC participants, Trevor Manuel, subsequently South Africa's finance minister, appeared with a battered face and a black eye, acquired in efforts to calm a nascent riot).

The procession carrying Hani's body to its final resting place had to endure the indignity, all captured on television as we watched, of passing a demonstration by members of a white supremacist group who had sworn they would prevent the burial of a black man in a previously pure "white" cemetery. (They failed.) Also captured on our television was another remarkable bit of symbolism. As the casket was lowered into the ground, a flock of white doves, symbolic of hope and peace, was released. One of the doves, however, failed to fly away and instead flew down into the newly dug gravesite; one of the attendants had to descend into the hole to bring it out.

8 AERC: Macroeconomic Background and Early Days

One of the activities I most enjoyed, and one that may well have been among the most useful, was my support of the development of African macroeconomic expertise in the face of growing macroeconomic difficulties across the developing world in the early 1980s. What eventually became the much-praised African Economic Research Consortium (AERC) began as an IDRC-supported "network" of African economists who met periodically to exchange experience and develop collective approaches to the building of African capacity in macroeconomics. I'd like to think that I had a hand in its earliest beginnings. In late May 1981, I wrote David Steedman, then director of the Social Sciences Division in the IDRC, as follows:

It has been increasingly worrisome to me in recent years that there is so little research, knowledge, expertise on African macroeconomic issues and problems, which are now horrendous. In work I have recently done for the G-24, and in a variety of related conferences that I have been attending, the examples are invariably drawn from Latin America, with the occasional reference to Asian cases. The telephone is ringing with appeals to send macroeconomic expertise to Tanzania, Ghana, Uganda – must this be so? And must the staff of the IMF and/or the World Bank be the sole source of wisdom on these matters?

I think that a potentially quite major contribution might be made by the IDRC if it were to organize/orchestrate a coordinated assault upon ignorance and inexpertise in and on Africa with respect to inflation, exchange rates, monetary management and financial policies. The macroeconomic scene in many parts of Africa is going to get worse before it gets any better. Who understands what is happening or is likely to happen, or what kinds of policy options lie before the macro-managers? Governments (particularly Treasuries and Central Banks) are bound to welcome work and training in this area. I'm not sure how many research institutes or university people are equipped for it. A role for the IDRC?[32]

I wrote to Steven Langdon and Jeffrey Fine, both former students of mine then working at the IDRC, shortly thereafter in a similar vein and offered any support that might be necessary, both personally and from the University of Toronto where Richard Bird, then director of its Institute for Policy Analysis, was very supportive. I drafted a memorandum arguing the case for a new network of individuals or institutions within Africa to encourage the support of macroeconomic research and policy modelling, and offered the backup support of the University of Toronto as might be required.

At the same time, economists in the University of Dar es Salaam put together a proposal requesting IDRC support for economic research and the development of a macroeconomic model for Tanzania. It was to be constructed jointly with the University of Toronto, and in particular with me. (I was not exactly an authority on macroeconomic modelling, but I did know a lot about Tanzania.) Two of the Tanzanian economists who happened to be on leave in the United States, Samuel Wangwe in Boston and Delphin Rwegasira at the IMF, travelled to Toronto to develop their plans with me early in January 1983. Unfortunately a few days before their arrival, I had to undergo some emergency surgery. Together with Steven Langdon, they all came to my room in Sunnybrook Hospital for what can only be described as a highly unusual planning meeting. These plans were to be further developed at a workshop on Tanzanian economic policies in Arusha in April 1983; unfortunately I fell ill again in London on the way to the meeting and was unable to attend. The agreement between the University of Dar es Salaam and the University of Toronto was nonetheless eventually approved, and quite a good macroeconomic policy model for Tanzania was constructed. But my appointment to the board of the IDRC shortly thereafter required me to give up my role in it; and my colleague at the University of Toronto, Sue Horton, very ably and efficiently took over from me.

Fortunately I was able to remain involved in the effort to construct a broader African effort in macroeconomic research. Funding for it was approved by the IDRC in the second half of 1983. Its Nairobi office, in the person of the incredibly energetic and imaginative Jeffrey Fine, who had relocated from Ottawa to Nairobi in January 1984 primarily for this purpose, went quickly to work on it. Suleiman Kiggundu, a Ugandan economist in exile in Nairobi, was appointed the project's initial research coordinator. By April/May 1984 a "macroeconomic research network for Eastern and Southern Africa" had been launched. I was very pleased to be involved in the early meetings, first in Lusaka (mainly on macro modelling in April 1984) and then in Nairobi (on exchange rate analysis in December 1984). I played a role in the planning and preparation of the latter meeting, as well as making one of the major presentations at it.

At the same time that these efforts were being initiated, I was engaged in parallel efforts to draw attention to African countries' macroeconomic plight and their difficulties in addressing it. These included speeches, and writing and editing a volume on the IMF in Africa (see chapter twelve). It was also at this time that I was involved in the abortive attempt to mediate in the conflict between Tanzania and the IMF discussed in chapter five.

Jeffrey Fine, later ably assisted by Benno Ndulu, who eventually took over the leadership of the AERC, quickly built an enthusiastic network of keen African economists, some in universities and others within governments and central banks, who came together regularly to exchange papers and ideas. Every effort was made to build the morale of otherwise isolated economists who were badly in need of support for their valiant efforts in extremely difficult environments. Not only were these previously isolated economists provided with an opportunity for professional interchange, supported by high-powered international expertise, but they were also supplied with current materials from the international literature on the subjects on which they were working. No less important was the deep sense of ownership of the network program on the part of its participants. A program committee composed primarily of senior African economists made recommendations as to what was to be done next. This "network approach" proved far more effective than the previously dominant model of "centres of excellence" for the building and maintenance of African capacity in the field. By 1988 the overall effort had become so successful that plans were made to extend it to all of Africa and to involve far more donors in its support. The IDRC macroeconomic network at this point "morphed" into the more formalized multi-donor African Economic Research Consortium (AERC). I think it fair to say that virtually all of the well-known economists in Africa during the 1990s and thereafter to the present day have been associated in one way or another with the AERC and its

8.1. Working meeting at Conference of the African Economic Research Consortium (AERC), with William Lyakurwa, later its head, Nairobi, circa 1988

predecessor IDRC network. Jeffrey and Benno deserve enormous credit for the AERC's achievements.

Two other international experts were especially active in the support of all of these early activities: Tony Killick of the ODI in London and Mohsin Khan, an old friend of Jeffrey's, by now (and long thereafter) at the IMF, who came in his personal capacity rather than as an IMF representative. The three of us attended virtually all of the meetings, read all of the papers and proposals, often staying up much of the night during network and AERC meetings to do so, and offered what we hoped was constructive criticism and advice to all the participants. We worked very hard during the meetings and also served as a "sounding board" for Jeffrey as he developed the program. Although we did not always agree on everything (as was to be expected since Mohsin had very IMF-like views as to macroeconomic policies), we developed a powerful esprit de corps and, I think, offered one another profound professional respect. We invariably left the meetings totally exhausted. I recall one occasion when our flights home were delayed and we all slept on the floor in the Nairobi airport for several hours before finding an ingenious way to break into the Air France lounge, where there were comfortable sofas upon which to sleep a little better. At a later stage, after the AERC got going, its board decreed that the members of the program advisory committee, as we were now formally designated, were to have a fixed and limited term. We drew straws to determine which of us would leave first. I drew the short straw and was the first to depart. I was warmly rewarded by wonderful farewell speeches at my last conference and two Kenyan soapstone carvings presented to me at the traditional conference farewell dinner at the Carnivore restaurant in Nairobi.

Of course, this "last" conference did not totally terminate my association with the AERC. I tried to take my farewell to the organization seriously. But Benno and his successor, Delphin Rwegasira (another Tanzanian), kept inviting me back. I always told them that Georgia found it difficult to understand how I could return to the AERC when it had given me such a pleasant goodbye and to which she had been a witness. I tried to help as best I could at a distance – reading papers, commenting upon plans, recommending personnel, and even serving on committees. When the AERC embarked a little later in the 1990s upon a new project on Africa's role in the international trading system, I participated in it, attending conferences in Accra and Mombasa, and writing a paper jointly with Ibrahim Elbadawi, now the organization's research director.[33]

I was deeply moved when, at a conference in Uganda in 1997, Benno presented me with the first volume of a new AERC book series on trade, containing a fulsome dedication – of the entire four volume series – to me for my support of the AERC and "for drawing the attention of the international community to the plight of SubSaharan Africa's development."[34]

In later years the AERC expanded its subject matter well beyond its original focus on macroeconomics. It also did its best to engage much more of Africa than its East African origins.

Despite its reliance on networking rather than in-house staff, AERC has long been generally regarded as the foremost economic research and capacity building institution on the African continent.

9 More African Capacity Building: ACBF

One of the most intense but ultimately satisfying board experiences came for me in an African context after my formal retirement from academia. It brought me new knowledge and new experiences, and, most important, some firm new friends. I was elected to the executive board of the African Capacity Building Foundation (ACBF) late in 1997, shortly before my retirement.

Following extensive international consultations spearheaded by the World Bank in the late 1980s on a proposed African capacity building initiative, a foundation to implement it was formally launched early in 1991. The idea was to make a concerted international effort to build African expertise and institutions that could more effectively manage economic policies for African development across the entire continent. This initiative was to be far more ambitious than the earlier IDRC/AERC efforts described in the previous chapter. It was agreed that the ACBF's headquarters would be in Harare, Zimbabwe, at that time seeming a stable and relatively prosperous and well-served location. A two-level governing structure was established. The donors would ultimately be responsible for the foundation via their governing board, but the details of program and operations would be advised by an eleven-person executive board comprised primarily of eight independent professionals, four from Africa and four from elsewhere, together with representatives of the three sponsoring bodies: the World Bank, the African Development Bank, and the UN Development Program (UNDP). There were many eminent names on the initial executive board, including friends: Ojetunji Aboyade from Nigeria; Harris Mule from Kenya; Sir Douglas Wass, whom I had known in the UN group on African debt (see chapter ten); Elliot Berg, the University of Michigan economist who had written the controversial World Bank report guiding its structural adjustment lending; Ellen Johnson Sirleaf, later Liberia's president; Senegal's Jacques Diouf; Nigerian political scientist Claude Ake; Sweden's Lennart Wohlgemuth; and the World Bank's vice president for Africa, Kim Jaycox.

The ACBF had very rough beginnings. As one could well imagine, there were fierce disagreements in a board with this many "luminaries" and independent thinkers. There were also said to be scandals and/or mismanagement in the secretariat, leading to early dismissal of the first two executive secretaries. Difficulties arose with the appointment of the next executive secretary, leading to the temporary (acting) appointment to this post of one of the World Bank's lead persons in the ACBF initiative, Kenya's Dunstan Wai. Even before this appointment, there had already been, by many accounts, an inappropriate degree of external involvement in the ACBF's affairs on the part of Wai and a heavy-handed World Bank. I had also heard of an unfortunate "bust-up" between a blustery Wai and my friends in the AERC. Few had confidence at that time that the ACBF could overcome such an inauspicious start.

Still, after a few very difficult years, it got more effectively under way with the financing of a number of new research/training institutions in the sphere of economic policy analysis and management in several African countries. Not everyone, myself included, was convinced that the ACBF was doing the right kind of work or that it was anything, in effect, other than a subsidiary of the World Bank, at a time when the Bank was increasingly seen as both less than fully effective and too intrusive in African affairs. Many saw it simply as a World Bank attempt to direct the longer-term future of African economic policymaking. Ole Moelgaard Andersen, my friend in the Danish Foreign Ministry, now a governor of the ACBF, shared with me, when it was completed, a highly critical (and controversial) independent assessment of ACBF activities. Not for the first or last time, Ole now set out to involve me in some complex and fascinating further African adventures.

The time-limited terms of most of the ACBF executive board's initial members had expired by 1997–8. It was time for a major renewal – five independent posts were to fall vacant within a year. To his Scandinavian colleagues' apparently considerable distress (so he told me), Ole nominated me for the Scandinavian "slot" on the executive board. (In the end, the Danes got another member anyway.) At the same time he nominated Kwesi Botchwey, a former finance minister in Ghana, as its chairman, the first African chair. To learn more about what board membership entailed and what the ACBF was now doing, I requested, and got, a long telephone conversation with Lennart Wohlgemuth in Sweden. It was broadly reassuring. He told me that there would be no more than two or three meetings per year, that the board had real independence, and that the ACBF's work had considerably greater potential than it had yet realized. The new board and new chair, it now seemed to me, offered promise. Although I was on the point of retiring for health reasons and was cutting back on everything else, I agreed to give it a try. If it didn't seem worth doing, I reasoned, I could always step down after my first three-year term, or even earlier if necessary.

My first executive board meeting in November 1998, in the World Bank's Paris office building, was more than a little worrying. This meeting was also the first for the new chair, Kwesi Botchwey. As we milled about before its beginning, Kwesi asked me, without any prior warning, whether I would agree to serve as the board vice chairman. Still full of doubts and fairly ignorant of the ACBF, I really didn't see how in good conscience I possibly could. A few minutes later we duly elected Joan Corkery, from Ireland and Maastricht, instead; she must have had even less time to think about it than I did. This process all seemed rather a casual style of governance. Moreover, the papers for the meeting were not all in very good shape, and some, including the proposed budget for the coming year, were not available in advance at all. Since these papers were not at that time very numerous, this inefficiency seemed to call into question the competence of ACBF's management. When the late-arriving new Danish board member, Poul Engberg-Pedersen, while still taking his seat and being welcomed, complained somewhat grumpily about the inadequacy of the papers, I was at first quite shocked at his bluntness. I approved of the polite reprimand he received from the chair, but Poul was right. The executive secretary seemed a pleasant and honest enough person, but efficient or dynamic he was not. Within a year we learned that he was not well and would be taking early retirement on medical grounds at year-end 1999. It was also distressing to learn that the ACBF had not been able to attract its expected funding, and that this budget uncertainty had generated almost total paralysis in its commitment authority for new projects and a freeze on its administrative expenditures. In many respects, then, it was not an auspicious start for the new board. When the draft minutes of the meeting were circulated shortly thereafter, further problems arose. I wrote a somewhat cranky and detailed critique, expressing dissatisfaction about

many of its elements: inaccuracies and/or vagueness about key decisions, including spending authority, management defensiveness, and
other deficiencies.

But the African capacity building agenda was certainly important,
and the issues it raised were fascinating. It was clear that the ACBF secretariat had attracted some very able African professional staff, and that
the organization had already been engaged in some significant capacity
building activities. Even at my first board meeting, despite my anxieties and the sense that the organization's administrative leadership was
weak, I could see the potential for further useful ACBF contributions. It
was clear that I was not alone in the new board in my wariness about
World Bank motives and approaches. I liked the board chairman and
approved of his stated principles, notably his insistence on our independence and his declaration that our meetings should henceforth normally be held in Africa, not in Paris or Washington. The substantive
discussion at that meeting had already been quite exciting.

At the World Bank, with its management's encouragement, a group
of African governors, backed by some African heads of state, had for
the past few years been vigorously pushing still another new initiative:
the Partnership for African Capacity Building, known by its acronym
as PACT. The PACT was to have a much broader mandate than that of
the ACBF and considerably greater funding. It was proposed that the
PACT should address capacity building requirements in the private sector and civil society in Africa as well as those to which the ACBF had
been confined in policy analysis within the public sector. This proposed
new capacity building venture was creating considerable confusion on
the part of both potential ACBF donors and potential beneficiaries. Its
broad ambitions and lack of focus made aid donors nervous by creating
the potential for many overlaps with existing educational and institution-
building activities. On the face of it, the PACT seemed, to many people,
to pose a particular challenge to the already existing ACBF. At a minimum, the relationship between the two needed significant clarification.
Together with the launch of a search for a new executive secretary, the
new board had its hands immediately full.

After much politicking, the basic (and happy) outcome of the much-
touted PACT initiative was that the ACBF acquired greatly expanded
funding from the World Bank and a broadened mandate. Within a few
years, the PACT terminology had been forgotten.

A key element in the "new" ACBF, it soon became apparent, was to
be the energetic newly hired executive secretary, Soumana Sako. The

full executive board interviewed all of the half dozen shortlisted candidates, and a self-assured fluently bilingual (in French and English) Soumana seemed to stand out. Sako, a forty-nine-year-old Malian with a US doctorate, had previously served in many official capacities, including even, for a transitional period, prime minister, a post of which he was very proud. He assumed his new post in January 2000 and set determinedly to work on the newly broadened ACBF agenda.

The immediate task was to persuade donors and particularly, in the immediate future, the World Bank, that the ACBF could make concrete sense out of its expanded agenda. This agenda could only be achieved by quickly developing a focused approach and identifying enough projects of high quality within it as to merit the expanded funding that was now, in principle, to be made available. The Bank had promised a first tranche of increased support, but it was conditioned on a demonstration that there were sufficient justifiable and viable projects that needed funding. Since the word was out that there could be expanded ACBF funding, literally hundreds of project proposals now flooded in to the ACBF, projects of every conceivable kind. The ACBF staff worked wonders and with prodigious effort succeeded in narrowing them down to about thirty. Our next executive board meeting was held at the headquarters of the World Bank in Washington in May 2000. It was hoped that, despite the earlier declared determination to hold meetings normally in Africa, by meeting in Washington the new management and the board could both make necessary contacts and build confidence in what we were now setting out "fresh" to do.

The executive board's operations committee, of which I had become acting chair (and I remained in that capacity for the rest of my term with the ACBF), had the difficult task of winnowing the projects down to a limited number that could be funded with some agreed rationale and criteria for doing so. The operations committee was responsible for advising the full executive board as to the acceptability of projects suggested by management. Normally, by the time a project had reached this board committee, it had been quite fully explored by professional staff; but, in this case, this vetting had not been possible. Given the unusual circumstances, all board members participated in this winnowing meeting (with the exception of the chair and the executive secretary, who were busy interacting with senior World Bank staff).

We decided that it was important that the ACBF signal what kinds of projects it would support, and also signal the importance of eventual self-sustainability in newly supported projects. We suggested that the

ACBF should, in the first instance, only normally support three further categories of project, other than the traditional ones on the strengthening of economic analysis, statistics, and administration. These three new categories were the following: projects strengthening the functioning of parliaments as they related to economic management and policy; projects strengthening civil society's capacities to make effective inputs into the economic policy discussions; and projects strengthening the interface between the private and public sectors in economic policy matters. A small further "catch-all" category was added to permit occasional support for unusually promising special cases. Once we had agreed on that narrowing of the expanded ACBF agenda, decision making became much easier for us. At the same time we agreed to adopt a consciously flexible "learning-by-doing" mode of operation in which a degree of risk-taking was inherent and acceptable, to avoid "great leaps" into risky new situations, to seek a role as catalyst and signaller rather than principal financier, to consider the eventual need for sustainability, and to keep a special eye out for potential regional cooperation. With these guidelines we were already able to agree on immediate support for a number of promising proposals. Many others were referred for further investigation and development at a later date.

Evidently satisfied with what we had done, the World Bank paid up as promised. The newly led and greatly expanded ACBF was now on its way. At the next executive board meeting, in November, the operations committee refined further the principles and criteria for future ACBF support in "complex" (for example, post-conflict) environments, program support, and support for regional proposals. At the same committee meeting, which stretched over two long days, it approved fully twenty-four new projects, making commitments of about US $50 million, far more than had ever been contemplated, let alone approved, before. Over half of these new projects and commitments were in ACBF's traditional line of activity – the public sector. A new and ambitious medium-term plan – with a clear focus on six "core" ACBF areas of competence – was soon developed and, at the following executive board meeting in the spring of 2001, the plan was agreed and passed on to the governing board.

It was the new management's aspiration to have projects in literally every country in Africa. We were aware that the ACBF had now become a very different organization. No longer simply managing a limited number of projects, all of a somewhat similar character, it had become a larger, more diversified, and more complex organization with responsibility for the Africa-wide collection, assessment, and dissemination of knowledge about capacity building in a variety of fields. While many donors, not least the World Bank, were heavily involved in parallel efforts – with far more money – the ACBF was unique in its capable, experienced, and 100 per cent African management and staff. We now aspired to be the African-owned and African-trusted leader, catalyst, and knowledge repository for all such activity on the continent. After the initial burst of project approvals, "my" operations committee settled into a more sustainable routine, typically approving commitments of US $10 to $15 million at each meeting.

We soon learned that there were some unexpected costs to our apparent successes. Our dynamic new executive secretary proved to have some problems. We had been aware that the ACBF staff had been working flat out before our Washington meeting in order to meet the World Bank's deadlines for fresh funding. Indeed we had both praised the professional staff and expressed anxiety about their workload. We had not realized, however, the extent of the pressures being felt by ACBF staff at all levels. We began to hear more about them. By the following executive board meeting in April 2001, almost all of the staff was in full revolt over all manner of issues. It is difficult now to convey the degree of malaise in the institution at that time. Secretaries in tears came to speak in private to Kwesi, our chair, describing impossible demands upon them and the absence of appreciation or worse. Senior personnel took us aside to whisper of anti-anglophone conspiracies or dictatorial management or the workload or unfair performance assessments. Grievance procedures appeared to be non-existent. Distrust of the senior management seemed universal. In our own meetings, Soumana still gave the impression of firm and confident leadership, but now we could see his staff looking away, or at each other, or at the ceiling, whenever he spoke. It was evident that we had an institutional crisis, or at least a management crisis, on our hands. To make matters even worse, the board at this time received a letter from the former (Zimbabwean) senior financial officer, recently dismissed, accusing the executive secretary of a number of specific procedural, financial, and diplomatic improprieties.

One positive externality that this crisis undoubtedly brought was a degree of bonding among executive board members as we attempted to address the ACBF's problems. We now ate all our dinners together and talked freely and frankly. As we spent more time together, discussing these and other issues, we also inevitably talked about many other things and got to know one another much better. In retrospect, I see these dinner gatherings as having been extraordinarily rich: Kwesi Botchwey telling us about Ghanaian politics, Winnie Byanyima describing her past in Museveni's struggle for Uganda, Brian Levy on some of the machinations within the World Bank, Poul Engberg-Pedersen on the running of a research institute, Joan Corkery with strong views on just about everything. Out of it all came a remarkably successful strategy – one of which I was initially very sceptical. Brian Levy had some experience with consultants on management problems and, in particular, on "change management." (The ACBF had certainly now changed!) He and Ibrahim Diallo, our acting representative from the African Development Bank, agreed to explore with knowledgeable others in their respective organizations the possibility of recruiting a good management consultant for the ACBF.

At the same time that these problems were bedevilling the ACBF, Soumana and his staff were developing plans for the first Pan-African Capacity Building Forum, a meeting that had long been suggested by the PACT backers. As now being developed, it was to be a huge Africa-wide conference on capacity building, to be held in Bamako, the capital of Mali, Soumana's home country. Many members of the executive board, myself included, had profound reservations about the value of such an expensive event relative to its cost. With the concurrent anxieties about Soumana, some of our members saw it as a step toward a political career he sought to build at home after his, perhaps quite early, departure from the ACBF. It was certainly intended to put the ACBF on the international and African map in a new way. I was among those who actively sought to shift the content of the draft program toward more technical discussions, away from the proposed pomp and prominent personalities. Apart from the inherent value of a substantive conference, it was only by demonstrating our capacity to assemble and exchange real experience and knowledge, it seemed to us, that donors would see the ACBF as uniquely deserving of support. In the end the conference was indeed quite a grand affair, held in the splendour of Bamako's enormous new conference centre in late October 2001. It had some good sessions, but there was more ceremony than substance. It featured some behind-the-scenes dramatics, in particular, fruitless and disappointing discussions with the deputy managing director of the IMF and his team on the terms of their planned support for capacity building in Africa. The IMF would cooperate with the ACBF, they said, as they undertook their own programs in Africa, but, sadly, they would not themselves become donors to the ACBF. At the concluding session, an attempt was made to agree on a conference declaration drafted by ACBF staff. Negotiations over the wording of a critique of technical assistance failed to resolve differences before the clock ran out. But the ACBF nevertheless subsequently circulated a version of the (unagreed) text as a conference document. One of the conference recommendations that was implemented – though to no great effect – was its call for the Organisation of African Unity (OAU) to declare the next decade the "African Capacity Building Decade." Such declarations are always easy to agree on.

In the meantime, a two-person team of reputable change management consultants was identified. They began to work within the ACBF in the summer and presented a full-blown (and very expensive) plan for change management to the next board meeting near the 2001 year-end. I was unimpressed with their presentation, which seemed to me to be a "boilerplate" offering. Most of it was offered by an American who, while evidently full of experience, was not on the face of it very knowledgeable about African circumstances. His African colleague seemed pleasant enough but didn't say very much. The presentation of their plan for further work with the ACBF seemed to me to be just so much standardized sales talk in support of new contracts for themselves. The board nonetheless agreed that, in the ACBF's difficult circumstances, we should give them a chance. In the end, I was proven quite wrong. Over the next year and a half the consultants achieved remarkable results.

Changes came fairly slowly at first. My notes record continuing staff tensions at year-end 2001 and during much of 2002. But progress began to be made. Clear procedures for performance assessment, grievances, communication, training, monitoring, and other matters were established. At a staff retreat facilitated by the consultants and in the subsequent period, remarkable new ACBF vision statements were developed in an open and participatory manner. Rather than the usual sort of aspirational generalities about the building of Africa's future and the like, they included matters of organizational culture, management obligations, and operating processes; and specific follow-up was set in motion. One could by late 2002 begin to see the change in the staff's mood. No doubt professional morale was also bolstered by the board's decision during this period, after much discussion and delay, on a final attractive remuneration package. It was also encouraging that an independent consultant to the British Department for International Development (DFID) had delivered a basically favourable verdict, shared with other donors, on the ACBF's progress in early 2002. Another midterm evaluation on behalf of the World Bank, about a year later, was also fundamentally supportive and encouraging. By the time I left the ACBF in 2003, morale within the ACBF seemed to have reached a new high.

During this period, our twice-yearly visits to Harare permitted us to see the steady deterioration of the Zimbabwe economic and political scene. Protected in our five-star (Meikles) hotel and the air-conditioned ACBF offices, we did not personally experience problems. We and the ACBF staff, like diplomatic personnel, received preferential treatment in every way. But it was heartbreaking to see the accelerating inflation, the long queues at gas stations, the closure of the only independent newspaper, the decline in the number of tourists, and the collapse of official foreign exchange arrangements. The accounts in the government newspaper, by 2002 the only one left, became ever less credible. The real statistics made it quite clear that the vast majority in the country were, by the early 2000s, already hurting badly. The situation in Zimbabwe thereafter unfortunately went from bad to worse.

My two terms on the executive board expired in mid-2003, as did those of chairman Kwesi. Immediately after our final executive board meeting in May 2003, the ACBF held a retreat at the Sheraton Harare hotel for all of the staff and board members. It was a wonderfully collegial affair, combining two days of open and professionally facilitated discussion of major issues for the ACBF, with a particular focus upon board performance and board-secretariat relations. During the first morning, our change management consultant presented a fascinating report of the results of his latest staff opinion surveys, now generally very favourable in just about every respect. Breakout groups gave everyone, from clerks and drivers to senior staff and board members, an opportunity to speak – and they did so. There were also professionally run get-to-know-each-other events, which created a relaxed atmosphere. On the very last evening a band was brought in, and staff and board danced the night away. I told several people there that if all the meetings ended like this one I would be happy to continue to serve in some advisory capacity (as Soumana and others had repeatedly asked me to do), though, of course, I had little real intention of doing so. It was a warm, wonderful, and memorable way to end my association with the organization. I had the distinct feeling, and some pride, that our board had carried it successfully through some very difficult times.

PART III

An International and Development Economist in International Organizations

10 UN Activities: Satisfaction and Frustration

I have devoted quite a lot of time and effort over the years to activities of the United Nations and its various agencies, most notably to UNCTAD and UNICEF. The UN has many problems, and working with it generates many frustrations. But it remains the only institution of its kind that the world has. As others have said, "If we did not have the UN, it would be necessary to invent it." A lot of resources have gone into the UN's creation and maintenance. I believe it is important to try to make it work.

I have no illusions about the size of my own contributions to the UN's activities or their possible accomplishments. They were minuscule. Still, when the UN Intellectual History Project was launched a few years ago in an effort to record the role of the UN in the creation and dissemination of ideas, I was one of the seventy-three individuals interviewed as part of its oral history component. So I can at least say that some people thought I was involved in some of the UN's intellectually interesting activities in a significant way.

UNCTAD

In the early 1970s, when I began to conduct more research on international economic questions and the proposed New International Economic Order (NIEO) was attracting great attention, I began my long association with UNCTAD staff. My sojourns at the Institute of Development Studies at the University of Sussex in 1971–2 and the summer of 1975 provided occasions for repeated visits to Geneva, UNCTAD's base. In these and subsequent years I developed particularly close relations with Alfred (Alf) Maizels, the principal economic advisor to its secretary-general (at that time Gamani Corea). I wrote, at his request, a number of advisory memos, comments on draft papers, research suggestions, and the like. I also advised on and wrote for UNCTAD's new journal, which Alf was editing. I interacted in a similar way with Surendra Patel, who at that time was directing UNCTAD's pioneering work on international technology transfer and intellectual property issues, long before these became the "hot button" issues of recent years. At the same time I was invited to a series of international conferences organized by UNCTAD in Geneva (and once in New York), frequently designated as meetings of "eminent persons" or "high-level experts," terminology that made me squirm but which seemed de rigueur as justification for the meetings. They frequently produced impressive-looking reports, for example, on economic cooperation among developing countries (in 1975) or a new program of action for the least developed countries (in 1979), but they never seemed to have much policy impact. I often found them frustrating. Following the 1979 meeting, which I had to leave before it finished, I wrote to Alf as follows:

> I hope the least developed expert group eventually finished up. I have had it with these things myself. Never again, I swore, as each sentence was negotiated Friday morning – after I'd been up until after 4 AM doing silly redrafting. There are no new ideas contained in the report so far as I am aware. One really does wonder what the point of these exercises is.
>
> Fortunately you have some good work going on within the building which always allows me to carry home useful papers, materials, and ideas. These externalities keep me coming to Geneva. The "politics" increasingly turn me off.[35]

One particularly memorable and useful Geneva meeting, however, financed by Canada's IDRC (see chapter seventeen) in 1975, brought together directors of developing country research centres to discuss their research priorities and other issues. There *were*, from time to time, some good meetings there.

One of my UNCTAD acquaintances, John Cuddy, a Canadian, gave my name to the government of Norway when they approached him about the possibility of organizing a conference that they very much wanted. Their idea was to convene a well-informed group of economists to consider the role of economic theory in North-South negotiations and disputes. The result was an excellent meeting at a quiet rural hotel in Norway (Refsnes Gods) in the summer of 1980, which I put together and chaired. At the opening dinner I spoke of the hope that in later years people might ask of participants, in wonder and admiration, "Were you at Refsnes?" Some years later my Oxford friend, Frances Stewart, reported that someone *had* actually asked her that question. But, outside of the usual circles in which our group worked, the conference did not appear to carry great influence. Its papers did nonetheless make a quite interesting book, which I edited, *For Good or Evil: Economic Theory and North-South Negotiations.*[36] The book called attention to the frequent bowdlerization, or misuse of theory, and the role of political influences in these processes. My introduction appeared as an article in the journal *World Development.*[37] I believe it may have been in this meeting that my friend Carlos Diaz-Alejandro first so aptly described the role of economists like us as "lawyers for the South." It was also there, as I recall, that he first publicly (and so memorably) accused some Northern economists of using the prestige of their theoretical expertise to influence North-South disputes by saying to Southerners, in effect, "Hocus-pocus, mumbo-jumbo. Therefore you are wrong." The Refsnes conference was not an UNCTAD event but several UNCTAD staff participated, and I would never have been involved in it had I not been associated with that organization.

I never was able, in this period, to respond to the repeated suggestions that I take on a formal consultancy and/or spend a summer at UNCTAD. Nor was I inclined to respond to the efforts to recruit me as Alf Maizel's successor in 1979–80. In 1981–2, however, I agreed to join, with Carlos Diaz-Alejandro and a couple of others (one was Ajit Singh from Cambridge, who was at this time opposing our "wise men" exchange rate policy in Tanzania), a formal "advisory group on trade" to assist the new director of the Manufactures Division, Renaldo Figueredo, to develop policy in his new post. We commented on his division's draft programs, wrote memos of our own, attended another "eminent persons" conference, and met three times as a group. I have fond memories of these meetings because they provided me with occasions to see my old friend Carlos. A vivid memory of one of these meetings revolved around a bright junior economist (still without a doctorate at the time) who was temporarily working at UNCTAD. Having heard a suggestion from me in the meeting as to a better methodology for estimating developing country imports than the one being used in the paper under discussion, he came back from the lunch hour with the results of an econometric test of this alternative approach. This kind of intellectual curiosity and speed was not the norm, to put it mildly, among UNCTAD staff at the time (or since). His name was Dani Rodrik, later to become a major global figure in international and development economics.

UNCTAD came under increasing pressure from the United States and others in the 1980s, as balance of payments problems, the debt crisis, and the Reagan-Thatcher administrations moved the IMF and World Bank more dramatically to centre stage. It was clear that the United States would have preferred to close UNCTAD down entirely. When asked, with other independent scholars, to contribute to a twentieth anniversary issue of the *UNCTAD Bulletin* in 1984, I wrote:

> UNCTAD will face increasing pressure from some of the industrialized countries to cut back on its activities in favor of research and action by the IMF, the World Bank and the GATT. There are some legitimate reasons for disquiet with UNCTAD's recent performance. But if there were no UNCTAD it would now have to be invented. The best response to such pressures is to continue to improve the quality of its research and information output; and to develop better ways of mobilizing world effort than the present quadrennial conference system. The world requires alternative sources of research and pressure in the fields of trade, finance and development; and it requires an institution in which trade and finance issues are addressed with the particular interests of the developing countries always uppermost. Quality of output, focus of effort, and institutional imagination will be the key challenges before UNCTAD in the coming years. This is no time for cutbacks in UNCTAD activities.[38]

I am afraid that this assessment is just as relevant today as it was then. UNCTAD continues to get "under the skin" of the United States and some other Northern governments; they continue to try to cut it back and rein it in.

In subsequent years I continued to appear on UNCTAD panels and to comment on its drafts, when requested, from time to time; but I did so at a much less "furious" pace, and I visited Geneva much less frequently. When in the 1990s I managed the G-24 research program (see chapter fourteen), which was administered through UNCTAD, I resumed regular interaction with some of its staff, notably Yilmaz Akyuz. Now my interactions with UNCTAD staff had to do much more with macroeconomic and financial policies than, as in earlier years, with primary commodities, manufactures trade, or technology transfer. I also spoke to the UNCTAD Trade and Development Board a couple of times: once on Africa, once on portfolio capital flows. I had reason to believe as well that my comments had significant influence on the quality of a couple of later UNCTAD reports on the least developed countries.

One of the more bizarre elements of my association with UNCTAD came with the arrival in my mail of one of their (ostensibly refereed and quite widely distributed) discussion papers, on African debt, in the 1990s. I thought it was very good, and I wrote to Yilmaz in its praise; but I had to add that most of it had been stolen, word for word, from a piece I had written a couple of years previously. It was hastily withdrawn.

In 2000, I was greatly honoured by UNCTAD's invitation to deliver the tenth lecture in memory of Raul Prebisch, its eminent first secretary-general. My lecture, "Markets, Politics and Globalization: Can the Global Economy be Civilized?" delivered in Geneva on 11 December 2000 seemed to be well received and was reprinted widely.[39]

UNICEF

My involvement with the United Nations International Children's Emergency Fund (UNICEF) stemmed from my personal friendship with Richard Jolly. I had known Richard since Yale graduate school days, and our friendship was later renewed when I spent a sabbatical year at the Institute of Development Studies (IDS) at the University of Sussex in 1971–2 (see chapter twenty-one). Richard had left the directorship of IDS Sussex to become UNICEF's deputy executive director at the beginning of 1982. Jim Grant, UNICEF's energetic head, gave Richard plenty of latitude to develop a research and advocacy program, and he used it very effectively. It eventually included the launch of an annual series of influential reports on *The State of the World's Children;*[40] first-ever publications on the impact of IMF stabilization programs upon children, and eventually an impactful book, *Adjustment with a Human Face.*[41]

In the spring of 1984, Richard called me from his New York office. "I'm going to take on the IMF," he proclaimed. "Will you help?" I first asked him whether he was out of his mind, or words to that effect. But I readily agreed to help prepare a paper for Jim Grant and Richard to carry to the meeting they had arranged with the IMF's then managing director, Jacques de Laroisière. There was very little time before this meeting, and I had a prior commitment to a conference in Korea, but I rerouted my ticket so as to be able to spend a weekend working at UNICEF in New York en route to Seoul. We began with a meeting in which Richard and Andrea Cornia, UNICEF's sole working economist, briefed me as to why they were meeting the IMF and what they hoped

to achieve. I quickly produced a rough outline for another brainstorming session among the three of us, following which Andrea and I went
off, separately, to draft portions of the paper. My main object was to
address, in advance, the reservations and objections that the IMF was
likely to offer in response to any attempt to move them toward greater
attention to the implications of their programs for the poor and, particularly, vulnerable children. We stressed that we did not question the need
for stabilization, did not question the IMF's mandate or their skills, and
did not expect them to acquire new skills. We asked merely that they
address the implications of their own and alternative policies for poverty, especially for the poorest children; monitor what was happening
to these children; and use the knowledge already available in UNICEF,
WHO, and other knowledgeable agencies. The paper was done by Sunday afternoon, and I flew to Korea that evening. Richard and Jim did
some further editing and refinement before it was presented.

The meeting with the IMF's managing director went well. Our paper
was not provided to him or his staff until near the end of the meeting,
and by all accounts it was appreciated, particularly the section addressing the IMF's anticipated concerns. Richard delighted in recounting
what had transpired at that meeting. At one point, as he told it, de
Laroisière, in response to the UNICEF argument that further thought
needed to be given to distributional issues, protested that the IMF, after
all, only had 600 to 700 professionals. Richard had to resist the tempta-
tion, he said, to tell him that the much-praised UNICEF policy paper
had been drafted by two friends working in their spare time, without pay, on a weekend. Further meetings and seminars on UNICEF's
themes were held in both the IMF and the World Bank. They took the
issues very seriously; and the continued UNICEF research and writing,
which was energetically supported by its board and by NGO and aid
agencies everywhere, placed the financial institutions very much on
the defensive. The original paper was never intended for publication.
(In fact, at the meeting with the IMF, the managing director sought and
received assurances that it would not be published.) It was nevertheless eventually published, ten years later, purportedly for its historical
interest, in a special section of an issue of the journal *World Development*
on "adjustment with a human face."[42] Andrea, Richard, and I are listed
as co-authors, but, at their insistence, my name came first.

For the next several years I served as a member of a small steering
committee that met from time to time in New York, helping Richard to
plan UNICEF strategy and tactics in the promotion of "human face"

research and approaches to adjustment policies. Its other members included Andrea Cornia, Rolph van der Hoeven, and Eva Jespersen (UNICEF economists); Frances Stewart (who also worked full-time at UNICEF for a period); and (usually at a distance, since they were all at IDS Sussex) Reginald Green, Hans Singer, and Stephany Griffith-Jones. Per Pinstrup-Andersen of IFPRI and Cornell, Sidney Dell, and Joan Nelson, a political scientist then working at the Overseas Development Council (ODC) on the politics of stabilization, also attended some meetings. (Carlos Diaz-Alejandro was to join us, but his tragic passing in mid-1985 ended that hope.) We offered advice, read drafts, and prepared papers of our own. On one occasion I made a presentation to UNICEF resident representatives from around the world as part of a two-day training session for them. I also had a hand in the paper on international dimensions of "adjustment with a human face"[43] in the subsequent basic volume, which some referred to as the human face bible (although it attracted more criticism from the right than the Bible ever did), published by Oxford in 1987. My name appears as the paper's co-author, together with Frances Stewart. In actual fact, all that I did was (hurriedly) prepare an annotated outline, which I had done at Richard's insistence one morning at his home in New York. I had spent the night there, following a meeting, before flying off somewhere else. Frances did all the final writing, and I was flabbergasted to see my name as an author when the book came out. Later, I contributed a section to a UNICEF staff working paper on the need for African debt relief at a time, in the early 1990s, when it was still a controversial idea; and it received widespread circulation.[44] At about the same time, after presenting a paper to a conference on adjustment issues in Africa at the new UNICEF Innocenti Research Centre in Florence in November 1992, Richard and Andrea (now working in Florence) persuaded me to join in the editing of the resulting volume. I was most reluctant to take this on, but, with Andrea's promise to do all the detailed dirty work, I finally agreed, and I also agreed to write the introductory chapter. (In the end, Andrea wrote an introduction to the introduction!) Published as a UNICEF study in 1994, the volume titled *From Adjustment to Development in Africa: Conflict, Controversy, Convergence, Consensus?*,[45] which was released in paperback as well as hardback, attracted quite a lot of (favourable) attention, and I was glad to have put the effort into it.

This activity in support of UNICEF complemented some of the other work I was doing at roughly the same time. Early in 1985 I wrote a paper on "Stabilization and the Poor" for a conference at the University of Toronto organized by Sue Horton and Richard Bird. (Its discussant was the director of Fiscal Affairs at the IMF, Vito Tanzi, who differed with me on many points, particularly on interpreting Tanzanian experience.) At a time when the issues it addressed were only beginning to be discussed, the paper attracted quite a lot of attention when circulated in mimeographed form, and was first published in *World Development*.[46] In 1984–5, I was also serving on an advisory committee for a new Overseas Development Institute project, led by Tony Killick, on the impact of stabilization policy on income distribution, which was also far out in front of the international discussions.

During the second half of the 1980s and the early 1990s, UNICEF had a profound influence upon international thinking about stabilization and adjustment policies. It influenced policy debates and decision making within aid agencies, finance ministries, international financial institutions, and developing countries themselves. It demonstrated that, even with limited resources, it is possible for determined, focused, and intellectually sound efforts – particularly when grounded in strong ethical convictions – to have policy impact. Unfortunately, after the departure of Jim Grant and Richard Jolly, and with the UN's overall effort to mollify a United States government that seemed to be losing interest in it, the UNICEF research and advocacy effort was abandoned.

Many years later, long after Richard had left UNICEF, I participated again in a major UNICEF think-tank activity at the Carter Center in Atlanta. Carol Bellamy, the new executive director, assembled some of the very best of UNICEF country resident representatives and an interesting external group to plot strategy for the upcoming (second) UN Children's Summit, planned for September 2001. (It eventually had to be postponed because of 9/11.) The first UN Children's Summit in 1990, through the extraordinary efforts of Jim Grant, had been a resounding success, attracting heads of state and political leaders from around the world and generating agreement on the UN Convention on the Rights of the Child. (This convention has since been ratified by all UN members except the United States.) As is often the case, a second meeting on the same subject, since it was "old news," was much more difficult to make successful. Not for the first time I was tremendously impressed with the quality – the expertise and dedication – of UNICEF personnel. I made a strong pitch for the resumption of UNICEF research and advocacy in the sphere of development policy and an attempt to restore its voice for the vulnerable in international policy discussions. Many of the UNICEF staff were enthusiastic. At higher levels, however, there was evidently continued caution about the resumption of such potentially "boat rocking" (especially as seen by the United States) activity. One of my contributions to this event was an attempt at a summary of the global record since the first Children's Summit. It was taken from the old Anglican *Book of Common Prayer*, and it found its way into the final summary session: "We have left undone those things that we ought to have done, and we have done those things that we ought not to have done." People of every faith seemed to agree to that much! And I subsequently enjoyed telling about this when I later delivered a homily on global justice to an Anglican congregation in West Toronto.

UN Secretary-General's Task Forces

I served on two advisory groups for the secretary-general of the United Nations. Both related to African problems.

The first was chaired by Sir Douglas Wass, previously the head of the UK Treasury and civil service, but by that time the chairman of Nomura International, a Japanese investment bank in London. Following the UN General Assembly adoption of a "programme of action" for African development in mid-1986, our group was asked to address possible means of resolving the financial crisis facing African countries at that time. It produced its report, *Financing Africa's Recovery*, in February 1988.[47]

Its origins lay in a private meeting to discuss Africa's financial problems, convened by Stephen Lewis, then Canadian ambassador to the United Nations, in his New York apartment in 1986, to which I was invited. When I arrived there I found, among other officials and assistants, Richard Jolly of UNICEF and Kim Jaycox, vice president for Africa of the World Bank. Jaycox, Lewis, and Jolly did most of the talking. There was general despair about the prospects for Africa. It seemed unlikely that Africa would be able to meet the internationally agreed program targets. In particular, the prospects looked bleak for obtaining the external finance necessary for even minimal progress or indeed the avoidance of regress. Jaycox was refreshingly candid about what the World Bank could and could not do. Although he and his staff could see that Africa's external debt load was a very serious impediment to Africa's prospects, it was not politically possible, he told us, for the Bank to push debt relief for Africa in public. Someone else, he said, would have to do that; and he was very supportive of the idea that this might be done through the UN. For credibility, it would be necessary, it was agreed, to involve thoroughly "sound" and "reputable" analysts from the international banking community in a well-publicized independent assessment of Africa's situation.

Following consultations with key member governments and with the IMF and World Bank, the secretary-general appointed an advisory group of, to use his language, "eminent persons with particular competence in the area of international financial flows." The group, numbering thirteen, included three prominent private bankers from the industrial countries, in addition to Sir Douglas. They included Robert Hormats, vice president of Goldman Sachs from the United States (whom I had briefly encountered ten years previously when he was a graduate student seeking to conduct research in Tanzania) and the heads of prominent Dutch and German investment banks (ABN and Warburg, respectively). There were three Africans, one of whom was my old Kenyan friend Philip Ndegwa, formerly governor of the central bank but now the chairman of a private financial institution. The others were Alwyn Taylor from Sierra Leone, director of the African Centre for Monetary Studies in Dakar, and the head of the principal caisse in Côte d'Ivoire. Apart from the chair of the Japanese Institute for International Economic Studies in Tokyo, who never did say very much, I was the only academic. Goran Ohlin, a Swedish friend and former academic, now the chief economist at UN headquarters, headed our group's very capable research staff.

Our meetings in New York and London went well. As anticipated, when the facts were pointed out to them (the non-Africans, including Sir Douglas, had previously known little about them), all agreed, bankers included, that Africa's financial situation was impossible. The chairman was a quick learner and, I believe, took some pleasure in reaching his own progressive conclusions. In order to show that we had had some direct contact with Africa, a subgroup of us – Sir Douglas, Alwyn Taylor, Goran Ohlin, and I – joined Philip Ndegwa in Nairobi to discuss some of the issues "on the ground." Among others whom we met, on Philip's insistence, was the Kenyan president, Daniel arap Moi. This "audience" was, as is so frequently the case, a highly stilted and formalistic occasion. Very little of substance transpired, and a disproportionate amount of time was spent waiting and setting up the required official photograph. I do remember, however, the tension surrounding the revelation to the president that Ohlin was from Sweden, whose Parliament had only recently condemned the abuse of human rights in Kenya. Goran had to explain that he was an international civil servant

10.1. With President Daniel arap Moi, Sir Douglas Wass, and members of the UN Secretary-General's Advisory Group on Financial Flows to Africa, Nairobi, 1997

and was not there to represent, in any way, his country of origin. During our stay in Nairobi, I had an opportunity to get to know Sir Douglas a little better and, in the end, at his suggestion, I drafted an outline for him of what I thought the report should contain.

It was quite a good report,[48] well received at the IMF and World Bank, among other places. It called for the urgent conversion of earlier concessional loans to grants, the rescheduling of other official (bilateral and multilateral) loans at highly concessional interest rates, relief of commercial bank debt on a case-by-case basis, and significantly increased official development assistance. Unfortunately the United Nations' press relations and publicity machine pressed entirely the wrong buttons when the report was released. To my mind, the real news was *not* in what was highlighted in their summaries: the size of the increased financial flows to Africa that were required. That was already an old, familiar, and sad African story – no surprise to anyone. The *real* news was that eminent private bankers and international financiers were joining in the call for increased financial flows to Africa and, even more remarkably, were calling for significant write-downs of African debt.

It would be several years before any debt relief was actually offered for Africa, and when it came it wasn't enough. An increase in net financial flows was eventually realized as well, but it wasn't nearly enough either. Our group did nevertheless contribute something, I believe, to the evolution of official thinking about Africa's financial problems.

The experience with the other secretary-general's advisory group was rather less satisfactory. In response to African pressure and a UN General Assembly resolution at the midterm review in late 1988 of the 1986–90 UN program of action for Africa, the secretary-general appointed another "expert group" to assess and make recommendations concerning the problems associated with Africa's extreme dependence upon primary commodity exports. It was controversial from its very beginnings, most notably because of the appointment of Malcolm Fraser, formerly a conservative prime minister of Australia, as its chairman. When I arrived at UNCTAD in Geneva for its first meeting, as an appointed member of the group, I found its staff abuzz, and horrified, at the apparent conservative hijacking, as they saw it, of the project. The remaining members constituted quite a motley collection, ranging from Ismail Sabri Abdalla, the Egyptian chairman of the Third World Forum, on the left, to Saxon Tate of Tate and Lyle, sugar barons, and Fraser himself, on the right. Richard Cooper from Harvard, Richard Webb of Peru, Norway's Martin Huslid, and I were somewhere in the middle. Five out of our fifteen were Africans, of whom one was Nigerian General Obasanjo, who was shortly to become Nigeria's elected president.

This group's final report[49] was not completed until the middle of 1990. In part, this lengthy time was because of the complexity of the subject and in part because of the difficulty of reaching agreed conclusions within such a diverse group. To reach agreement we had to meet six times – in Geneva (twice), New York, Addis Ababa, London, and Oslo. Indeed the whole venture nearly collapsed at the final meeting in Geneva over the chairman's unwillingness – until the last minute – to compromise and agree to the draft's recommendations on the possibility of international producer agreements for cocoa and coffee. Unfortunately General Obasanjo never did sign the report; and Abdalla and Huslid insisted on attaching letters of qualification to the final published document.

In part the report's long gestation period was also because Fraser took it upon himself to consult and travel extraordinarily broadly. He also pressed members to undertake exploratory and educational travel on behalf of the group, and report back on our findings. I undertook to travel with Abdalla to Tanzania and Mauritius. Unfortunately my colleague backed out at the last minute, and I was left to be received alone, on my arrival in Dar es Salaam, by a visibly disappointed bevy of UN officials and representatives of the Egyptian embassy. Illness at home forced me to cancel the visit to Mauritius that was intended to follow. Fraser travelled, in his capacity as the group's chairman, throughout Africa as well as to Japan, Europe, and North America. Some of this travel, particularly travel within Africa, was widely attributed to the fact that he was at that time also actively campaigning to be the new secretary-general of the Commonwealth. (He did not succeed.) All of this took a lot of time, and, of course, probably cost the UN considerably more than they had originally budgeted for this expert group.

Backup for this group was to be provided by the UNCTAD secretariat, the UNDP, and UNECA, at that time headed by a determined Nigerian, Adebayo Adedeji. The latter proved to be a source of considerable annoyance to the chairman. Shortly after our initial meeting, and without the authorization or knowledge of the chairman or anyone else within the group, UNECA, in apparent collaboration with UNCTAD, circulated what they described as an early draft of some introductory chapters of our report. It reached Washington shortly before visits that Fraser had arranged there with the World Bank, the IMF, and other experts and authorities, at some of which he had asked me to join him. The draft was a weak piece of work, full of "passionate intensity" (to use the language of W.B. Yeats) but with little analytical content. A World Bank official described it to Fraser, he angrily told me, as "sophomoric." Certainly the paper should not have been circulated before coming before our group or at least the chairman. Fraser was, in fact, absolutely furious at the implied discredit to his own reputation, and he did not fully trust UNECA, or to some degree UNCTAD, to draft anything from that point on.

At the first meetings, Obasanjo, to whom the normally rather irascible, impatient, and abrupt chairman was quite deferential, spoke repeatedly and at length about the shortcomings of African governments and their need to reform themselves. His inputs were consistent with the sterling global reputation he had earned as a military leader who had voluntarily transformed his country into a democracy and as chairman of the corruption-fighting NGO, Transparency International. To Fraser, who had known Obasanjo from their earlier work together in the Commonwealth's effort to find a way through South Africa's morass, all of this was just the kind of music that he wanted to hear. At later meetings, however, when commodity issues were finally discussed in greater detail, the famed Nigerian statesman took less interest. He did not express views or objections at the final meeting at which the last details of the report's recommendations were tortuously negotiated. Yet he subsequently refused to sign the report (the only member of the group to do so). He wrote no minority report and offered us no explanations, although he subsequently wrote two letters to the UN secretary-general expressly dissociating himself from the report. Among his complaints was that too much emphasis had been directed to Africa's own mistakes, an emphasis that he had himself originally insisted upon. Adedeji (and UNCTAD) had very much wanted a recommendation for the establishment of a "diversification fund for Africa." Our group could see no reason to believe that additional financing for it would materialize and therefore did not recommend it.

The group's meeting in Addis in July 1989 was timed to coincide with a meeting of African heads of state in the Organisation of African Unity (OAU), the predecessor of the African Union, which was also attended by the UN secretary-general, Javier Perez de Cuellar, who also took the occasion to meet us. I have never forgotten the scene in front of the ornate Africa Hall where I joined a crowd of the local curious to watch the arrival of the various political leaders in their limousines. (In those days security was not as tight as it would be today.) The crowd was polite but silent as each of the leaders, some magnificently attired in traditional dress, got out of his (they were all male) official car and, with his entourage, went into the hall. The only leader to receive applause, and it was quite vigorous, was Perez de Cuellar. I was mightily impressed by the fact that he was recognized at all but, even more, by the respect for the United Nations that the warm reception for him seemed to reflect.

Our report was widely regarded as a "conservative" one. This label was probably because it began with the need for continuing reforms within Africa and the recommendations for more effective use of African commodity export potential and the development of a "commodity strategy" within each country. These messages were taken by some, quite incorrectly, as advocacy of continued reliance upon primary commodity exporting as against diversification and structural change. This conclusion was inaccurate and unfair, and it was painful for me. The recommendations for the international community were actually quite far-reaching, including vastly expanded resource flows to Africa, commodity agreements at least for coffee and cocoa, further debt relief for Africa and IMF gold sales to support some of it, reduced agricultural protectionism in the industrial countries and an end to their subsidized food exports to Africa, and "human face" measures in adjustment programs. When Hans Singer (together with Adrian Hewitt) attacked the report on specious grounds in a letter to the *Financial Times*,[50] although Hans was a friend and intellectual ally, I felt I had to reply with some vigour (as did Fraser):

> I am at a loss to recognise the ... report Messrs. Hewitt and Singer say they are attacking. They cannot have read the report in which I was involved ...
> The Fraser Report makes a large number of recommendations that deserve discussion. It seems a pity to waste effort on debates that do not stem from the contents of this report.[51]

There followed a lively exchange of personal letters with Hans, who had again written in a similar vein (in the UN's *Africa Report*) to which I also took very strong exception:

> [Y]our assault upon the Fraser Report is again way off the mark ... you have once again grossly distorted the message of the report ... I do not know why you have decided to launch these attacks upon straw men in this way. It is my confidence that we do not disagree significantly on any of the important issues that holds me back from challenging your account again in print.[52]

To his credit, Hans replied that, after my letter, he had re-read the report. "I still have my doubts," he wrote, "but I now accept much of what you say and will now keep quiet in future on the report."[53]

Committee for Development Planning

Established in 1966 by the UN Economic and Social Council (ECOSOC, as it is colloquially known), the Committee for Development Planning (CDP) is an advisory body of independent "experts" that is asked to assess, in annual reports, world development trends and prospects, and to formulate appropriate policy recommendations for the use of the international community. Membership is spread widely so as to be broadly representative of the international community. The experts are appointed for three-year (renewable) terms. I was first appointed to the CDP in 1984 and resigned in November of that same year. Much against my better judgment, I accepted another appointment in 1987–90.

Originally, under the intellectual leadership of Jan Tinbergen, the meetings were probably quite exciting and fruitful. By the time I joined it, however, they were mostly rather tedious and frustrating. Usually held at UN headquarters in New York, they always created pleasant opportunities for picking up the latest UN documents (and gossip), catching up with "expert" friends, and meeting new ones. The experts included excellent people, and still others were often invited to attend and/or contribute on matters of their special expertise. But the formal meetings themselves were, to me, pretty much a waste of time. They typically consisted of two or three days of rambling discussions on some pre-agreed theme, in which the contributions varied enormously in their quality and relevance. The Russians and East Europeans could be counted upon (although there were sometimes surprising exceptions) to offer denunciations of Western approaches and policies, while offering little of substance to the subject under discussion. Westerners were sometimes little better. Despite the difficulty of finding commonalities upon which all could agree, these discussions were followed by drafting sessions in which a rapporteur was delegated, sometimes with others' assistance (I was often one), to try to cobble together some kind of report, usually working late into the night. There followed another, usually very difficult, day (by that time the drafters were tired and irritable), in which the members offered line-by-line complaints about the draft and argued at length over the details of the final text. After our departure, the UN Secretariat was left to put the final report together for subsequent publication and circulation. Another task of the committee was to define and to identify (by name) what were to be recognized by the UN as "least developed countries"; this job was not the most fascinating or intellectually challenging of tasks either. I dare say that none of the CDP reports made any significant contribution to the world's stock of knowledge. Nor did the world's development practitioners or experts take much notice of them; most of them probably did not even know of their existence. Whether they had any influence upon the UN diplomats to whom they were sent would be difficult to say.

I made some efforts and exerted some pressure toward the reform of the CDP. It seemed to me that if it had a significant research budget (it had virtually none), it could perform a very useful function by commissioning expert research on frontier development policy questions, which it could be the function of the CDP to identify. As a small foundation, with an international expert board, it might in this way at last have both intellectual and political impact. Goran Ohlin of the UN Secretariat, with whom I engaged in a useful exchange of letters about it after my initial resignation, had some sympathy with my views; but these ideas eventually went nowhere.

At the time of my first appointment, the UN Secretariat was trying to raise the profile of the CDP by appointing some better known and more "political" members. Sonny Ramphal, Commonwealth secretary-general, became its chairman; and Robert McNamara, former president of the World Bank, now chairman of the ODC in Washington, became the American member. Advice was sought from prominent journalists as to how more effectively to "market" its reports. All of this eventually came to nothing. But the McNamara presence did help to precipitate my resignation following the CDP meeting in Geneva in November 1984.

At the previous CDP meeting (my first), I had agreed to serve as rapporteur for a subcommittee that would prepare a report, for the use of the committee, attempting to make the case for multilateralism in policy approaches to international economic problems. At that time multilateral approaches were being seriously challenged, particularly by the United States under the Reagan administration, and it seemed to all of us that some kind of international "call to arms" in defence of multilateralism was required. The subcommittee held a quite productive meeting in Geneva following which, although I was heavily burdened with other obligations, I prepared the promised draft report. I was more than a little surprised when the Yugoslav member of the subcommittee, who until that point had been a vigorous and productive contributor to its deliberations and upon whose contributions I had in large measure drawn in what I thought was quite a good report, registered objections to nearly every paragraph in his very long written commentary on the draft. I found this very discouraging. With very little time before the plenary CDP meeting, I had neither the time nor the inclination to attempt a redraft. It was therefore not presented and, to all intents and purposes, vanished forever.

At the Geneva meeting, however, the CDP seemed to make major progress on another front: addressing the problems of Africa, including, most recently, famine in Ethiopia. The chairman had prepared the ground well, having invited some extra experts (including Reginald Green, an old friend from Yale, Tanzania, and Sussex days) to attend the meeting as specialized backup should it be required. McNamara made an impassioned plea in the meeting for international action to address Africa's longer-term problems and forestall a succession of further food crises in the future. We decided to issue a special short emergency report on Africa. I was asked to draft it in the evening after the meeting. I stayed up half the night doing so, and, with only minor amendments, it was adopted (and it was subsequently printed as a pamphlet and widely circulated in the UN system[54]). It was decided that, for maximum effect, chairman Sonny Ramphal and McNamara should hold a press conference the following day to release the report; and Sonny asked that I come to back them up in case they needed it.

To my mind, the press conference was a disaster; and McNamara helped to make it so. After Sonny's introduction of the CDP's recommendations for action on Africa, the floor was opened for questions. They all came to McNamara rather than to Ramphal. None had anything to do with Africa or the CDP; and McNamara seemed to enjoy responding to questions about the US automobile industry and its problems, and other American issues, apparently totally insensitive to what was happening to our project and the purpose of the press conference. I was disgusted – and angry.

To make it worse, my association with the CDP was already under some stress. During the previous day's meeting, Sonny had, without prior warning, publicly sprung a request upon me: that I take on the job of "rapporteur" for the CDP, succeeding Goran Ohlin, who was moving to a new high-level job (assistant secretary-general) in the UN. The rapporteur carried prime responsibility for the preparation of the CDP's reports. Although I had already been a significant contributor to their drafting, my professional workload was already very heavy. Moreover, I had just been through an unfortunate experience with the subcommittee report, and was very tired from the previous night's drafting of the African report. I was in no mood for such surprises. My (equally public) declining of his request was probably too testy. It included the unfortunate phrase, "I have much better things to do with my time." This incident alone was probably reason enough to offer my resignation.

Also of great concern to me was the decision, led by the chairman, that the next meeting of the CDP would focus upon "domestic policies," a topic so broad and so inappropriate for an international body such as the CDP, or so it seemed to me, that it could only generate a report that was even more useless than the already dubious norm. When the date for the next meeting was agreed, I did not bother to say that, in fact, I was unlikely to be able to attend at that time, for my interest in it was already at low ebb.

As I angrily left the press conference, I felt it necessary to tell Janet Singh, Sonny's trusted assistant and personal secretary (and by now a good friend, in consequence of all of my work with the Commonwealth Secretariat, detailed in chapter eleven), of my intention to resign. I wrote Sonny a short formal letter of resignation and a much longer personal letter. In retrospect I think the letter is quite interesting, so I will quote from it at some length:

> Do not think for a minute that I have acted lightly or without considerable regret – even personal anguish – over what I should be doing. Nor should you think that your pressure tactics in the final meeting had any significant impact upon the decision that I was bound to make; they merely triggered a faster decision.
>
> Let me try to give you some of the reasons for my resignation:
>
> – The time input required of me has proven far greater than anticipated and, even with the best possible future scenario before the committee, it looks like being greater than I want to put into it.
>
> – I see my own prime responsibilities and capacities in terms of teaching and research in a scholarly context. The fact that I involve myself in analysis of policy questions and even participate in some political processes does not alter the fact that the contribution that I want to make is as a "resource person" rather than a diplomat or civil servant.
>
> – The technical and political support for the CDP, however energetic and dedicated may be its chairman, is so weak that I question seriously whether it can be an important vehicle for the sorts of professional inputs that I want to make to the discussion of policy.
>
> As you yourself most certainly know, able people must continually make difficult choices as to how to allocate their energy and time – what people, issues and institutions to support (and sometimes even carry). I suppose that, most important of all, are some directions and priorities to guide the daily decisions. We share some – you and me – but we do not share them all. No doubt we may also judge some prospects differently. In particular, I now see the CDP and the UN itself (especially now that I had seen them

a little closer up) considerably lower – in my overall rankings – than many other potential outlets for my limited time. The thought that I too could be "sucked into" the UN maw, like some others of my acquaintance – including the last two CDP rapporteurs – terrifies me. I have no aspirations whatsoever to "rise" in some overall international hierarchy (whether UN or other). If there are reserves of time and energy available for my personal redeployment, they presently are likely to go to family and the world of the handicapped in which we at home are deeply involved ...

One last reflection – even more personal, and perhaps even idiosyncratic, than the rest. I have been annoyed by the two changes of date for CDP plenary meetings, both made to accommodate the same member. I enjoyed meeting and listening to Robert McNamara, and I agree with much of what he has to say and am glad that he can so vigorously express his views to the world. But, all things considered, I was offended by his behaviour, particularly at the press conference. One cannot blame McNamara for his insensitivity to those with non-American concerns or his disrespect for the CDP; they are part of his personality. But the CDP is in some danger of becoming known – especially perhaps in the US – as a vehicle for McNamara's views. And the staff and membership of CDP will have only themselves to blame for their "asymmetric interdependence" if they continue to jump every time one of the members squeaks. I, for one, will in future be quite careful regarding involvements in which so dominant and insensitive a personality is involved ...

Let's just put this CDP affair down to a youthful (!) error. We all make mistakes. The trick is to recognize them quickly.[55]

In the end, I was persuaded to attend the next meeting as an external expert invitee to help them put together their report, not on domestic policies, but on "the challenge to multilateralism," a topic on which I had already put in some effort on the CDP's behalf.

When I was persuaded to rejoin a totally reconstituted committee in 1987, we got off to a very rocky start in the selection of a new chairman. One of the new CDP members seemed to assume (he had probably been led by the UN Secretariat to believe) that he would be the logical choice. Mahbub ul Haq, then a Pakistani cabinet minister, had been a vice-president of the World Bank, had been active in North-South circles, and had established something of a reputation as an iconoclastic economist. Instead of the usual pro forma election of a pre-agreed new chair and immediately getting down to business, however, the CDP meeting was almost immediately and rather awkwardly adjourned, pending further consultation among members. We then returned with agreement on a new chair: Abdlatif Al-Hamad of Kuwait (whom I had come to know and like as a member of the Wass committee on African finance). No one commented on the incongruity of the fact that the chair of the UN's independent committee on development was also one of the world's wealthiest men and came from a country in which democracy and women's rights were, to put it mildly, somewhat limited.

The new American appointee to the committee, replacing McNamara, appeared to be a sop to the Republican administration – Henry Nau, a conservative political scientist with ties to the administration and no prior background, so far as we could discover, in development. Just Faaland, a colleague from Norway of whom I was to see much more in later years (see chapter fifteen), became the rapporteur. The CDP reports of this period were no more significant than before. But under the influence of our Kuwaiti chairman, one of them focused upon the issue of the future availability of water, and at the time this was quite original and proved prescient.

In deference to the changing political and intellectual environments, the CDP has since been slightly renamed. Instead of a Committee on Development Planning, it is now a Committee on Development Policy. I suspect that its problems have not changed much.

International Labour Organization

The International Labour Organization (ILO), established in 1919, is the oldest of the multilateral organizations concerned with economic matters. Its unique tripartite governance system provides for equal representation from government, labour, and employers in each of its member countries. For much of the postwar period it had concerned itself primarily with union-management issues and labour rights. In the 1970s, however, under a dynamic director of the relevant division, it began to take a leadership role in international research on poverty and efforts to address employment problems in developing countries. In the international development community at this time there was considerable disillusion with the apparent ineffectiveness of previous governmental efforts to reduce poverty by stimulating economic growth in developing countries. In the face of rising urban unemployment and continuing mass poverty, there was much talk of "dethroning GNP." Much of the intellectual stimulus for these revisionist approaches derived from a group of economists at the newly created Institute of

Development Studies (IDS) at the University of Sussex, then directed by Dudley Seers. They included, among others, Richard Jolly, Hans Singer, and Michael Lipton. The Sussex group led a series of ILO employment missions, emphasizing the new approaches, first to Colombia and then to Sri Lanka and Kenya. Many other such ILO country missions followed, often challenging more conventional advice such as that received from the IMF and the World Bank; but the earliest ILO reports generated the most excitement. When I arrived at the IDS Sussex for a sabbatical year in 1971, there was still a great buzz there about the recent success of the Colombia mission. Shortly after my arrival, I was vigorously pressed to join, as a leader, the forthcoming mission to Kenya. I managed to protect my sabbatical, and relations with my family, and declined; although, to overcome my guilt, I wrote many pages of comments a few months later upon the early drafts of the Kenya mission report. (The report, with its emphasis upon the "informal sector" proved to be highly influential within the development community, if not in Kenya.) I suppose, then, that this was when my association with the ILO really began.

The leader of this new ILO employment initiative, called the World Employment Programme (WEP), was Louis Emmerij, an energetic Dutchman who was great company if you got along with him, as fortunately I did. Sensitivity and patience were not his strong suits. But he certainly got things done! He was ably supported by his research director, Dharam Ghai, a Kenyan Asian friend from my Yale and East African past. (He had directed the Institute of Development Studies at the University of Nairobi when I was doing a somewhat similar job in Dar es Salaam.) In personality, Dharam was Louis's polar opposite – quiet, mild-mannered, polite. I liked Dharam very much and respected his work. (He subsequently became the very successful director of the UN Research Institute for Social Development, UNRISD, in Geneva.) Together they made a formidably effective pair.

In the summer of 1975, while I was again at the IDS Sussex for a couple of months, Dharam invited me to prepare a paper for the ILO on the role of multinational corporations in the development of manufacturing for export from developing countries, a subject on which I had been doing research for some time. It was to constitute one of the background research papers in support of a forthcoming global ILO conference on employment and development. For me, such a paper was a labour of love, and I happily wrote a long survey paper and got it done on time. (It was later published in the ILO volume containing all of the conference background papers, and, still later, in French translation, in an academic journal.[56]) I next heard from Dharam in the fall when he asked for my help, as a consultant, in the preparation of the basic conference document. Earlier in the year the WEP had gathered together a small group of "progressive" economists, including many friends of mine, to advise as to the appropriate thrust of a World Employment Conference, planned for 1976. One of the outcomes was a decision to emphasize not merely "employment" but, rather, "basic needs." During the months that followed, draft chapters began to be prepared and circulated.

Evidently there had been trouble over the proposed chapter on the role of multinationals in employment and basic needs provision. Always a controversial topic, it had proven difficult to prepare a draft that was sufficiently "balanced" as to pass muster with both labour and employer representatives, not to speak of the governments of both developed and developing countries. Dharam argued that, with my knowledge of the subject (at that time I was on top of the relevant literature and was writing quite a lot on multinationals) and with my "openness" and "balance," I would be the perfect person to prepare this draft chapter, apparently the only chapter still giving them serious trouble. I had my doubts, but he persuaded me to give it a try, so I came to the ILO in Geneva for about ten days in January 1976 to interact with others and help put the final conference document to bed.

My draft chapter, put together in the first three to four days, seemed well received. A small group of ILO economists (Dharam Ghai, Louis Emmerij, Keith Griffin, Ajit Bhalla, and Keith Marsden) then repaired for the rest of the week, with a couple of secretaries, to a small motel on the northern outskirts of Geneva to pull together the overall draft conference report in a final "crash" effort. Louis insisted that I join them. In a large room set up with a number of desks, we drafted sections, paragraphs, whole chapters; rapidly got them typed; and exchanged them with one another for comments. It was a real team effort and, although I was not part of the ILO, I was treated as a full member. By Friday we had it done, and Louis treated us to an exuberant celebratory dinner at a nearby restaurant, followed by a much-too-boisterous party (some of the other residents complained) in one of the rooms back at the motel. The complete draft was then made available to employer and labour representatives, and to the ILO management, for them to read over the weekend. On Monday they all gathered with us to offer their comments, chapter by chapter, on the overall draft report. I was shocked by the reception accorded my chapter on multinationals. After describing it as "clever," the employer representative proceeded to quarrel, almost on a knee-jerk basis, with all the statements in the draft that might be interpreted as critical of multinational corporations. My draft had not been directly critical; rather, it had tried to lay out the agreed knowledge and some of the pros and cons, drawing on such empirical literature as there was at that time. I thought I had leaned over backward in order to be fair and to forestall such possible attack. To my astonishment, the labour representative made little effort to come to the draft's defence. On the contrary, after the morning session, he went off to lunch with the employers' representative at an expensive restaurant. It was as if it had all been fixed in advance. There were some healthy exchanges of view. But the ILO director-general, Francois Blanchard, who chaired the meeting, showed signs of accepting these comments and recommendations at face value. Coming from an academic tradition, I was quite disillusioned by this experience. Before returning home the next day, and with Louis's encouragement, however, I decided to make one last stab at saving the report's section on multinationals. I wrote a personal letter to Blanchard:

> I am writing to you in my personal capacity, not as a member of your staff or as the temporary consultant to the ILO which until today I have been ... to express my deep concern as to the possibility that the ILO may take a "wrong turn" on it [the subject of multinational enterprises].
>
> In my work as a consultant to the United Nations, the UNCTAD, the OECD and the Government of Canada – as well as in my own academic experience – I have had considerable exposure to the debate on multinationals. I can truthfully say that the views which were being expressed to us in yesterday's meeting are quite out of touch with the present high-level discussions. It did not seem appropriate to document the various "assertions" in the draft chapter but I can assure you that they were, in every case, not "views" but facts (appropriately and carefully qualified where necessary). In high-level discussions in the UNCTAD committees on the transfer of technology and restrictive business practices, in the OECD discussions of a possible code of conduct, and at the governmental level in Canada, such facts are taken as given and the discussion proceeds as to what is to be done about them. They are not taken as "views" which others (employer spokesmen) are invited to rebut through presentation of other "views."
>
> If the section on multinationals is emasculated in the manner being suggested yesterday, I fear the ILO will find itself in the peculiar position of

bringing up the rear in the international discussion of the subject, more conservative even than the majority of OECD member governments. Apart from the effect this would have on the ILO's credibility in the Third World, particularly in Latin America, I believe it would also severely damage its reputation and credibility in the overall discussion of development issues at the international level. The effect would be particularly devastating if such a conservative approach to this issue were taken in a document which at the same time offers so much advice to the governments of developing countries.[57]

Unfortunately, my advice was only partially heeded. The section on multinationals was significantly "softened" (made more bland) to mollify the employers. Perhaps in compensation, I was invited to contribute a short paper on multinationals and employment creation in the developing countries for publication in *ILO Information*, the in-house bulletin.[58] The conference background report, *Employment, Growth and Basic Needs*,[59] and the conference itself nevertheless proved influential in moving the international development community away from its previous focus upon economic growth toward greater emphasis upon poverty and distributional objectives. The ILO and UNICEF successfully "pushed their envelopes" in this respect, helping to drive aid donors and eventually the World Bank and even the IMF in a more poverty-focused direction. It was good to be part of these efforts.

I stayed in touch both with Louis, who left the ILO the following year, and with the ILO over subsequent years. When the ILO launched a research program on "alternative stabilization programs," I contributed to it. As at UNCTAD, I had the dubious honour of having another of my papers on Africa plagiarized and submitted to the ILO as an original piece of research; as at UNCTAD it was hastily withdrawn. In more recent years, I served as a member of the editorial board of the *International Labour Review* (the ILO journal), although, truth to tell, this involved very little work.

11 Sonny Times at the Commonwealth Secretariat

For many years, and certainly during my years of living in Africa, I had a deep scepticism regarding the role of the Commonwealth. It seemed to me a relic of the British Empire, deserving of an early retirement. I remember attending a conference on the future of the Commonwealth held at Laval University (of all places, a francophone institution in Quebec), probably in the early 1970s, where all of my doubts seemed to be confirmed by what seemed to me to be the preponderance of "old Commonwealth hands" in attendance. But I was to change my mind.

During the tenure of Sir Shridath "Sonny" Ramphal of Guyana, its second secretary-general (1975–90), successor to Arnold Smith, the Canadian who subsequently became the first chairman of the board of the North-South Institute (see chapter eighteen), the Commonwealth Secretariat aspired to become a significant actor in international economic debate relating to development issues. The membership of the Commonwealth not only straddled the North-South divide but also shared common language and certain cultural characteristics, making it possible for Ramphal to argue that it could often serve as a useful bridge across this worldwide divide. Its relative informality made it possible for him fairly quickly to launch, with a minimum of the usual diplomatic niceties, a number of constructive initiatives in search of global economic progress and reform at a time when the world badly needed them. I was honoured to be asked to play a significant role in some of these efforts.

The first record in my files of any contact with the Commonwealth Secretariat was a request in December 1973 from J.P. Hayes, director of its Trade and Finance Division, to discuss their plans for research regarding the role of foreign direct investment in developing countries during one of my stopovers in London en route to Africa. I was happy to oblige. I had myself been working in this field for a couple of years, notably during my sabbatical at the IDS Sussex in 1971–2. Further contacts led to an invitation to participate as a resource person in a regional seminar on the subject held in Port Moresby, Papua New Guinea, in March 1976. This opportunity was too good to miss, particularly since I had played an intermediary role in the appointment of Papua New Guinea's then chief economist, David Beatty, and I was anxious to see how it was working for him. It was a good seminar and a good trip. In addition to my expected duties, I enjoyed interacting with the principal government economists and a brief trip into the highlands.

My principal contributions to the work of the Commonwealth Secretariat, however, had to do with the series of "expert" reports that it commissioned over the subsequent years. These reports were typically formally commissioned either by the Commonwealth finance ministers or by the Commonwealth heads of state, in both cases usually jogged by Sonny Ramphal and his secretariat. A representative group of Commonwealth experts, supported by the secretariat and other consultants, and acting in their personal capacities, met and produced agreed reports, which were then printed and widely circulated. The first – on the New International Economic Order (NIEO) – was the product of a group chaired by Alister McIntyre from the Caribbean (born in Grenada) and appeared in 1977.[60] The Canadian member of this group, an official of the federal government, evidently had a difficult time agreeing to it all, but eventually signed on to a report that was highly sympathetic to the aspirations of the developing countries. So did the British and Australian members. It received quite a lot of attention. Evidently here was a device that could be used again.

The next expert group to be formed, in 1977, addressed a more specific controversial issue: the common fund for primary commodities that had been recommended by UNCTAD as the central pillar of the proposed NIEO, being pushed by the developing countries at the UN at the time. The industrialized countries, led by the United States, were bitterly opposed to any such new fund. I was honoured to be invited to join this group, which was chaired by a British businessman with interests in sugar, Lord Campbell of Elkan. My principal contribution was to argue vigorously for a stress upon its "second window," which was to finance commodity-related development (storage, processing, and the like), rather than upon the stabilization objectives of the "first window." Remarkably, the group was able to reach agreement with only two meetings in London. Again, the report was much more sympathetic to developing countries' interests than were the Northern member governments of the Commonwealth. From the Commonwealth Secretariat's standpoint, this new instrument thus seemed to be working well, although still carrying little policy influence with the governments of the United Kingdom, Canada, or Australia.

At about this time, a much higher-level and more ambitious version of this instrument was deployed to explore North-South disagreements and global needs. At the suggestion of Robert McNamara, and under the chairmanship of Germany's former socialist chancellor, Willy Brandt, the Brandt Commission included, among its eighteen members, Britain's ex-prime minister Edward (Ted) Heath, the United States' Katherine Graham (publisher of the *Washington Post*), Sweden's Olof Palme, and, on the developing country side, among others, Sonny Ramphal. (Canada was represented by national union leader Joe Morris.) It had a very professional secretariat headed by Goran Ohlin and Drag Avramovic, and including Robert Cassen and Justinian Rweyemamu (from Tanzania) among others. Shortly after its creation, Sonny Ramphal used the occasion of an "eminent persons" meeting at UNCTAD (Geneva), which was addressing various international development issues, to invite a number of participants, all economists and all from Commonwealth countries, to a side meeting to discuss some of his own concerns and needs. Half a dozen of us assembled in his room at the Intercontinental Hotel, where we were greeted by his personal assistant and secretary, Janet Singh, of whom we were soon to see a great deal more. Sonny explained his need for a Commonwealth "think tank" of people who could offer him, on an informal and voluntary basis, expert independent opinions, comments, and assessments of economic materials and issues (he was a lawyer) with which he had to deal. I do not recall any reference specifically to the Brandt Commission, but perhaps he did mention it. It was easy for us all to agree in principle. Thus was born the informal group that he (and others) later enjoyed calling the "Commonwealth t'inkers."

In 1978–9, as the Brandt Commission deliberated at a series of meetings around the world, considering staff papers, outlines of its report, and chapter drafts, Sonny drew liberally on his "t'inkers." We received all of the commission's background papers, and as many of us as could make it met with Sonny before each meeting. Those who couldn't attend sent comments. Sonny had invariably read the material carefully and was always ready, and made the time, for detailed discussion. I was very

11.1. With Sir Shridath "Sonny" Ramphal, receiving an honorary degree from the University of the West Indies, November 1997

impressed with his seriousness and professionalism. On one occasion, dissatisfied with the draft outline of the final report that the commission secretariat had prepared, our group settled into a villa on the shores of Lake Geneva for a weekend in November 1978 until we had thrashed out what we considered to be a better one. In mid-May 1979, I prepared for Sonny a fairly detailed outline of what I believed should be the principal recommendations of the commission report. Mike Faber and I also did a paper that Sonny presented to the commission on the need for new financing arrangements for international minerals exploration to "socialize" its risks and reduce the prospect of conflict over its returns. I'm not sure whether other commission members or the commission secretariat even knew of the existence of our group at first. Its membership was like-minded, professional, and good humoured. It included Alister McIntyre (then at UNCTAD, later vice chancellor, University of the West Indies), Dharam Ghai (Kenya, then at the ILO), William Demas

(Trinidad, at that time president of the Caribbean Development Bank), Manmohan Singh (India, later to become finance minister and prime minister); and from the Commonwealth Secretariat, Mike Faber (UK), Frank Rampersad (director of Economic Affairs, Trinidad and Tobago), and Vishnu Persaud (Barbados, Frank's eventual successor as director of Economic Affairs). Janet Singh (Guyana) was also always there looking after all the details of travel and accommodation. It is easy to see why some described the dominant group around the Commonwealth Secretariat at the time as "the Caribbean mafia." I like to think we had an important impact upon the Brandt Commission's progress. But I know that we all, in any case, enjoyed the experience of working together.

In the end, the Brandt Commission members had great difficulty reaching agreement on a report. A split secretariat didn't help matters: Ohlin and Avramovic were unable to agree on several issues. At what he had apparently hoped would be a final meeting, an exasperated Willy Brandt finally washed his hands of the whole business, abandoned the commission secretariat, and instead agreed to leave the redrafting of an agreed final report to the two principal protagonists in the commission's debates, Ted Heath and Sonny Ramphal. It was evidently assumed that if these two could agree, the others would follow. The effective commission headquarters was moved to London, to the Commonwealth Secretariat, and one of the commission economists, Robert Cassen, came along to lead the redrafting. There followed an all-out "push" in the fall of 1979 to complete a revised draft. It was agreed that the principal message would be that it was in the mutual interest of the North and South to cooperate in global development. But the specifics as to what exactly needed to be done were still in considerable dispute. Heath appointed his former assistant, Archie McKenzie, as his representative as the redrafting proceeded. Sonny appointed me as his, at least on some of the more difficult issues. Our principal task was to reach agreement on the specific recommendations that were to be made. Both of us drafted sections. I completely rewrote, for instance, the chapter on international monetary issues (originally drafted by Rweyemamu with help from Avramovic). From time to time, when differences arose, as in the case of the section on transnational corporations and foreign direct investment, Archie and I met to iron out the agreed text. Archie was a perfect gentleman and, with compromises on both sides, we were always able eventually to find agreement. I flew across to London every other weekend for these activities. Sonny's chauffeur with his beautiful Silver Cloud limousine (licence plate: CSG 1) met my flights and, later, delivered me back to the airport. Jet lag was obviously a serious problem for me on these flying weekend visits. Sometimes I grabbed a catnap at my desk in London. Once I used a sofa at Sonny's residence. I was supported in every possible way. We got it done.

At a final commission meeting in December in Leeds Castle, Kent, to which the two "representatives" were not invited, Willy Brandt rammed it through to unanimous approval. The report was presented to the UN secretary-general in February 1980, and it was published to widespread acclaim shortly thereafter.[61] The *Times* of London declared it to be the most significant document of the twentieth century (or words to that effect). It elicited heated debate around the world. The left criticized its emphasis on "mutual interest," declaring it to be naive and hopelessly reformist in the "real world" of conflict and power. The right regarded it as wildly idealistic and impractical. The Brandt Commission held further meetings from September 1980 onward to consider later developments and follow-up. The "t'inkers" were again enlisted as backup, but this time without physical meetings. I wrote more memos and recommendations for Sonny and, on one occasion, prepared an outline of questions for him to take to his Brandt-related meeting with Robert McNamara and others at the World Bank, a meeting about which he seemed to be unusually nervous because of his lack of professional background in economics. Another Brandt report was eventually published two years later,[62] this time written by its own staff, basically Robert Cassen, but it did not receive anything like the same attention as the first one.

The Brandt Commission model was subsequently followed by a number of others: the Brundtland Commission on the environment, the Palme Commission on peace and security, the South Commission, and the international Commission on Global Governance. Sonny was a member of all of them. Only in the latter two cases, however, did he call upon my services at all – for ideas and comments on drafts – and then only sparingly. In the case of the South Commission (chaired by Julius Nyerere, with the secretariat run by Manmohan Singh), I attended one meeting in London on North-South relations, and also offered it a critical paper on the World Bank's approaches to adjustment.

In mid-1979, while the Brandt process was still under way and I was on sabbatical at Oxford, Sonny called on my help in another endeavour. This time it was to help with a Commonwealth-sponsored mission to Uganda, following the Tanzanian army's eviction of the Idi Amin dictatorship. (I told this story in chapter six.) My later 1988–9 participation, at

Sonny's request, in the Commonwealth-sponsored "wise men" mission to Guyana (together with Alister McIntyre, Mike Faber, and, eventually, Chandra Hardy) is told later in this chapter in the "Guyana – Mission Impossible" section.

In 1982, I was invited to join another Commonwealth expert group, this time on protectionism and its impact upon developing countries, chaired by (Sir) Alec Cairncross. Manmohan Singh was an active member, as was Stuart Harris of Australia. We met three times in London and produced quite a good report.[63] Although it was unusual for group members to do extensive drafting themselves, I wrote a chapter on which I took some pride on the "new protectionism" and its dangers.

But my most significant and time-consuming involvement with Commonwealth expert groups was still to come. At the annual meeting of Commonwealth finance ministers in London in August 1982, immediately prior to the annual IMF/World Bank meetings, the prime minister (and finance minister) of New Zealand, Robert Muldoon, called for an expert independent review of the entire international financial and trading system. The global economy had just come through the second "oil shock," was experiencing a severe recession, and the Third World debt crisis was already at hand. The Bretton Woods institutions were forty years old and seemed to be showing some signs of middle age: slow response to new circumstances, uncertainty as to their future, creaky structures. It seemed an opportune time for such a comprehensive review, even if the idea came from a populist politician whose own economic management skills were in some question. To my utter stupefaction, Sonny called me up – I had not even heard about the proposed review at this time – and asked whether I would chair it. Obviously I had no prestigious titles or affiliations, and I had never actually chaired anything very serious before, so at first I tried to beg off. But he was insistent. I then sought assurances as to the necessary backup, including a significant research budget, research and secretarial assistance for me in Toronto, the full support of the Commonwealth Secretariat, and (it now seems a hilariously inconsequential request) an immediate year's subscription to the *Financial Times* (FT), *New York Times*, and *Wall Street Journal* so that I could stay on top of current developments. All were immediately granted. (It was during that year that I learned that the FT was a far better guide to international economic and political events than the other two; indeed I don't know how I ever got along without it before, and I have been a subscriber ever since.)

Sonny had a masterful way of involving prestigious Brits in all of his expert groups. In this instance he really outdid himself, catching (Sir) Jeremy Morse, formerly the top official in the UK Treasury, the chair of the C-20 deputies who had pursued international monetary reform during the 1970s, and now the chairman of Lloyds Bank. He was the epitome of the best of the British public service: an Oxford first in classics, a chess grandmaster, and, as I was to discover, an intelligent and charming companion and host. (Typical of his humour, when he had the group to his residence for dinner one night, he required us, as an early bit of entertainment, to uncover the precise logic of his seating arrangement.) His name lent considerable prestige to our enterprise both in the United Kingdom and in international financial circles. But there was power in the rest of our group as well. It included I.G. Patel, former governor of the Reserve Bank of India, who had been to the Indian civil service more or less what Sir Jeremy had been to the British, and was later to become the head of the London School of Economics; Lal Jayawardena of Sri Lanka, who had been prominent, with Sir Jeremy, in the C-20 deputies, and who was to become the first director of UN University–World Institute for Development Economics Research (UNU-WIDER, see chapter sixteen); Ken Dadzie of Ghana, at that time high commissioner in London, later to become secretary-general of UNCTAD; Willie Demas, president of the Caribbean Development Bank; and again Stuart Harris of Australia; together with a couple of others from Nigeria and New Zealand.

We worked well together. By the end of our first meeting in London in late January 1983, we had agreed on an annotated draft outline of the report (which, on the basis of our first few days of discussion, I had worked long into the night to draft). We also divided up responsibility among ourselves for the preparation of early draft chapters as a basis for further discussion.

We commissioned a number of state-of-the-art papers by leading authorities of the day (including John Williamson on exchange rate regimes; Richard Cooper on the possible functioning of a global central bank; Chuck Frank on the role of commercial banks; and Hans Singer, Drag Avramovic, and John Loxley on topics relating to development finance), which were eventually made more widely available in a separate bound (but unfortunately unpublished) volume. We solicited cooperation and views from all of the major international financial institutions. The secretariat circulated to all of us a wide range of relevant reports and papers, and drafted many issues papers of their own for our consideration. In April, a small subcommittee of the whole, including Sir Jeremy, visited the IMF and World Bank in Washington for discussions with staff and executive directors, which were surprisingly unhelpful to us. I was able to see the great respect in which Sir Jeremy was held there. (The IMF's economic counsellor *cum* chief economist at the time, William Hood, on the other hand, while friendly to me, delighted in telling people that he used to pay me to shovel the snow from his sidewalk on Cottingham Street in Toronto – which was true. He also later taught me undergraduate courses on money and banking, and econometrics.) On our last evening there, Sir Jeremy suggested that we do a straw poll among ourselves as to the five most important matters that we should address in our report. We all scribbled them down on separate pieces of paper so as to ensure that we did not influence each other. And, lo, there was already almost total agreement. From Washington we flew on to a meeting of the full group at the Caribbean Development Bank headquarters in Barbados, where we discussed some of the draft chapters and began to achieve a broader consensus.

A warm and abiding memory of that visit to Barbados was the wonderful trip all around the island to which Willie Demas treated me on my last day there while I awaited my evening flight home. He drove me in his black official bank car. On the back streets where little boys were playing scruffy cricket matches (cricket stars were a source of great Barbadian pride), the unmistakable six-foot-six (or thereabouts) president of the bank in his black car was greeted with enthusiastic shouts of "Willie! Willie!" He modestly ascribed this to his frequent appearances on local television. But it was quite clear that they knew him well and had a genuine affection for him. I was able to reminisce about this tour when, many years later, in St Lucia, in the presence of his wife, I delivered a lecture honouring his memory at the annual meeting of the Caribbean Development Bank.

The secretariat thereafter set earnestly to further work on the draft report. The early drafts done from the secretariat were frequently much too long and verbose. As they sent them to me (not yet to the rest of the group), I chopped and revised quite mercilessly, and my "editing" was received remarkably graciously. At our final group meeting in London in early July, we went through each chapter carefully, making further revisions, and all but agreed on everything, including its title: "Towards a New Bretton Woods, Challenges for the World Financial and Trading System."[64] The final revision of one section had eventually to be left to Stuart Harris, who was to send it in as soon as he could. My final approval of the whole text came in a couple of telephone calls to Australia and London from our cottage hideaway at Big Bay (near Owen Sound, Ontario). And off it went to the finance ministers in August. I travelled to their September meeting in Port of Spain, Trinidad, to present the report to them formally.

The report did not call for a huge new conference, as its title might suggest, and we were careful to say that. Rather, in pursuit of the same economic objectives as had motivated those at Bretton Woods and in the same spirit, we argued, it was necessary to take account of the numerous changes in the international system since that time and to undertake appropriate changes in the exchange rate system, provision of adequate international liquidity for all, mobilization of required development finance, the international trade regime, and the like. Its analysis was much more focused and detailed than that in the Brandt Commission report. In retrospect, I think the report was remarkably good considering the time we had available for its preparation. The only key issue that – at Sir Jeremy's insistence – we did not address was the issue of the governance of the international financial institutions themselves, the voting and power structures. Ours was an ambitious agenda, but the report was a reformist rather than a revolutionary document. Perhaps more significant than the specifics of our recommendations was the fact that they had the unanimous support of all of the group's members, and particularly, of course, that of Sir Jeremy Morse.

In his introductory speech to the Commonwealth finance ministers' meeting in Trinidad, Sonny made a big point of the importance of our report. Actually, there was an amusing incident as he was speaking. Sonny's reputation for eloquence in oratory was well known and well deserved. And he fussed a lot over the preparation of his speeches; I had seen him do so over this one during the previous evening. Unfortunately, when he was in full flight before the finance ministers, and the television cameras, he suddenly discovered that the next page of his speech was missing. He stopped, a little flustered, shuffled his papers looking for the missing page, and finally called for assistance: "Can anyone help me with this?" An aide (probably Janet Singh) soon got him the sheet of paper he needed, and on he went. The next day the local paper headlined: "Ramphal at a Loss for Words." Everyone chuckled. Shortly thereafter I made a presentation to the meeting with a plea for early action, concluding: "If not now, when?" I subsequently learned from friends that this phrase had a long history and traditionally had even theological significance.

The government of Canada's response to the report was less than enthusiastic. Meeting an official from the Department of Finance on the Air Canada flight to Trinidad, I was disconcerted when all he seemed to want to discuss were our recommendations concerning exchange rates and macroeconomic coordination among industrial countries. These issues were not at all what I thought were the most important matters in the report. As I was to see repeatedly thereafter, this reflected the (usual) myopia of most Canadian Finance Department personnel on international monetary matters. Finance Minister Marc Lalonde, as he introduced his comments to the conference, made a jocular off-the-cuff remark to the effect that our report showed the fine tradition of free speech in Canada. Mrs Thatcher's British government was, of course, even less receptive. We were told that when she saw the title of our report, she set it aside completely untouched.

Early in November I was invited to Ottawa to discuss the report with high-level officials from the Departments of Finance and External Affairs, the Bank of Canada, and the cabinet office. A number of questions were prepared for me in advance as the basis for some of the discussion. Internal governmental confidential commentaries (doubtless not all of them) were made available to me. A formal luncheon was held in my honour in the Lester B. Pearson building. Everyone appeared to be trying to be constructive and was friendly, but I learned from my moles within the government that it was actually looking for ways to distance itself from our report. The finance ministers had forwarded it to the next Commonwealth heads of government meeting in New Delhi in December; but Northern ministers (United Kingdom, Canada, Australia) were clearly uneasy about it. Sonny invited me to New Delhi to make a fifteen minute presentation to the heads, but I declined, believing it to be a long way to travel for a short and dubious purpose. The report could certainly stand on its own, and its arguments were unlikely to be improved by a short presentation. (In the meantime, Sir Jeremy was active in trying to sell the report in the United Kingdom, about which he wrote me in friendly and supportive fashion. Evidently his signature on the report had not been a mere polite formality. But this was not an easy sell during the Thatcher years.) According to the enthusiastic letter I received from Sonny after the New Delhi meeting, the report was well received and extensively discussed. An eight-country consultative group was established to carry the discussions forward. As so often happens, however, nothing much was ever heard about either this group or our report thereafter.

At the Commonwealth's request, Alec Cairncross and I attended a conference in Glasgow a couple of years later, at which we promoted our respective reports and argued that they had not aged and deserved more attention. In my view they both still read very well.

That was the conclusion of my Commonwealth expert group career. Sonny delighted in telling me (several times actually) that the next time he sought to create an expert group, and consulted the government of Canada as to a possible appropriate Canadian member, he was firmly told, without his even asking, that he could not have Helleiner.

* * *

Guyana: Mission Impossible

In 1988–9, I was involved in an independent advisory group on adjustment issues under Commonwealth auspices in Guyana. Sonny Ramphal, the secretary-general of the Commonwealth, was a citizen of Guyana; indeed he had once held cabinet positions in its government. He was therefore very familiar both with its deteriorated economic situation and with its imperfect political leadership.

During the 1980s Guyana had entered a profound downward economic spiral. Real GDP was declining at an estimated 6 per cent per annum; its per capita income had descended to a level below that of Haiti, previously the lowest in the Western Hemisphere. Inflation raged. Both fiscal and balance of payments deficits were out of control. Its debt load was among the highest, relative to exports or GNP, in the developing world; debt service obligations amounted to 75 per cent of the value of exports. Informal and illegal activities had overtaken in importance the overregulated and imperfectly functioning formal economy. Massive emigration, especially of the young and skilled, amounted to 3 per cent of the working age population every year. Complicating all else was a history of strained racial relations between those of African and those of East Indian origin, which was reflected in its political parties. Despite its enormous natural resources – and a tiny population of only 600,000 – its future looked very bleak.

Early in 1988, with the support of the government of Guyana, Ramphal created an advisory group to report directly to the president of Guyana, (Comrade) Desmond Hoyte, on the possible path to a more satisfactory longer-term economic future. By that time Guyana was already actively engaged in discussions with the IMF and the World Bank as to an adjustment program that could attract their support. It was not intended that our group intervene in any way in these discussions, although its members did in the end make some relevant inputs to them. (Agreement was not reached with the IMF until March 1989.) The idea was, rather, that careful – and independent – thought now had to be given to issues and concerns of a longer-term nature, longer-term than those with which the international financial institutions typically concerned themselves.

Appointed chairman of the group was Alister McIntyre (at that time vice chancellor of the University of the West Indies, UWI). The other members were Mike Faber (formerly director, IDS Sussex and, before that, at the Commonwealth Secretariat in London) and me. Later, a fourth member was formally added – in recognition of her major inputs to our report – Chandra Hardy (Guyanese, formerly a member of the staff of the World Bank, and, importantly, sister to Sonny's long-standing personal assistant, Janet Singh). All were well known to and were, I believe, fully trusted by Ramphal. The work of the group was to be supported and complemented by Commonwealth-supported staff working in Guyana both for the group and for the government of Guyana under technical assistance contracts.

We began our work in April/May of 1988, travelling to Guyana as a group to familiarize ourselves with the current problems of the country. The support staff arrived only some months thereafter. We met President Hoyte and others of his cabinet, and began to gather data and to discuss what needed to be done. The challenges certainly seemed enormous.

By February 1989, many months later, our effort seemed to be drifting a little. The support staff in Guyana was undoubtedly doing useful work for the government, improving the statistical base and conducting studies, but did not seem to have clear direction as to how to contribute to our project. It was decided that Chandra Hardy and I should go to Guyana, try to move the project forward, and provide some direction to the staff. We spent a productive week in Georgetown, the capital, and I learned much more about the country and its problems in the process.

Arriving in Georgetown this time on my own, rather than as a member of a VIP delegation as in the previous visit, I got an immediate taste of the horrendous overregulation under which the ordinary citizen suffered. I was accustomed, from much overseas travel in Africa and elsewhere, to the filling out of numerous forms upon entry and exit. At that time it was quite normal in many countries to be required to declare all currencies, travellers' cheques, and so forth when entering a country. At Georgetown airport, however, they really outdid themselves; in addition to the usual immigration forms, we were required to declare not only currencies and travellers' cheques but also absolutely everything of possible monetary value – wristwatches, jewellery, pens, and the like – and to do so, without benefit of carbon paper, in duplicate. The forms were not available until we reached the inside of the (rather rundown) airport, and there were at first not enough to go around. It was after dark, and the lights were dim and flickering. It took most of us the better part of three-quarters of an hour to acquire and complete the forms.

Arrival at the hotel provided another indicator of the realities of life in Guyana at that time. Shortages of foreign exchange and resulting shortages of fuel and spare parts, among other things, created many problems in Guyana as in many other places. There was no electric power when I arrived, a problem with which I was again quite familiar from travel in Africa. But, in this case, it had been a very long day, my bags were extra heavy, my room was on the fourth floor, and there didn't seem to be anyone available at that hour to help. The clerk on the front desk lent me a candle, and that was very helpful. But I remember it as an exceedingly long climb. I remember literally falling into bed, exhausted.

I met with a lot of people during that week, developed some concrete work plans for our support staff, gathered more data, and wrote a couple of policy papers. One paper was on exchange rate policy, advocating a "crawling peg" with a detailed explanation of how to do it. Another proved, I think, extremely important – on highly specific policies to address the social impact of the coming adjustment program. I drew on my knowledge of UNICEF experience with its efforts to introduce a "human face" to adjustment programs elsewhere. Elements of both of these papers found their way into government policy and into our final report. High-quality policy papers were at a premium within the Guyana government at that time. One of the most striking elements of the government scene was the scarcity of professional staff. Many desks and offices seemed to be empty. Many of the best and brightest had evidently fled the country. Inevitably, those who were left were working flat out.

In fact, there was a very depressing atmosphere – a feeling of hopelessness, of despair – that seemed to pervade everything in Georgetown at that time. Government wasn't functioning very well, and those who worked for the government knew it. There seemed even to be a certain paranoia at the upper levels of government and in the state-controlled press. One evening, as we were discussing some of Guyana's problems over dinner at the hotel, a cabinet minister (I have forgotten what her portfolio was) came over to our table to inform us that "people could hear us" and that such discussions should not take place in public. The atmosphere in the primary foreign exchange black market – an area known colloquially as "Wall Street" – was downright sinister: very tough-looking characters congregated in bunches or walked the street, all in broad daylight, exchanging what seemed to be enormous wads of greenbacks and local currency. We were warned not to walk about there, or for that matter anywhere else, alone. I saw very few police officers anywhere. On my last morning, I went into a gift shop and bought some attractive salad bowls made of local hardwood; the proprietor was so grateful for my business and seemed so anxious to talk freely about the country's problems that I actually felt guilty I couldn't buy more or stay longer. There seemed to be many, like him, who felt trapped in an impossible and apparently hopeless environment.

When I left Guyana at the end of that week, I had a remarkable sense that I was leaving many decent and hard-working people behind, people who were trapped in a hopeless scene and unable to leave in the way that I was. There have been many other places and occasions when I might legitimately have felt similarly. But I had never felt this sense of hopelessness so strongly before; nor did I ever feel it so strongly again. It had been an emotionally draining experience.

Because Alister couldn't get away from his university responsibilities, our group travelled to his home on the UWI campus in Jamaica to work on our final report in late April 1989, and then to London to complete it (nearly) in June. Chandra did a final rewrite in August, and we submitted it to the president in September. Happily, he accepted our recommendation that it be made public. We had written the report in such a way as to engender debate and discussion. It was quite short and written in a punchy style. As we had hoped, the "McIntyre Report" elicited much public discussion both in Guyana and elsewhere in the region. Although the report was hard-hitting and critical in many respects, Hoyte evidently liked it; and a couple of months later, to my great embarrassment (this should not have been a high priority in a desperate country), he sent me, special delivery, two bottles of fine Guyana rum for Christmas. The report was published by the Commonwealth Secretariat in 1990: *Guyana, the Economic Recovery Program and Beyond.*[65]

The country's economy has since somewhat recovered, but many of its underlying problems, of course, remain.

* * *

I did further work for the Commonwealth Secretariat thereafter from time to time, including papers to conferences on negotiating with the IMF, foreign direct investment, and the problems of small countries, among other subjects. After Sonny's departure from the post of secretary-general, however, my contacts with it were far less frequent.

In 1996, during the regime of Sonny's Nigerian successor, Chief Emeka Anyaoku, I agreed to do a paper on the benefits and potential costs of liberalizing the capital account (of the balance of payments) in developing countries, a topic on which I had organized a significant G-24 research project that had recently been completed. My paper was to be presented to the Commonwealth Finance Ministers Conference in Bermuda in September; and it was. But some of the events surrounding it were rather peculiar. Our research project and my paper concluded that capital account liberalization in most developing countries was probably, at their current stage of development, unwise – this at a time when the IMF and its major members were promoting it vigorously (indeed even calling for a change in the IMF's articles of agreement in order to grant it greater power to promote it). The Commonwealth's then director of Economic Affairs, Rumman Faruqi, with whom I had earlier worked closely in Washington when he was in the Pakistani executive director's office in the World Bank and who had now commissioned my paper, seemed rather ill at ease with my conclusions. I received critical comments from members of his staff, and what I can only call vigorous representations on the eve of my presentation to the finance ministers, seeking to "tone down" my sceptical approach to the official line. When the paper was made available to the ministers, an appendix was attached which I had not written, containing views contrary to my own. My paper was very well received by the ministers from developing countries and most of their staff. A representative from India made a strong presentation describing their own experience, which had not been included in our research, but was consistent with our general findings and conclusions. The Ugandan finance minister approached me, after my session, and asked if he could get a copy of my excellent paper because, he said, his staff (which was in the process of liberalizing his country's capital account) had not allowed him to see it. Paul Martin, then the Canadian minister of finance, had asked to lead off the discussion of my paper. Like Marc Lalonde before him, he

11.2. With Finance Minister Trevor Manuel, Republic of South Africa,
Commonwealth Finance Ministers Conference, Bermuda, 1996

began by joking about my role as a critic of his government before going
very critically on with the general IMF line on the subject. The UK and
Australian ministers spoke vigorously and critically as well.

There followed a remarkable delay in the publication of my paper.
Another paper on the same topic by a couple of British authors without experience in developing countries, which had not been presented
at the meeting and must have been commissioned subsequently, and
which extolled the benefits of capital account liberalization, was now
published by the Commonwealth Secretariat. I wrote and asked what
had happened to mine and was told that the delays were due to a short-
age of funds. It finally appeared almost two years later. I expressed my
genuine disappointment to Faruqi at a subsequent meeting at the IMF.
He denied that there had been any funny business in all of this. But I
found that difficult to believe. This kind of toadying to (presumably
British) pressure would never have occurred during the Ramphal years.

It is always nice to have the last laugh. After the Asian financial crisis in 1997–8, the conventional wisdom shifted markedly in the G-24's direction, and even the IMF was forced to back off, conceding that controls over international capital movements can indeed be useful instruments of macroeconomic policy in the context of some developing country circumstances.

12 Cool Relations with the IMF

My relationships with the IMF have often been a little strained, although I have at times enjoyed cordial relations with individuals within the organization (including some of my former students). I have been consistently quite critical of the IMF's policies toward low-income countries, finding them inadequate in terms of funding levels and inappropriate in their conditionality. But I have never been a "root and branch" critic of the type that ran the "Fifty Years Is Enough" campaign, believing as I do that the IMF has had a potentially important role to play, if only it could have played it better.

For a time I wrote and advocated vigorously on the need for expanded low-conditionality finance for low-income countries facing exogenous balance of payments shocks. The enormous need for this type of finance was demonstrated at the time of the two great "oil shocks" *cum* recessions in 1973–4 and 1979–80, when commercial banks stepped into the stabilizing role for middle-income countries but were unwilling to do anything for the poorer countries, which they deemed less creditworthy. Perhaps illustrative of the mainstream legitimacy of my arguments at the time was my (short) paper on the IMF's limitations in the May 1983 *American Economic Review, Papers and Proceedings*.[66] As reported in chapter eleven, in 1982–3 I also chaired a group reviewing the IMF and the World Bank for Commonwealth finance ministers.

Instead of expanding and loosening its finance for low-income countries, as many of us argued was necessary, the IMF, under US and others' pressure, was at this time tightening conditionality on the Compensatory Financing Facility, which had previously been the main instrument for the provision of near-automatic credit to "shocked" countries. My struggle then shifted, defensively, to the terms of the

IMF's conditionality, which had always tended, and still does, toward a uniform and unbending demand for fiscal and monetary restraint. In the early 1980s I delivered a somewhat passionate, but factual, invited lunchtime lecture at the annual meeting of the Canadian Association of African Studies (CAAS) in Toronto in which I tried to explain (and, to some degree, attack) the greatly expanded, but still little recognized, role of the IMF in Africa. It was very warmly received, generating not only intense immediate interest from many of those who were there but also early requests for its publication from the editors, who were there, of both the semi-popular *Canadian Dimension* and the academic *Canadian Journal of African Studies* (CJAS). As was my custom in those days, I had spoken from notes, but, although that had never originally been my intention, I decided I had better convert them quickly into a written text for publication. It appeared in 1983 in two slightly different versions, because of different editors' stylistic preferences, in the CJAS and, probably much more significantly, in the more prestigious *Princeton Essays* on international finance, edited by Peter Kenen.[67] The latter was the first ever, and perhaps still the only, essay in the Princeton series devoted exclusively to Africa. It seemed to establish me as one of the very few critical academics with knowledge of the IMF's activities in Africa at that time. From then on I did my best to remain current on the Bretton Woods institutions' activities in sub-Saharan Africa, and wrote critically on this topic regularly. In March 1982, at John Williamson's important conference on IMF conditionality at the Institute for International Economics (IIE) in Washington, when the scheduled African panelist for the concluding session failed to appear, I was hastily inserted as a substitute, alongside Arnold Harberger, Dick Cooper, and the IMF's representative. My paper on IMF conditionality at the IIE's conference on African debt and finance a few years later in 1986, which I thought (and still do) was pretty good, dealt with the same theme.[68]

Tensions between African governments and the IMF in the early 1980s generated a suggestion from the Association of African Central Banks (AACB) that they organize, jointly with the IMF, a symposium that might lead to a better mutual understanding of the design and implementation of adjustment programs. At that time the chairman of the AACB was Charles Nyirabu, governor of the Bank of Tanzania, whom I knew a little. Nyirabu was advised on many issues by Reginald Green, an old friend and colleague. It was undoubtedly Reg who suggested my name as an appropriate moderator for the symposium. The IMF, principally in the person of Azizali Mohammed, then its director of external relations, agreed. I was both flattered by the IMF/AACB invitation and stimulated by the prospect of its potential importance and eagerly accepted.

The IMF representative responsible for putting together the details of the program, Ahmed Abushadi, thereafter consulted me regularly as to its makeup. Presumably he was also in regular contact with the AACB. I was able to insert some modest improvements in the draft program, notably a paper on "Alternative Approaches to Stabilization in Africa"[69] by John Loxley, another friend from Tanzania days, by this time at the University of Manitoba. But the program's main outlines were determined by the IMF. One element of the program discussions, of which I am not proud, stands out in my memory. When I suggested an old friend, Frances Stewart, as a potential contributor – I think it was for the paper finally contributed by John Loxley – Abushadi let it be known that, in his view, the African governors would not be comfortable with a woman in such a prominent role in the program. These were not necessarily his views, he assured me, but he thought that we should take them into account. I expressed some surprise but, in the end, to my shame, acquiesced. The program eventually contained not a single woman. It is striking how quickly things changed in the years to come. Anxiety is now more typically expressed with respect to the inadequacy of gender balance in international organizations' conference programs.

I believe that the symposium, which took place in May 1985 in Nairobi, and the subsequent conference volume, which I spent inordinate amounts of time editing for publication were, in the end, quite successful.[70] But the symposium was extraordinarily stressful. As its moderator, I felt it my responsibility to ensure that African voices were heard in a set of exchanges which were bound to be unbalanced in that the preparatory "firepower" in the IMF far exceeded anything available to the African governors. The symposium got off to a very bad start, as I saw it, when the introductory IMF paper by Richard Erb, deputy managing director, proved to be a no-nonsense and thoroughly standard IMF presentation that made no concessions to the African context or to the African governors' previously expressed concerns. It was as if the IMF had not heard the reasons for the decision to hold a symposium. As I told him later that day, his paper could have been written by a machine in the IMF basement. To make matters worse, as IMF staff saw it, during the sessions of the first afternoon the moderator (me) was less than "balanced" in his conduct. I had done my best to clarify, on behalf of some of the African voices from the floor, the nature of their concerns

12.1. With Philip Ndegwa, governor of the Bank of Kenya, Conference on the
Role of the IMF in Africa, 1985

in order that the speakers being questioned could speak clearly to them.
I had also placed on the table at the back of the room a recent paper that
I had myself written on aspects of IMF policy in low-income countries,
to which at an appropriate point I invited the participants' attention.

At a reception that evening I learned how upset the IMF staff were
with my "unbalanced" conduct of the meeting. My friend John Williamson (who was an independent participant in the program) informed me
that the IMF staff were going to hold an emergency meeting that evening and that it might be wise for me to speak to Erb or others before it

took place. Azizali Mohammed, visibly upset, informed me that he had gone out on a considerable limb on my behalf when others in the IMF questioned my suitability for the role of moderator and asked, "What are you trying to do to me?" I therefore felt it necessary to speak directly to Erb and asked him what he considered to be the problem. I told him what I thought of his introductory paper and the damage it had done to the atmosphere at the beginning of the meeting. I also tried to explain what I thought my role as moderator entailed. He was somewhat evasive about the specifics of my allegedly inappropriate conduct. I do not know what transpired at the IMF staff meeting that evening. Evidently they allowed the meeting to proceed as originally planned. Obviously I do not know what options they might have considered. (I do not think they could have had many.) In any case, there was quite a useful and vigorous exchange of views during the next couple of symposium proceedings.

At the conclusion of the meeting, it fell to me to try to summarize the discussions. (This summary, in more or less its original form, appears as the introduction to the conference volume, *Africa and the International Monetary Fund*.) I did so in as balanced a fashion as I could, and spoke, among other things, of the difficulty that monetary managers everywhere have in being understood by the broader public. In the published version I said:

> There was a remarkable degree of agreement among Governors that Fund staff, missions, and management have not always responded to their problems with the understanding that they believe they have a right to expect. Many, including some with reasonably successful Fund programs, suggested that the Fund staff is inadequately informed or insensitive with respect to local conditions and objectives, patronizing in their relationships with local professionals, and rigid or powerless or both in their negotiations with African governments. Whether or not these perceptions are accurate, their persistence must be a matter for profound regret ... Increased Fund awareness of these perceptions and the range of countries in which they are held was an important outcome of the symposium.[71]

Unfortunately, Azizali Mohammed had fallen ill by that time and was not present for the final session. Other IMF staff must have reported to him on what I said in some detail because when I saw him next, at the concluding dinner, he spoke to me in very supportive terms. Indeed, when he rose formally to thank me for my role as the meeting's moderator, he actually apologized for having misjudged me during the early stages of the event. Several in attendance commented thereafter that it was the first time that they had ever heard the IMF apologize for anything!

I am happy to say that in later years, after his retirement from the IMF, at which time Azizali went to work for the Group of 24 (G-24), we became good friends. I might add, in this connection, that I had been favourably impressed with him when I first met him a few years previously – when we were both discussants of the paper by Walt Rostow at a conference on development pioneers organized by the World Bank. Azizali had publicly wrung his hands on that occasion about the difficulties experienced by citizens of developing countries who worked within the international financial institutions, a problem of which I had not previously been so aware.

When the AACB and the IMF held their next joint conference, in 1991 in Gaborone, Botswana, I was again invited, but not this time as its moderator. I learned that the IMF had vetoed the AACB's suggestion that I serve as moderator again. Agreement was reached upon a more "neutral" (and older and more experienced) personality, but one who knew little of Africa, I.G. Patel of India. (I liked and respected I.G., who had been a member of "my" Commonwealth Bretton Woods group.) I was nevertheless invited both to present a paper and to participate in the concluding panel. I happily did both. In doing so I found myself much freer to speak my mind than I would have been had I been serving as moderator. In the final panel I had the opportunity to present my own summary view of the meeting's most important points.

There was a curious incident surrounding the subsequent publication of my (constructively) critical paper on IMF and World Bank activities in Africa. A very, very careful reader might have noticed (but I am sure no one has done so) that there is a paragraph in the article published in *World Development* shortly thereafter that does not appear in my otherwise identical chapter in the Patel-edited volume containing the conference papers, which appeared later. (I hasten to say that this omission was the product of an IMF editor and was not I.G.'s editorial decision.) The missing paragraph reads as follows:

> There is also, in non-Washington perceptions, considerable "inbreeding" in the Washington policy community, limiting the variety of sources from which consensus views there are developed and subjecting them to periodic "herd" behaviour. Certainly the IMF and the World Bank both have

established ways of looking at things – implicit models – and therefore what some (both inside and outside these organisations) call "party lines." This has led some aid donors and many developing country governments consciously to seek alternative views and, in the case of donors, to make them available to skill-scarce low-income countries. Greater efforts could be made to obtain independent assessments of alternative policy possibilities as a matter of course, and thus to improve the quality of both donors' and African governments' performance.

African governments or donor agencies, of course, may have their own "party lines." So may other international institutions, some of them African ones – UNICEF, ILO, ECA, etc. – but their influence has been much less.[72]

I thought this was quite a useful thing to say. Similar thoughts later led others, initially John Williamson who popularized the terminology, to speak of a "Washington consensus." Its recommended policy components were at that time quite explicitly described. Obviously there were differing views as to the desirability of alternatives to such a consensus. The Japanese, among other governments, found some of its elements difficult to accept. So did a great many developing countries and NGOs.

One of my most memorable IMF occasions was the 1987 conference, sponsored jointly by the IMF and the World Bank, and held in the IMF's main meeting hall, on "growth-oriented adjustment." At that time there was a growing sense that sheer demand restraint, of the kind advocated by the IMF, could only be a short-term response to macroeconomic imbalance and, as my colleagues and I had long advocated, supply-side expansion would be required to achieve sustainable balance and restoration of normal growth. I was the official discussant for the lead-off IMF paper, written in this instance by Manuel Guitián, a senior staff economist, in the opening conference session. While the World Bank's opening paper was quite promising, I found the IMF paper severely wanting; and I said so with some vigour. Before the session began I made a point of speaking with the author, and I warned him that I would be highly critical; he told me that he expected no less. In retrospect, in my public commentary perhaps I used language that was too strong. I began by saying that the paper showed certain Bourbon qualities, the Bourbons having prided themselves upon "learning nothing and forgetting nothing." I went on to discuss the details of the paper's deficiencies. Its principal problem was that it showed no sign of any alteration in IMF approaches to adjustment to take account of the need for continuing or re-establishing growth. It simply underlined the need for price stability and overall macroeconomic restraint in support of growth, and the repayment of arrears on debt. I concluded my comments by suggesting that if the IMF had no more to contribute it should at least get out of the way.

The chairman of the session, Ernie Stern of the World Bank, was evidently sufficiently annoyed with me to interrupt before my allotted time had expired (I have never experienced such behaviour on the part of a chair either before or since), and I was forced to stop before I had finished. Most of the assembled participants seemed to be quite upset with the tone, as well as, no doubt, the substance, of my criticism. Apparently it had not been customary for such vigorous criticism to be offered within the hallowed halls of the IMF building – at least not of papers written by senior staff members. The executive director for India, Arjun Sengupta, although he knew me to be a friend, in his subsequent commentary made a point of saying what a fine economist Mr Guitián was. Marcel Masse, the Canadian executive director, took the floor and spoke similarly. The feeling I had was very much as if I had broken wind in church. There were only two immediate exceptions: Stan Fischer, at that time the senior economist in the World Bank, who passed me a supportive note in which he told me, quite unnecessarily, that he had liked my recent book on Africa; and an executive director (for Iran, Ghana, and others) who invited me to lunch and told me that I had been "a breath of fresh air." A couple of friends in attendance later told me that they "admired my courage." Guitián, the author, was livid and did not deign to speak with me. (One staff member who did engage me briefly and courteously, and by that time I very much appreciated it, was Jacques Polak, the dean of the IMF's research staff.) When, that evening, I joined a group of young economists from the Canadian executive directors' office for dinner (this had been arranged before my "misbehaviour"), I learned that prior to my arrival they had been debating among themselves as to whether my comments in the opening session had been justified. I found the whole experience totally foreign to my experience of academic conferences in which, to put it mildly, vigorous exchange was entirely normal.

I was never invited to another IMF-sponsored conference. On the other hand, to the IMF's credit, they did publish my comments in full in the volume reporting upon the conference proceedings.[73]

My interactions with the IMF and World Bank ramped up significantly in the 1980s and 1990s. As already noted, many of my academic writing and papers included criticism of IMF (and World Bank) policies, particularly in Africa. My analyses of the newly expanded IMF activities in Africa were among the earliest such works in the field (which subsequently became quite crowded).

In the 1990s my considerable continuing interaction with the IMF (and the World Bank) took place primarily through the medium of the G-24, for which I then served as research director. My experiences with the G-24 are recounted in chapter fourteen.

In the late 1990s and thereafter, the IMF at last joined the World Bank in emphasizing, at least in its rhetoric, the need for country "ownership" of their stabilization and adjustment programs. There was also increased recognition of the positive role that could be played by independent inputs and evaluations. I had myself, of course, been plugging both of these themes – the need for ownership and the value of independent evaluations – for years. There remained significant differences in what was really meant by national "ownership," but this discussion and debate represented something of a change in mindset on the part of Bretton Woods technocrats. On the value of independent assessments there was amazingly rapid progress. I joined others in signing (I was not involved in its preparation) an independent report, written by a prestigious group organized by the ODC in Washington, advocating the creation of an independent evaluation unit for the IMF. The Independent Evaluation Office, initially headed by Montek Ahluwalia, was established soon after; and it has played a very constructive role.

Over the years, although I was probably better known as a trade economist, I think I may actually have devoted more time and effort to international monetary and financial affairs than to trade issues. I was surprised, moved, and, yes, delighted when one of the volumes in the Washington-based (Jesuit-sponsored) Center of Concern's series on international monetary and financial aspects of development (volume 4) contained the following dedication:

> This volume is dedicated to Graham Bird, Gerald Helleiner, Tony Killick and John Williamson, in appreciation of their work on the developing countries' concerns with the international monetary system.[74]

13 Ambivalent Relations with the World Bank

My relationships with the World Bank have been long standing and complex. At a meeting in the 1990s, called by enthusiasts within the Bank who sought to transfer greater ownership over Bank-financed programs to borrowing countries, I described my approach to the World Bank as having been historically one of "love/hate." I think that about summarizes my situation. It has been the most important global institution working in the field of development and, more particularly, in Africa. Its professional staff included many for whom I had the greatest respect. It also, however, has at times been infuriating in its promotion of ideologically driven development bromides.

My first exposure to the World Bank came as I prepared to travel to Nigeria for the first time. The then relatively new report of a World Bank mission to Nigeria, led by John Adler, was the first detailed country study of its kind, and it was enormously useful to me. But Bank economists did not thereafter figure prominently in my work on Nigeria, either in Washington or in Lagos. At that time the World Bank focused primarily upon projects and did not yet play the dominant policy role it was later to acquire in Africa.

During the early 1970s, while Hollis Chenery was the World Bank's chief economist, I was periodically invited to Washington with other academics for conferences and/or informative discussion sessions about development and the Bank's policies. From time to time, I was even invited to consider employment there.

I had some modest interactions with World Bank staff during my initial work in Tanzania and thereafter. I actually led a Bank-financed mission there in 1978 to advise on export promotion, a story which I told in chapter five.

In the early 1980s, as also recounted in chapter five, I was appointed a member of the three-person "wise men" group, financed by the World Bank and promoted by its president, Robert McNamara, to seek accommodation, vainly as it turned out, between the IMF and the government of Tanzania. In the 1990s in Tanzania, I was again financed in part by the Bank, although primarily by the government of Denmark, as I worked on the improvement of aid relationships there.

At the same time, my work with the Brandt Commission and with the Commonwealth finance ministers had also addressed World Bank issues fairly directly. My primary concerns with developing country finance from the 1970s onward were twofold: first, the provision of greater liquidity – short-term, low-conditionality finance from the IMF to enable low-income countries without access to commercial bank finance to ride more easily through temporary exogenous shocks from changes in the terms of trade or weather, and therefore necessitate less draconian demand restraint; and, second, expanded longer-term finance from the World Bank to assist in supply-side restructuring (toward tradeables – export and import-competing activities) necessitated by more permanent adverse external shocks.

Existing IMF/World Bank financing conditions severely prejudiced the prospect of longer-term growth by impacting severely upon the investments, including those in education and health, upon which future growth depended. When exogenous shocks, rather than domestic mismanagement, had caused current imbalances, it appeared to me that it was both unrealistic and unfair that the entire burden of stabilization and adjustment should be borne by their victims. The G-24 and others had been promoting the provision of such supply-side structural adjustment financing throughout the late 1970s and early 1980s. But the World Bank, backed by its Berg Report (named for its principal author, Elliot Berg) on Africa in the early 1980s,[75] had now completely hijacked the supply-side approach and the "structural adjustment" terminology. It did so by adding privatization, financial and import liberalization, and reduced state activity to the supply-side policy package that it now actively promoted through the conditionality in its greatly expanded African program lending. These oversimplified and ultimately damaging loan conditions had to be resisted. I also continually emphasized, in my work with UNICEF, the importance of analysing the impact of stabilization and adjustment programs upon poverty and income distribution.

The increasing intrusiveness and ideological content of the condition-ality of World Bank lending to desperate African (and other) govern-ments, and its leadership of aid donor thinking there, became a very serious problem in the 1980s. Though it has since backed off some-what in these matters, not least because of the advice of some of its new senior African staff, the World Bank's reputation in Africa has yet fully to recover. Its workings there were once succinctly described by an experienced senior African economist (who subsequently worked for a time in the Bank) in more or less the following terms:

> The first Bank mission recommends a study of a policy area. How can anyone object to that? The study is then conducted but senior policymak-ers in the country are much too busy to read it. The next Bank mission makes recommendations based on the study. The next thing you know the recommendations have become conditions on the next loan.

One of my more memorable early direct "assaults" upon World Bank activities came in the form of an essay on policy-based program lending in the collection published in 1986[76] by the Washington Overseas Devel-opment Council (ODC), purportedly intended to guide the incoming president, an inexperienced Barber Conable. John Sewell, ODC's pres-ident, had appointed me a member of the ODC's program advisory committee, and I had called attention to the need for such a paper in their planned volume; the suggestion eventually had the predictable result: I was asked to write it. In it, I called attention to professional disagreement on some of the elements of development strategy being actively promoted by the Bank in its structural adjustment lending and the anti-state and pro-liberalization imbalance (as I saw it) in the Bank's research program. I thereby earned the enmity of the Bank's chief econ-omist at the time, Anne Krueger, who, at a subsequent conference at Yale, vigorously (privately) berated me for the damage I had done to the prospects of funding for her research program. (It should go without saying that I did not back down. Nor did she seem to lose any finance.) I was told by several sources that my paper had been widely discussed within the Bank. I don't doubt it, because the Krueger research divi-sion had by that time earned many enemies within the Bank as well as external to it.

From that time onward, I found myself repeatedly pitted against the World Bank in public events – for example, against Berg himself in tes-timony before the US Congressional Subcommittee on Africa; against

Kim Jaycox, the Bank's VP for Africa at a Scandinavian conference on Africa in Copenhagen; and against a Bank spokesman in Paul Volcker's evening graduate seminar at Princeton. At the last, much to my exqui-site social democratic discomfort, I was picked up in a black stretch limousine, complete with uniformed chauffeur, dark windows, bar, TV, and the works, for the trip from Newark airport to Princeton. The Bank man irked me, and I probably went further than I should have in my criticisms of the Bank's approaches and "Anglo-Saxon" staffing and image. At one point, I was moved to say that borrowers needing the finance "held their noses" when dealing with the World Bank, which seemed to anger him. The after-seminar drinks were rather tense.

At this time, indeed for most of the time, and particularly after Krueger's departure, I seemed to be considered an "acceptable" critic of the World Bank. I was repeatedly invited to Bank conferences and placed in prominent positions in the programs. I was a member of the concluding panel in both of the Bank's major conferences on adjust-ment lending in 1989 and September 1990 (with Joe Abbey, Stan Fischer, Manuel Guitián, Pedro Malan, and Moeen Qureshi in the first, and with Edmar Bacha and Arnold Harberger in the second). Oddly, although I was a contributor, I was asked (and agreed) to be an external assessor in the publication process for the proceedings of one of these conferences. I was also asked to be an external reviewer for other important World Bank reports. Although I almost invariably agreed, my recommenda-tions and strictures were not always listened to. Particularly galling was the Bank's 1993 report on adjustment in Africa, when the external advi-sory group (Paul Collier, Tony Killick, Benno Ndulu, and me), after hav-ing been left entirely in the dark throughout the report's preparation, were given only a couple of weeks to comment on an entire long draft. We all nevertheless did so, in considerable detail and at some length, and were all extremely critical – so much so that we even consulted with one another at one point as to how to avoid any appearance of support for the report. Our critical comments were totally ignored. Not only that. I was subsequently informed by a Danish friend that Bank staff had told him and others that, although I had helped to "destroy" an ear-lier Bank report, I had supported this one; when I heard this I immedi-ately protested to a relevant official at the Bank (to whom I had already complained about the failure to address our criticisms) and received a letter of apology. The following year I nevertheless offered detailed comments on the (much better) 1994 report on Africa, this one led by Ravi Kanbur, an excellent and sympathetic analyst who had become the World Bank's chief economist for Africa. (He was later to direct the preparation of the Bank's flagship World Development Report 2000, with its innovative approaches to poverty and development, only to resign over efforts to "doctor" his next-to-last draft. Shortly before, I had been on an Ottawa platform with him, both praising and lightly criticizing his initial draft.)

In the preparation of the 1999–2000 World Bank Report on Africa in the coming century, the Bank tried to involve the AERC, the UNECA, and the African Development Bank in its preparation, and I was again recruited as an external advisor and reviewer. Again, I was fairly critical of the draft report, expressing disappointment that the purported collaboration with African institutions had not generated better results. My critique was welcomed by the Africans, I was told, who evidently had had difficulty influencing the draft, and this time it did have some effect on the final product. I was, when asked, able to endorse it (for its back cover) as a "must read" report, even if, as I noted, agreement on all points was unlikely.

Professional critique of World Bank draft reports was always problematic. Whatever the merits of the Bank's professional staff – usually they were extremely competent, though sometimes, as in the Krueger years, highly ideologically tinted – the published reports were subsequently "massaged" by management in a quasi-political process, so it was difficult to know whether the final published products constituted the product of research or political negotiation or some varying combination of the two. A group of NGOs pertinently asked for clarification of these matters, with particular reference to the annual World Development Reports, in a later letter to then chief economist Joe Stiglitz, and I added my name to the list of signatories.

Individual papers within the Research Division were easier to handle. One such paper by Ibrahím Elbadawi, whom I had come to know through the AERC where he was research director for several years (on leave from the World Bank), nevertheless generated great problems. When in 1991 he sent his empirical (econometric) paper on the effectiveness of World Bank adjustment lending for African development to me in draft form for comment, I noted that, although his text certainly did not emphasize it, its most significant result was that the Bank's finance appeared to be, statistically speaking, unhelpful – no effects on growth or inflation, negative association with savings and investment rates. He then changed his account and modified the title to "Why World Bank Adjustment Lending in Africa Doesn't Work" (I may have that title slightly wrong), and, before anyone at higher levels caught it, it was circulated widely in this "final" form. It created consternation, and was soon withdrawn.

In my own areas of expertise, most notably in trade, I found the World Bank's publications simply ignored academic research that was unsupportive of its general policy stance of liberalization. Even when the missing items were pointed out, as on one occasion I ensured through a developing country executive director, the bank authors continued to ignore them. (In that case, the executive director had requested my comments on the draft 1991 World Development Report on trade and development, and I had supplied the missing references.) In later years, when they at last, and only grudgingly, began to acknowledge contrary evidence, they continued to preach orthodox liberalization and to ignore or downplay much of the empirical literature. The same had been true of the official line on the (purportedly positive) effect of higher interest rates upon saving in previous years; despite much controversy, it was many years before it was permissible for World Bank reports to admit that any such relationship might be questionable. For some time, according to friends within the Bank, empirical studies generating the "wrong" result had actually been suppressed.

Once I caught the Bank in a simple, but serious, technical error. In the 1987 World Development Report there appeared a box purporting to explain the meaning and significance of the "real" (that is, inflation-adjusted) exchange rate, a concept quite critical to an understanding of stabilization and adjustment issues. As presented, its definition was incorrect. The authors had somehow dropped "the inverse of" at a critical point in the account. Picturing scores of students, and even conceivably their teachers, carefully copying down and trying to understand this upside-down definition from the fount of all development wisdom, I hastily wrote David Hopper, the new VP research, suggesting the insertion of an *erratum* slip to rectify the damage. In his letter of reply he said, "You are the only one who has spotted it and our faces are red." Since 90 per cent of the distribution was already done, he said, a correction was not likely to be useful.

In 1989–90, Robert McNamara, Kim Jaycox, and Jan Pronk (at that time, Dutch aid minister) sought to build upon the World Bank's latest report on Africa by creating a Global Coalition for Africa (GCA) to direct more aid and other supports to the beleaguered continent. It was to be launched with a huge international conference in Maastricht. The background papers were to be assembled by Ram Agarwal, a Canadian at the Bank who had been instrumental in the preparation of the Bank's very well-received 1989 long-term perspective study on Africa;[77] that study relied to a unique degree, for the time, on consultations with African scholars and practitioners on the ground, and in consequence came to more sophisticated and realistic conclusions than other Bank analyses. He now prevailed upon several Bank critics to help him in this new venture. Despite some reservations, I spent a few days working in the Bank on a draft on economic cooperation within Africa, a subject that many within the Bank, believing it relatively unimportant or even harmful, treated with disdain. Its material was incorporated into the background papers for the conference. At his invitation I attended the (very well-orchestrated) Maastricht event in the spring of 1990, which was, ostensibly, co-chaired by McNamara and the president of Botswana; but I did not speak.

Everyone in the African aid "business," including UN representatives like Adebayo Adedeji and Stephen Lewis who had both been highly critical of the World Bank's activities, was there. The agenda was tightly controlled and, as it turned out, the "fix" was already in. At that time, for instance, although there had been an expert report for the UN Secretary-General recommending debt relief for Africa, it was still bad form to mention the need for it. Nowhere mentioned in the background papers, the issue surfaced only once in an unscripted intervention from the floor; and it did not appear in the final reports. On the final day at Maastricht, the launch of the GCA was duly announced together with the intention (previously unknown to us) to house its headquarters in Washington. I was stunned, believing this location to be a major mistake, a blow to the perceived "freshness" of the new effort. I perceived it as an "automatic abort" for the whole enterprise. Many of us had simply assumed that the Dutch, in the primary person of Jan Pronk, would carry this initiative and thus provide new energy and credibility, while reducing the Bank's domination of the African scene. Agarwal seemed equally upset and, to his credit, felt it necessary to apologize to some of us for having involved us in such a mistaken (and evidently totally Bank-driven) enterprise. I privately confronted Jaycox and McNamara on it in a corridor on the final day (Jaycox arguing that the Bank was the only available home), and I then wrote a strong letter to Pronk. In the end the GCA added little but further conferences. It probably didn't matter where its headquarters were.

For a few years I served, by invitation (by then-editor Moshe Syrquin), as a member of the editorial board of the *World Bank Economic Review*

(WBER), a scholarly outlet for some of the Bank's research papers. I was impressed with the care and thoroughness of the journal's refereeing practices, but did not enjoy the heavy paperwork. I resigned from this appointment shortly after my formal university retirement in 1998. My principal contribution to the WBER may have been to represent non-Bank scholars in a controversy involving the possibility of the journal's publication of articles based upon Bank data that were not available to "outsiders." My position was that

> any papers written on material that cannot be made available to external researchers who may want to replicate it or develop alternative tests of the hypotheses should not be published in our journal. Perhaps when you have external editorial board members taking a hard line on this issue, it will stimulate the Bank to be more open with its data.[78]

When Joe Stiglitz resigned, or was fired, from his post as chief economist at the World Bank in late 1999, I was among those who were upset. He had no doubt been in a difficult position there but, as I wrote him in December, he had

> brought integrity and honesty to the research function in the World Bank at a time when it was badly needed ... [and] managed to offset, at least to some degree, the hidebound and ideologically closed reputation for which the Bank and the IMF had become infamous.[79]

When in 1990 the Brookings Institution, with the support of the World Bank, initiated an independent history of the World Bank (actually its second such venture; the first, by Mason and Asher, covered the first twenty-five years[80]), timed to be completed by the time of the Bank's fiftieth birthday, I was invited to join the project's international advisory council. The co-authors were two friends, John P. Lewis of Princeton, former chair of the ODC's Program Advisory Committee and the OECD's Development Assistance Committee (DAC); and Richard Webb, formerly governor of the Central Reserve Bank of Peru. At its first meeting I argued strongly for interviews with non–World Bank institutions and people, rather than exclusive or even primary reliance upon Bank files (which, remarkably, were to be totally opened to them). At this meeting I met, for the first time, their young Indian research assistant, a political scientist with a keen interest in matters economic, a former student of John's, Devesh Kapur. He and I seemed to agree on many things. His role in the enterprise gradually expanded to the degree that he was graduated to the status of a full co-author and, because of academic conventions as to the (alphabetic) ordering of co-authors, their eventual joint book is generally cited as Kapur et al.[81] For whatever reason, and certainly Richard's methodical and meticulous writing style was an important one, the project dragged on. The book became longer and longer. The fiftieth anniversary came and went. Finally, with the agreement of the authors, Brookings appointed a "guidance and closure committee" to prod the authors with quarterly meetings to bring the project to fruition. I was the only member of the original advisory committee to be invited to join this one – I'm still not sure why. The other committee members had significant World Bank experience – William Diamond, Jonas Horalz (from Iceland, once the Nordic executive director), and Mervyn Weiner (an expatriate Canadian who had long lived in Washington working in the Bank). We met to hear reports on the authors' progress, read and commented upon draft chapters, and strategized on overall approaches and content. Presumably, we sped matters a little, but it was difficult to see much impact at the time. The volume eventually took seven years to complete. It is full of fascinating material but, inevitably, it is uneven and/or repetitive in places. Sadly, despite all of the effort that went into it, the World Bank more or less disowned it. Sometimes, its staff's comments on early drafts (notably in the case of Ernie Stern's reactions to the material on adjustment lending) had rivalled in length the draft chapter. Thereafter comments and reactions from the staff fell off. Within the Bank the decision had evidently been taken simply to ignore the project. When published, the book was priced (at $160) outside popular reach, and even the World Bank bookshop did not stock it. In April 1998 *The Economist* reported on "The World Bank's Hidden History" and the fury of its authors about the way it had been treated.[82] It remains a definitive source. I am proud of my association with it.

Late in 2003, and somewhat to my surprise, I received a call from the World Bank inquiring as to my possible interest in presenting a paper on the state of knowledge on trade and development to the forthcoming Annual Bank Conference on Development Economics (ABCDE, as it is colloquially known). The topic was one in which I had a long-standing interest, had something to say, and felt that the Bank's work had often been simplistic and misleading. My previous research and writing in this area had not received much play. Exposure in the ABCDE ensured a wide readership, much wider than in my other publications in academic

13.1. Last hurrah at the World Bank, ABCDE Washington, 2004

journals and elsewhere. I had certainly not planned to write a major paper on this (or any other) theme at this point in my career (five years after retirement). But I was greatly tempted, and agreed to discuss the possibility further. It emerged that if I were to agree to do it, I would have to submit an early draft in advance for comment and review. I had almost always sent early drafts of papers to others for their comments and suggestions, so I had no problem with that part of the requirement.

But I had myself chosen those reviewers from whom I welcomed comments. The Bank told me that my primary reviewer would be Richard Cooper, an academic and former senior US official for whom I have some respect but a person with known orthodox approaches and not a person with any special expertise in my assigned topic. It seemed to me a transparent attempt to ensure, because of my unpredictability, or even "unreliability," that I would not stray too far from the mainstream. If I were to do a paper on this important topic, I now reasoned, even if it were to get a wide readership, did I really want it vetted in advance by Richard Cooper or others in the World Bank? I thought not. I declined, and offered my services instead as a discussant for whoever else eventually agreed to do the paper. That offer was accepted, and I had a brief opportunity at the conference to identify the (many) holes in the paper on trade liberalization (not, in the end, trade and development at all) by Riccardo Faini. The paper and the discussants' comments were published in 2005.[83]

14 Life with the G-24

The G-24 (formally, the Intergovernmental Group of Twenty-four on International Monetary Affairs) was founded in 1971 to provide more effective voice for developing countries in the international financial institutions. Although its original membership numbered only twenty-four, its meetings have been open to all developing countries. Early in its development, it established a research program, funded by the UNDP, administered by UNCTAD, and run by Sidney Dell at the UN, as backup for its efforts. It sponsored studies that provided alternative views, reflecting developing countries' concerns, on international monetary and financial affairs during a period of intense international financial turmoil and negotiation. During the 1980s, I was approached by Sidney to undertake some research activities on behalf of the group, and I was honoured and happy to be able to do so. In particular, I undertook to help plan and then to synthesize and summarize two of the G-24 research program's major projects: one on the implications of the post-1971 (flexible) exchange rate regime for developing countries; and the other on the longer-term implications of the balance of payments crises in developing countries, which had been created by the severe exogenous shocks of the 1970s. Both of my summary/synthesis papers were first made available to the G-24 in mimeographed form, as was then the custom, and later published in more accessible outlets.[84] Both were very well received. During the course of these activities, I developed a firm respect for and friendship with Sidney. He took to consulting me on a variety of other matters in his work for the UN Centre on Transnational Corporations (he was for a time its director), the non-governmental North-South Roundtable in which we were both involved, and other issues. He frequently asked

14.1. With Sidney Dell at the Conference on the International Monetary System, New Delhi, December 1984

me for comments on his own draft papers, and he was kind enough to comment on many of mine.

In the mid-1980s, as part of a UNDP policy of limited grant renewals, and despite strenuous representations (from me among others) that the G-24 should constitute an exception to its rule, this excellent research program looked like it would run out of money. I was able to use my connections in Canada's IDRC (at that time I was a member of its board of governors, and the key program officer was a former student of mine) to induce them to provide a "rescue" grant in 1988 to keep it going. The IDRC provided support for the G-24 research program for many years thereafter and never had reason, I believe, to regret it. Sadly, Sidney Dell passed away, at the age of seventy-two, in December 1990, leaving many of his projects unfinished – not least important, his proposed complete history of the activities of the United Nations in the sphere of economics, to which he had devoted forty years of his life. Together with Edmar Bacha, a Brazilian economist with whom Sidney had worked, I had already been thinking of arranging a Festschrift for Sidney. Unfortunately, after his death, it had to become a memorial volume, eventually co-edited by five of his friends and published as *Poverty, Prosperity and the World Economy*.[85] Actually, I did most of the organizational and editing work on it. Roger Lawrence at UNCTAD and Pedro Malan, later to become the Brazilian finance minister, were among the other (nominal) editors. It contains a wonderful essay on Sidney's life and work by Shahen Abrahamian, at UNCTAD, who put in more work in this cause than any of the rest of us (and, sadly, himself died a very few years later). My contribution was a paper on African finance and debt.

Early in 1991, Roger Lawrence, who had worked closely with Sidney and carried administrative responsibility for the G-24 project within UNCTAD, called me to ask whether I would consider replacing Sidney as the coordinator of the G-24 research program. At that time, I considered myself already heavily committed in all kinds of directions, not least my university teaching and PhD dissertation supervisory responsibilities. During the previous year I had also become chairman of the board of the North-South Institute and, in a totally unexpected development, chairman of the board of the crisis-ridden International Food Policy Research Institute (IFPRI), which looked like it might take a great deal of time (see chapters eighteen and fifteen, respectively). At that time I was also heavily engaged in a UNU-WIDER–financed research project on trade and industrialization (see chapter sixteen). Although flattered by the invitation, I had considerable doubts. In the first place, I wanted some assurance that the G-24 membership, rather than just Roger Lawrence, sought my services. Roger and UNCTAD seemed to regard the G-24 research program as "theirs," for them to run as they saw fit. I saw my responsibility, if I were to take the job, as one to the G-24 membership rather than to UNCTAD. Roger undertook to canvass the G-24 members at their forthcoming spring meeting. Second, there was the matter of my limited time and energy. Roger asked me how much it would cost to buy my time and provide the necessary secretarial support. I tossed out some numbers, which I believed to be rather large – including about 40 per cent of my salary. He immediately declared them to be entirely reasonable. Then there was the matter of my potential conflict of interest as a member of the IDRC board, which provided the finance for the program. Obviously, if I took on this new responsibility I would have to resign from this board; and I had quite enjoyed my activities there.

Although I had some doubts as to how assiduously Roger had canvassed the G-24 members (and I subsequently discovered how difficult it always is to do so), I took him at his word when he told me that they were enthusiastic. The financing would free me from one-year–long teaching course and provide secretarial backing for all of my activities. When the IDRC began to approach me about leading a mission to South Africa, using IDRC funding, and IFPRI planners also talked of seeking IDRC support, I realized that my potential conflict of interest problems were, in any case, already getting out of hand. Involvement in yet another IDRC-financed project wasn't now going to make much difference. I decided to undertake the G-24 task. At the next IDRC board meeting, which by chance had a paper on board conflict of interest questions before it, I composed and circulated my letter of resignation. Some kind and well-meaning board members wanted to reject my letter and discuss the special circumstances that might overcome, in my case, apparent conflict of interest issues; but I quickly persuaded them otherwise.

I directed the G-24 research program for the next eight years. As I have said, UNCTAD tended to see this program as a project of their own, and to see me as their employee. They spoke of it as UNCTAD's G-24 project. UNCTAD handled all of the G-24 research program's administration – contracts, travel, accounting, editing, and publication – and did so very well, extracting a modest percentage of the funding in return for these services. Substantive cooperation was also excellent, extending to their provision of relevant papers to the G-24 program whenever appropriate and possible. But I regarded myself as answerable not to UNCTAD but exclusively to the G-24/G-77 membership, and I worked continually and assiduously to make the research program function more effectively in their interest. Happily, our financial supporters were also happy to leave UNCTAD, the G-24, and me with virtually total independence as to the details of the program.

The Group of Twenty-four (G-24) was, and is, a peculiar organization. Its membership consists of eight countries from each of the developing world's major continents: Africa, Asia, and Latin America. Its chairmanship rotated annually, and rotated among the three continents, each of which decided as a group which one would represent it in the chair. Representatives of the two continents not in the chair occupied posts as vice chairmen. The chairman and two vice chairmen together constituted the G-24 Bureau, which carried overall responsibility for G-24 activity. Unfortunately for the credibility of the group as spokesperson for the developing countries as a whole, the overall membership was not completely representative (there were no members, for instance, from East or Southeast Asia, or from East and Southern Africa), there were no provisions for changing its membership, and its constantly changing leadership was sometimes very weak. After the breakup of Yugoslavia, the G-24 formally numbered only twenty-three. When Mexico joined the OECD, it was required to drop its membership in the developing country G-77; but, although the G-24 was purportedly an offshoot of the G-77, Mexico remained a member of the G-24. All members of the G-77 were welcome to participate in its activities but few actually did. On the other hand, China and Saudi Arabia, neither of which were formally G-77 members, were active participants in the many G-24 meetings I attended. After the transition in government in South Africa, I worked to persuade the new finance minister, Trevor Manuel, to participate; and he did.

Relationships between the G-24 and the formal organization of the developing countries' G-77 were sometimes somewhat tense. Relationships between the G-24 and a later developing country group led by Malaysia, the G-15, were also somewhat uneasy. The G-77 regarded the G-24 as a product, or an offshoot, of the larger group. On the other hand, the finance ministries and central banks that were at the core of the G-24 preferred to see themselves as an independent group. The foreign ministry types, who functioned at the United Nations and in the G-77, frequently saw those who worked within the G-24 as too conservative and accommodating to the international financial institutions. Central bank and finance ministry types, equally, saw foreign affairs officials and the G-77 as too "political" and impractical. It was considered a major triumph when, in September 2001, G-77 and G-24 officials met together, for the first time, in New York (only days before the infamous 11 September) in order to coordinate and plan their positions in advance of the Monterrey Summit on global finance and development. I had a minor role, through behind-the-scenes representations within the G-24 and through my supportive 1997 address to the United Nations Second Committee,[86] in the decision to hold this unprecedented "summit" conference. Although by this time I had retired from my G-24 post, I was invited to this potentially very fruitful meeting and was a member of the summary panel at its conclusion. It was my last G-24 event.

As director of the G-24 research program, my responsibilities included attendance at all G-24 deputies' and ministerial meetings (and often G-24 Bureau meetings as well). These meetings took place immediately prior to those of the international financial institutions (the IMF and the World Bank) – both the spring meetings of the Interim Committee (now the International Monetary and Finance Committee) and the Development Committee, and the full annual meetings every September/October. The bulk of the time in these G-24 meetings was normally devoted to the finalization of the G-24 communiqué, which, like that of the much more powerful G-10 (the more significant industrial countries), regularly presented their "take" on the current state of the global economy and current issues before the forthcoming IMF/World Bank meetings. Normally, the first draft was prepared by officials of the country currently holding the chair (which, as already noted, changed every year). This draft was then "improved" in a couple of days of (excruciatingly boring) meetings of a larger group of officials from G-24 members, usually including some IMF/World Bank developing country executive directors. I quickly learned to avoid them if I could. Despite all of these preparatory efforts, the deputies of the ministers invariably spent further hours in their own meetings, which I was required to attend, fine-tuning the text. Those who had lost arguments during the previous preparatory meetings frequently used the deputies' meeting to resurrect their cases. Unfortunately the same thing often happened at the full ministerial meetings. The result was a great deal of wasted time. It was assumed by outsiders that I had a hand in the preparation of G-24 communiqués and, particularly when they were unusually short, I sometimes received compliments on their quality. Every now and then I did draft a paragraph or two, or suggested some form of wording to try to resolve overly long controversies, but by and large I avoided any substantive involvement in drafting of G-24 communiqués at IMF/World Bank meetings. I played a more significant role, however, at special G-24 meetings in Cartagena, Colombia, and Caracas, Venezuela, in 1994 and 1998, respectively (see below). At the regular G-24 meetings, I tended to confine my activity to the presentation of brief reports on research activities and plans, and the answering of questions about them. (But there were rarely many questions.)

G-24 ministers did not usually attend all of "their" meetings. They were most likely to be present at their formal beginning, at which time, after the gaggle of press photographers had left, presentations were always made by the managing director of the IMF, the president of the World Bank, and the representative (sometimes the secretary-general) of UNCTAD. These presentations were invariably interesting as advance summary statements of the subject matter for the meetings to follow. When the meetings were in Washington, and they usually were, I particularly enjoyed these opening statements because my chair at the table, beside the UNCTAD representative, was directly opposite – no more than ten yards away – from the IMF and World Bank chairs, and I was able to closely observe not only the IMF/World Bank leaders but also the behaviour and body language of their top officials. Michel Camdessus of the IMF, for instance, always tried to be charming and casual; but he always left immediately after his carefully prepared presentations, walking like sped-up royalty, very quickly, with a young assistant carrying his papers trailing obsequiously behind him. A more relaxed James Wolfensohn of the World Bank, on the other hand, rarely spoke from prepared texts, which offended some and delighted others. The UNCTAD presentations were invariably more pessimistic than those of the IMF and the World Bank; and, during my period, they were more accurate. I recall one occasion when a Mexican official came over after the meeting to thank the UNCTAD representative for his statement, describing the UNCTAD presentations as a most useful "reality check" on the others. Unfortunately, these interesting presentations were usually followed by a long and unhelpful one from the representative of the People's Republic of China, which wasn't even a G-24 member, but typically asked and received the privilege of making its own introductory statement. By that time, many of the key finance ministers (and sometimes also their deputies) had wisely left, leaving their chairs to be occupied by more junior officials or even executive directors, often the very people who had already been wasting their time in similar pursuits over the course of the previous few days. Efforts were periodically made to use the ministerial meetings more productively. On a couple of occasions, the chair sought to limit ministerial improvements to the text of the communiqué by such devices as requiring written suggestions in advance or attempting to "rush" the proceedings; but these attempts never succeeded. In short, it simply has to be said that these G-24 meetings were usually extremely trying.

At my first G-24 meeting, in Bangkok, as a newcomer to the IMF/World Bank meetings, I felt a little like a "fish out of water." But I used the occasion to begin to get the "feel" of the situation in the G-24, at that time chaired by Colombia, meet with UNCTAD's Roger Lawrence, make some other contacts, and solicit funding from the Dutch government via an old acquaintance who had become the Dutch executive director in the World Bank. My first proposed major research undertaking was a study of the role and effectiveness, after twenty years, of the G-24 itself. During subsequent months, in pursuit of this undertaking and to try to plan an effective future for the G-24 and, in particular, its research program, I sought advice from friends and acquaintances in the IMF (notably Mohsin Khan), the World Bank, and elsewhere, and commissioned a paper reviewing the G-24's history, experience, and potential from an American political scientist working on international monetary politics, Randall Henning.[87] I then arranged, with the strong support of a younger economist in one of the World Bank developing country executive director's offices, Rumman Faruqi (later to become the chief economist in the Commonwealth Secretariat), a special brainstorming meeting in Washington to review the role and effectiveness of the G-24 and its research program. I managed to attract some key developing country macroeconomists of my acquaintance (including Carlos Massad, Jose Antonio Ocampo, Azizali Mohammed, and Arjun Sengupta, among others), along with several developing country executive directors in the IMF and World Bank, including the irascible senior IMF executive director from Brazil, Alexandre Kafka, and Moisés Naím, then the World Bank executive director from Venezuela. There was a "free and frank" exchange of views – an extremely useful meeting. From this emerged a rough plan of attack for my subsequent research program. What seemed to be most needed were timely and professional second opinions on matters of current policy interest, with particular attention to the needs of developing country executive directors in both the IMF and the World Bank, and special efforts to draw upon developing country authors.

In the absence, at that time, of any sort of G-24 Secretariat and with little public attention paid to G-24 official communiqués, I increasingly realized – and more and more participants told me – that the research program was actually the core of the G-24's contribution, if there was one, to international monetary and financial affairs. It was critically important to link it more effectively to IMF/World Bank decision making and activity, and to make its output more visible and influential more generally. As a follow-up to the Washington brainstorming meeting, and with the support of the then head of the World Bank's developing country executive directors group (known as the G-9), in what may have been only a lucky triumph, I was able to arrange, in the spring of 1992, what I believe to be the first-ever joint meeting of developing country executive directors from both the IMF and the World Bank. The agenda consisted of a discussion of the role of the research program and the presentation of four of the first research papers I had commissioned, of which the one that seemed to attract greatest interest on the part of the participants was not on international monetary or financial affairs at all. That paper was the one by Jose Antonio Ocampo of Colombia, a critical account of developing country interests in the progress of the Uruguay Round of the General Agreement on Tariffs and Trade (GATT) trade negotiations, a topic specifically requested in the brainstorming meeting of the previous November. (The other papers were a critique of the latest World Bank World Development Report by Lance Taylor and Roberto Frenkel of Argentina; an analysis by Peter Pauly, now at the University of Toronto, using the UN's LINK macro model, of the implications for developing countries of increased financial flows to the former Soviet Union and Eastern Europe; and a paper by Nurul Islam, at IFPRI, on the implications for developing countries of some emerging environmental issues.[88]) The meeting was held in the top-floor board room in the IMF, and attendance both by the executive directors and their various assistants was, miraculously (as I was later to discover), nearly complete. I think the (enormously busy) executive directors were genuinely intrigued as to what such a meeting could achieve. It seemed to me that there was something of a "buzz" as they all trooped in. There was good discussion, and they seemed to enjoy it, but I sensed some possible disappointment at the "overly academic" character of the papers. The next meeting of its kind, about a year later, attracted far fewer participants. In the fall meeting of the G-24 later that year (1992), with my active encouragement, a formal decision was made to establish a "research studies advisory committee," to be chaired by the Bank executive director from the constituency of the current G-24 chair, to work with the research coordinator. It met for the first time, chaired by the Nigerian Bank executive director, in October.

The G-24 research program budget amounted, in total, to no more than about US $200,000 per year. From the earliest years, I managed to attract further ongoing support from the governments of the Netherlands and Denmark to add to the amounts supplied by the IDRC. In my later years, G-24 members also began to contribute significant amounts to the budget, as well as to the new Washington G-24 liaison office. Further grants were made by these and other donors for special purposes, notably a Bretton Woods fiftieth anniversary conference in 1994 in Cartagena, Colombia (which Norway and Sweden joined the others in supporting); an extra set of papers on capital account issues shortly thereafter (funded by the IDRC); a special conference on alternative approaches to economic reform in developing countries, organized jointly with UNU-WIDER and the World Bank, in Washington early in 1993; and an extra technical meeting on the reform of the international financial architecture at UNCTAD in January 1999 (also funded by the IDRC). In later years, the OPEC fund added its support to the program, but, annoyingly, insisted that its funds not be channelled through the account at UNCTAD. All of the papers were written by consultants or, in a few cases, by the research director (me). The program had no full-time staff and no office. It is perhaps a miracle that the G-24 research program had any impact at all.

Between 1992 and 1999, I commissioned over eighty papers, the vast majority of which were eventually published – in batches – in eleven volumes of a new UNCTAD series created solely for this purpose entitled *International Monetary and Financial Issues for the 1990s*.[89] Further unpublished issue papers were done in response to specific requests from developing country executive directors, particularly in the later years after the creation of the G-24 liaison office. Generally speaking, the papers were of high quality. I managed to attract many excellent authors, both from developing countries and from the more sympathetic elements in the development wing of the established Northern mainstream, including Jeff Sachs, John Williamson, Rudi Dornbusch, Lance Taylor, Dani Rodrik, Goran Ohlin, Tony Killick, and Reginald Green. (I recall Rudi Dornbusch, when he came to present his paper on the Tobin tax to one of our Technical Group meetings, telling me, not at all in an unfriendly way, that I seemed to be a "shit disturber.") There was no external peer review process. I was it; and I spent quite a lot of time suggesting revisions and improvements before allowing the papers to be presented at G-24 meetings or more widely circulated. In a few cases, I chose not to circulate them at all on the grounds that they did not meet the necessary quality standards and were unlikely to be salvageable through revision. Informing authors of this assessment was obviously a somewhat painful process, never more so than when old friends were involved.

The papers were always first made available in mimeographed form to the G-24 meetings, before later final editing and eventual publication. From my early consultations I learned that up until my time, few outside G-24 circles knew of the papers' existence, not even IMF and World Bank staff. After presentation, these often excellent papers apparently vanished, irrelevant and ignored. Sidney Dell and Roger Lawrence had managed to arrange, with North Holland, an academic press, a three-volume hardback (and very expensive) publication of previous G-24 papers; but this was years after they had been written. Although useful and quite well reviewed, these volumes were more in the nature of a historical record rather than a contribution to current policy debate. We now resolved to try to do better. In 1992 the chair of the G-24 (at that time Nigeria) wrote to the heads of both the IMF and the World Bank, requesting their assistance and support for the publication of G-24 papers. Although backup administrative support for G-24 activities was supplied by both institutions on a regular basis, both declined this request. UNCTAD responded to the need instead. We were well aware that far more attention would have been directed to our papers in the relevant policymaking circles had they been published under IMF/ World Bank auspices, but there was little we could do about it. UNCTAD published about 5,000 copies of each volume in our series, most of which were circulated free of charge to libraries and developing country embassies. Unfortunately, they were neither well publicized nor widely read, at least in Northern circles. In later years, when I finally saw the UNCTAD distribution list, I was genuinely appalled at the irrelevance and downright sloppiness of its composition.

I think (and I certainly hope) that individual papers may nonetheless have been influential, or at least helpful, in the formulation of some developing country positions. Our failure to get more attention for these potentially important papers, and thus greater voice for the South, was a constant source of frustration. (My successor, Dani Rodrik, achieved greater success, I think, by circulating each individual paper in a glossy working paper series with a Harvard University *imprimatur* alongside that of UNCTAD. But even then it was difficult to get much attention from mainstream sources.) On two occasions, we republished revised papers in edited books on more focused topics (international monetary/financial reform and capital account regimes) with a commercial publisher; but, sadly, they didn't receive much attention from the Northern mainstream either. Mere World Bank working papers and relatively minor documents from within the international financial institutions (IFIs) often receive attention from *The Economist* or the *Financial Times*. We could only get regularly reported in the Southern News Service (SUNS). There remains a fundamental problem here.

Only on rare occasions did these papers seem to get much attention from the IMF or World Bank either. Once, the president of the World

Bank, James Wolfensohn, heatedly devoted a significant part of his regular address to the G-24 ministers to an attack upon one of our new papers, by Devesh Kapur, which challenged the Bank's recommendations for the use of its net income and its arguments on the need for increased charges. I didn't think he persuaded any of us; but, of course, under the Bank's weighted voting system, he won the vote in the subsequent Bank meeting anyway. On another occasion, a senior member of the World Bank staff (Jim Adams, later, as resident Bank representative in Dar es Salaam, to become very helpful in my efforts to improve aid relationships in Tanzania) complained mightily to me in private about a paper, by Louis Emmerij, suggesting that the Bank's purported new poverty emphasis had not changed anything very much in Bank practice; he felt it was unfair. More typically, our papers were simply ignored by IMF and World Bank staff, while their own permanent research units, financed by budgets that were huge multiples of ours, continued to churn out papers.

Perhaps our greatest success was with the 1994 conference in Cartagena, Columbia. At one of the 1993 G-24 meetings, I had suggested the convening of an independent G-24 conference to review, on the occasion of the fiftieth anniversary of the Bretton Woods conference that created the IMF, the state of the international monetary and financial system from the standpoint of developing country interests. The idea was well received and, at the conclusion of the ministerial meeting, the Colombian delegation came to me and issued an invitation to stage it in their country. It proved to be quite easy both to find the necessary funding and high-quality developing country authors. Formally, I had an advisory committee consisting of Philip Ndegwa from Kenya, Richard Webb from Peru, and I.G. Patel from India (in keeping with G-24 practice, one from each developing country continent). Happily, the G-24 agreed that the meeting should be a technical one, rather than a political one; that it should be open; and that participants should be free to present their personal views rather than those of the institutions or governments with which they might be associated. We made it a matter of principle that all those on the program (both authors and discussants) were to be from developing countries. Ironically, when the chair of the G-24 at that time (the finance minister of Syria) was unable at the last minute to come, I found myself in a prominent substitute position on the platform – both at the beginning and at the end – as the sole participant who was not from the developing world. Our conference in mid-April 1994 was the first fiftieth anniversary conference of the Bretton Woods institutions' celebratory year. There were to be many more. Its papers were critical and they were good. The program had a truly stellar cast. Participants came from all over the developing world. It was truly a great success. I was able to provide a (personal) summary of its principal conclusions for the Washington G-24 ministerial meeting, which came immediately after. UNCTAD broke all speed records and got a publication of the proceedings finished in time for the IMF/World Bank anniversary meetings in Madrid in September. I was able to offer a summary of the G-24 conference findings as my contribution to a panel in the IFI-organized anniversary conference in Madrid. We then took a little more time, edited the papers more carefully, and produced an attractive book, *The International Monetary and Financial System: Developing Country Perspectives*.[90] The conclusions appear in my introduction to the volume, and they now look even better than they did then, anticipating, for instance, the later problems with volatile private capital flows, unserviceable IFI debt, inappropriate conditionality, and IFI governance.

On the last morning of the Cartagena conference, Dragoslav Avramovic, at that time the governor of the Central Bank of Yugoslavia and very proud of the early success of his new stabilization program there (it later foundered), asked me over breakfast what I really wanted from this conference. I told him (and others who were with us) that we needed to have some ongoing mechanism to carry on at an official level the discussions of reform that had taken place at this meeting and those that would undoubtedly follow in subsequent anniversary events later in the year. I drew an analogy with the Committee of Twenty, which had carried forward the discussions and proposals for international monetary reform in the turbulent 1970s. During the discussion in the final session of the conference later that morning, Drag took the floor and made exactly that suggestion for follow-up. There therefore appears in my summary the recommendation from the meeting that, as a step toward appropriate change, there should be established

> an intergovernmental committee with broad representation, along the lines of the Committee of Twenty of the 1970s, mandated to reconsider the functioning of the international financial institutions after 50 years and their future role in a changing world economy, with a view to achieving improvements in their overall efficiency and democratic governance.[91]

14.2. With Drag Avramovic, governor of the Central Bank of Yugoslavia, at
the G-24 Conference on the International Monetary and Financial System,
fiftieth anniversary of Bretton Woods, Cartagena, Colombia, 1994

Unfortunately, like so much else that we did, this volume received
very little attention. Despite its topicality and its high quality, I cannot
recall having seen a single review anywhere.

A major innovation in G-24 procedures originated from a special
meeting in late August 1994, organized by the new chair (Guatemala)
in response to the membership's request for a review of G-24 effectiveness. The meeting was held in the beautiful Guatemalan (Mayan)
interior town of Antigua, once a Spanish colonial capital before a devastating earthquake in the seventeenth century and now a centre for
Spanish-language classes for North Americans. (The Nigerian delegate
arrived late because his travel agent mistakenly sent him to the island
of Antigua in the Caribbean.) Our Central Bank hosts were gracious and
generous, and arranged for us all to be granted honorary citizenship

by the mayor of the town; but I couldn't help feeling uneasy about our hosts' whiteness in the context of the very recent history of oppression and violence against the indigenous Mayan people of the Guatemalan highlands.

The Antigua meeting was divided into two parts. The first, to which I was not invited, was to consider the overall functioning of the G-24, including its research program. The second was to consider the follow-up to the Cartagena conference and any recommendations to be made to the G-24 ministers in that regard. Both parts had significant outcomes. The latter agreed, after considerable debate, to recommend to the ministers the proposal to push for a new Committee of Twenty (C-20) or something analogous. The hosts appeared to want far more specific immediate policy recommendations, but they had had great difficulty drawing them from the various Cartagena papers and finally agreed to the C-20 proposal, which was purely a matter of process. As will be seen, this became a recurrent theme in subsequent G-24 communiqués, and in much of my own writing and speechmaking. When the 1995 G-7 conference in Halifax, for which there had been great hopes, failed to push this agenda forward, there was great disappointment in the G-24 as well as elsewhere. But the Asian financial crisis of 1997 brought it all back to the international front burner.

The Guatemala meeting led, among other things, to a decision on the part of the ministers to create a G-24 Technical Group to improve the relations between the research program (and its coordinator), the G-9 executive directors, and the G-24. From then on, this Technical Group would meet regularly (twice a year) to receive, discuss, and consider the policy implications of research papers in a systematic way, and, if appropriate, make recommendations to ministers. To improve link-ages between G-9 executive directors and the relevant officials in G-24 national capitals, and to connect the latter with the research program, it was suggested that meetings should be held regularly in G-24 national capitals as well as in Washington. It was also suggested that the research program should take greater advantage of developing country authors. Responsibility for the research program was assigned to a specific min-ister, the first vice chairman (the incoming chairman) of the G-24. I very much welcomed these recommendations, all of which were quickly put into effect.

The first Technical Group meeting took place in November 1994 in Washington. Technical Group meetings thereafter took place in Abidjan (February 1995), Islamabad (March 1996), Margarita Island, Venezuela

14.3. With friends after a G-24 Technical Group meeting – Azizali Mohammed,
Yilmaz Akyuz, Lal Jayawardena – at Lal's home, Colombo, Sri Lanka, March 1999

(March 1997), Algiers (March 1998), and Colombo (March 1999), as well
as every fall in Washington. I carried responsibility for the programs
and attended all but the one in Venezuela (which I was forced to miss
because I was in bed with hepatitis A, acquired on a visit to Tanzania).
All were characterized by lively and constructive debate. Attendees
included large numbers of executive directors and other officials from
Washington who appeared to relish the opportunities for interesting
travel. Apart from those from the host countries, however, there was
not great success in attracting more "technicians" from G-24 national
capitals.

The meeting in Algiers was memorable, though not because of its
usefulness. In fact it was rather lightly attended, both by authors and by
delegates, because of the severe security situation there. (A *fatwa* upon
foreigners had been declared by the militant opposition movement.)
Strenuous efforts were made by other G-24 members to persuade the

Algerians not to try to host the Technical Group meeting. UNCTAD offered its facilities in Geneva instead. But the Algerian government could not be moved. In the absence of authors (several of whom chose not to come), I was forced to make an unusual number of paper presentations myself. The Algerians seemed very grateful to those of us who did come, and our security was certainly protected. Upon arrival I was met, together with a couple of other delegates, at the base of the stairway of the Algerian Airways flight from Paris (other airlines no longer flew there), as if we were foreign potentates. We were taken directly to a group of cars already waiting on the runway, and whisked, at very high speed, to a modern hotel on the outskirts of the city, unusually characterized by tank barriers on the approach to its front doors. What sticks most vividly in my mind, however, is an evening in which entertainment was offered to accompany dinner – a troupe of about fifteen local musicians, singing and playing local instruments. I thoroughly enjoyed their somewhat monotonous and even lugubrious music, but a more mournful group of entertainers I have never seen. They did not smile, acknowledge applause, or show any emotion all evening long. We came away with the distinct impression that they were performing under duress. A planned excursion outside the city was called off, on short notice, because of security concerns. Political repression, high unemployment (quite visible as one drove through the city), and our hosts' obvious nervousness created an overall atmosphere that I was happy to leave as soon as the meeting ended.

The Asian financial crisis of 1997 created both new problems and new opportunities for the G-24. At the Hong Kong annual meetings in the fall of that year, the IMF still seemed supremely confident. One of its open sessions featured an all-IMF panel explaining the need for universal capital account convertibility and a change in the IMF Articles of Agreement to encourage it. By the end of the year, reality had caught up with it. The G-24 chair at the time (Venezuela) decided to organize a special "quasi-political" conference, funded in large part by itself, in Caracas to consider the wider implications of the Asian crisis. My principal role was to assist in the recruitment of appropriate speakers. When I arrived in Caracas a day before the conference was to begin in February 1998, I was also immediately put to work – together with Azizali Mohammed, now of the G-24 Washington office who had arrived earlier – drafting a "Caracas Declaration." Some of my draft's wording survived into the final version. The times were sufficiently fraught that, when invited, the managing director of the IMF, together with some of his senior staff, felt it necessary to attend this conference. The United Nations was also represented at a high official level, generating some protocol anxieties as to the order in which speeches could be made. There was also some diplomatic anxiety over the parallel ambitions of Malaysia and its G-15 but, in the end, a G-15 representative came to the G-24 event. It was a huge conference, and it succeeded in demonstrating G-24 interest and capacity in the building of what came to be called a better "international financial architecture." Among the most interesting elements to me was the complete unwillingness of some governmental representatives, notably one from the Philippines, to countenance the mention of the possibility of capital controls in our public declaration. That was soon to change. It was in Caracas that I heard for the first time, from the Brazilians, about the rumours of a US proposal for their own kind of Group of Twenty.

The Venezuelans also began at this time a G-24 effort to engage, informally, with the finance ministers of the G-7. Behind the scenes, meetings were conducted with G-7 "sherpas" (deputies to the summit heads), and G-7 representatives were invited to the next two Technical Group meetings. At the same time, G-24 research and public representations continued in support of some kind of broadly representative "Committee of Twenty" arrangement. In the end it went nowhere. An alternative "Group of Twenty" made up of finance officials (not yet heads of state) was eventually created, unilaterally, by the United States. But its limited mandate and its membership (encompassing only "emerging markets") bore little relationship to the long-standing G-24 proposal; and it is doubtful whether those who launched it were even aware of it. In 1998–9, the G-24 launched yet another effort to play a reformist role in the re-energized discussions of international financial architecture. Lal Jayawardena of Sri Lanka, who was now, as G-24 VP, formally responsible for the research program, argued for the creation of a "Bellagio process," analogous to that of the 1970s, in which academics and officials could gather informally to try to work out appropriate reforms. In the belief that one had to begin with discussions purely among developing countries, I arranged for IDRC support for a January 1999 meeting to that end in Geneva at UNCTAD, immediately prior to the annual meeting of the World Economic Forum in Davos. In what I considered to be a serious mistake, Lal expanded the meeting to include such key "outsiders" as Jack Boorman of the IMF and Joe Stiglitz of the World Bank. Rather than a strategy session, it became just another generalized seminar. And that was the end of that. I shifted my personal efforts – by that time I was getting ready to leave the G-24 – toward pushing for similar objectives via other non–G-24 channels, in what eventually became the IDRC-supported Global Financial Governance Initiative (GFGI; see chapter seventeen).

In 1997 the G-24 finally established a permanent office in Washington. The IMF offered rent-free offices, and the World Bank offered some secretarial support. Azizali Mohammed, acting in a voluntary capacity (he had by now retired from the IMF), ran the office, later replaced by William Larralde of Venezuela. This office made an enormous difference to my capacity to be useful and to the more effective utilization of overall G-24 potential. So did the increasing transparency, planned and unintended, of IMF/World Bank activity. I was at last able to respond reasonably quickly to at least some of the urgent G-9 executive director requests for "second opinions" on IMF/World Bank management papers. In my early days, it had been virtually impossible to gain access to board papers. Even the annual work programs of the two executive boards, to which a useful G-24 research program must at least partially relate, were at that time still confidential documents. (Now they are posted on the IFI websites.) When I began at the G-24, the G-9 executive directors, particularly those in the IMF, were unwilling to make internal papers available to me, much less to my authors, claiming that to do so would be in violation of the agreed rules governing their appointments. On one occasion, I was specifically asked by a meeting of G-24 deputies to pursue a purely technical matter (the calculation of member quotas under different assumptions as to the correct means of converting GNP data to a common numeraire) on which I learned that there were already such data available within the IMF. When I requested the relevant document, I was informed that I could only receive it if there were an IMF Executive Board resolution authorizing its release to me. We decided that this matter was not important enough to justify so extreme a measure, particularly since the relevant information was already available to those who had asked for further analysis of the subject; so we didn't make an issue of it. By the time my term ended, however, all kinds of unpublished papers and information about board discussions were available through NGO networks and increasingly on the Internet. It was amazing to me that Washington NGOs were usually better informed on current IMF and World Bank business than the G-24 research coordinator.

Even when G-24 research papers were right on topic, and were persuasive, there were limits to our capacity to influence G-24 members' efforts. On one particularly memorable occasion, an African executive director spoke to me, after the presentation of a paper on capital account issues, about his problems. Paraphrasing only slightly, his account ran as follows:

> I am completely persuaded by the analysis in this paper. But you must understand my position. If I place these arguments in my minister's forthcoming speech at the meetings, he will be denounced by the US and UK ministers who will tell him of his failure to understand economics, or worse. My minister will then come and denounce me. I therefore cannot make these arguments in my country's representations until the US and the UK declare them to be sound and make them themselves.

What was I to say to that? I had no answer. On another occasion, a bright young economist, working in an executive director's office in one of the IFIs on a two-year leave from a government post at home, complained bitterly to me. Evidently, whenever anything the slightest bit critical of the institution's papers or practices was inserted by this official into his executive director's notes for use in board meetings, they were omitted in his presentations there. Critical analysis, of the kind featured in our papers, was not welcomed and probably not even understood by this particular executive director. When finally brought to the point of complaining to him, this economist was told to relax, not rock the boat, and try to enjoy the two-year break away from home a little more. These incidents should not be taken as a reflection on all developing country executive directors. Some have been truly excellent. But many have not.

Despite some earnest attempts, I pretty much failed to develop good links between the G-24 and potentially supportive NGOs. My first effort took the form of a small meeting in Washington, immediately after the Cartagena conference and just before the spring IFI meetings, between some of the conference paper authors and NGO representatives. It went reasonably well and led to further contacts, at least between them and me. My most serious effort was the commissioning of a formal research paper, from NGO authors Nancy Alexander and Charles Abugre, on the potential for cooperation between NGOs and the G-24. G-24 representatives were, and probably remain, extremely suspicious and critical of NGO motives and activities relating to development policy. NGOs were seen by many developing country officials, who observe their criticisms of developing country governments, as Northern-financed agents with objectives of their own or ill-informed or both. Although the paper was well done, it was, to put it mildly, not very well received.[92]

My distinguished immediate successor, Dani Rodrik, promoted excellent research and improved the distribution of papers. He invited me to one of his conferences (at Harvard, on trade issues in the run-up to the Seattle meetings of the World Trade Organization, WTO, where in my concluding panel presentation I observed that it would not be a disaster if the meetings failed, which they eventually did). He also urged me to do a research paper for him on aid relationships. At first I agreed, but later, as part of my determination to institute a new "retirement regime" for myself, I decided against trying to complete it according to the required timetable. Dani had huge other professional commitments, and after only four years he was succeeded by Ariel Buira, formerly a Mexican executive director and the author of some excellent G-24 research papers, who took on both the administration of the G-24 office and the running of the research program at the same time. Earlier, I had approached him about taking on the responsibility for the G-24 Washington office, but it had not been possible at that time to work out mutually satisfactory arrangements. He succeeded, at a personal level, in generating new life in both the research program and the G-24 office. Through his own publications, participation in many conferences, and fresh links to NGO efforts, he brought increased attention to the G-24. At an early stage, he invited me to join an advisory committee, and I received repeated invitations to attend Technical Group meetings. Not having papers or up-to-date knowledge to contribute, I chose not to attend them. Apart from agreeing, when asked, to write a brief introduction to one of Buira's edited volumes, I was never called upon for, nor did I offer, other advice. By 2006 he too had gone. In subsequent years the G-24 research program expanded significantly, and distribution of its material was vastly improved with the arrival of the Internet and the creation of a G-24 website.

Much more could be said about my G-24 experience. I certainly do not regret the time and effort I put into its research program. Research in support of developing country interests and objectives in the IMF, the World Bank, and other international financial institutions must continue and be strengthened. But until the developing countries more effectively coordinate their international activities and positions (I once was even moved to write a desperate letter about this to a number of Southern leaders – Julius Nyerere, Manmohan Singh, and Sonny Ramphal), and until the industrial countries finally acquiesce in improved international financial governance arrangements, there will continue to be strict limits to what such research may be able to accomplish.

15 Interlude at IFPRI

The International Food Policy Research Institute (IFPRI), located in Washington, is the world's foremost research institution addressing the economic and social dimensions of food supply for the world's poorest people. It is the social scientific arm of the Consultative Group on International Agricultural Research (CGIAR), a consortium of aid donors initially organized by foundations, supporting a number of international agricultural research institutions in developing countries to the tune of over US $300 million per annum. Institutions under its wing did the fundamental research that generated the "green revolution" in rice and wheat in developing countries in the 1970s. The group is led by the UN Food and Agricultural Organization (FAO), the UNDP, and the World Bank, and is chaired by a vice president of the World Bank. Its research institutions cooperate closely with one another, but each is separately incorporated and has its own independent board of directors.

During my period on the IDRC Board of Directors in the 1980s, the president of the IDRC, Ivan Head, was a member of the IFPRI board. As his six-year term approached its conclusion, he approached me casually to ask whether I would allow my name to stand as his replacement. He assured me that membership in the IFPRI board would fit my interests well and would not require great inputs on my part. Meetings only occurred twice a year and, so he told me, the meetings were primarily devoted to professional discussion on matters of economic policy relating to developing countries' agricultural sectors and their development problems more generally. I would be better able to contribute usefully to them, he modestly asserted, than he had been able to. I equally casually agreed to let my name go forward and promptly forgot about it. I was abruptly reminded, however, by a telephone call to our Big Bay cottage (actually to my sister-in-law's cottage next door since we did not have a telephone at that time) in mid-summer of 1987. It was John Mellor, the executive director of IFPRI, whom I had known for some years, enthusiastically informing me that I had been elected to the board, telling me what it involved, and urging me to accept. I did accept. But my experience on the IFPRI board was utterly different from that which either Ivan or John had led me to expect. I was to devote enormous amounts of time and energy to IFPRI's affairs over the next six years or so. Parts of my time there were quite nightmarish. But when I left the board at the end of 1994, I did so with some sense of accomplishment and satisfaction.

The first two years were relatively uneventful. My international board colleagues were interesting. One was Nobel Prize–winning Ted Schultz, now in his 80s but still as sharp as ever. I enjoyed the staff as well, some of whom I had known before, including Nurul Islam, once the chief economist for a newly independent Bangladesh. IFPRI's research output was impressive and permitted me to return to the concern with agricultural problems, which had driven much of my work in Nigeria and Tanzania many years previously. John Mellor and his wife, Uma Lele, hosted very pleasant social occasions at their residence in suburban Alexandria during my first two years of our Washington meetings. I enjoyed travelling to Tokyo, where I had not been before, for a board meeting (originally planned for Indonesia but moved for fear of possible hostility there because of the Gulf War). Another board meeting and associated conference was planned for Abidjan, Côte d'Ivoire, but, at the last minute, President Houphouet-Boigny declared that the French member of our board, Claude Cheysson, was unwelcome in his country (they had evidently had some earlier policy disagreement); whereupon IFPRI did the correct thing, cancelling the conference and moving the board meeting to Paris. This cancellation was truly unfortunate because the staff had prepared an excellent set of papers on African agricultural issues for its use, and they were rather wasted on the board meeting.

In May 1990, when I had only been on the board for a couple of years, I received a telephone call from the CIDA (Canadian aid) representative on the consultative group. She asked me if I knew what was going on at IFPRI. I had no idea what she was talking about. I was soon to learn. Over the next few weeks I learned that accusations were flying within the aid donor community about financial mismanagement and other alleged misbehaviours on the part of both John Mellor and the then chairman of the board, who was from the Netherlands. Staff morale was said to be plunging. There was consternation within CGIAR circles. The CGIAR system of independent boards provided for a much looser rein than was normal for many donors. Here was the most visible of all the independent CG institutions, the one located in Washington, experiencing financial mismanagement and crisis. The whole system seemed to be at risk. An emergency meeting of the IFPRI board was called for Washington in early July. I had planned to be at the cottage at the time, but I obviously had to attend. What an extraordinary event it was!

One of my first tasks was to persuade the chairman, who offered no sign that he had previously considered this possibility, that he could not possibly chair this emergency session in which accusations against him would be heard. I succeeded – in conversations with him in the elevator and corridor en route to the opening session. The vice chairman, Harris Mule, an old friend from Kenya, then ran a very tense meeting. Most of it was conducted in camera, with the staff anxiously hovering around us whenever we emerged, trying to find out what was going on and sometimes lobbying for their favourite solutions. We spent the first day simply learning.

On the morning of the second day, John Mellor made a passionate and brilliant presentation on his work at IFPRI. The chairman agreed to resign, while continuing to proclaim his innocence. The next step was to decide on John Mellor's future. We were well aware that IFPRI had been built, from the beginning, through the vision and energy of this director. Despite some evident recent errors of judgment, he seemed just as capable as he had ever been. The argument that he had been for some time under severe pressure seemed, on the basis of our own recent experience with him, quite persuasive. Our decision was therefore to provide him with an immediate year's (paid) leave, allowing him time to restore his equilibrium and permitting matters to cool down. The next step was therefore to find an acting director to keep the institution going during his absence.

IFPRI happened, at that time, to be undergoing the regular CGIAR-sponsored external review of both its management and its program. The leader of the external management review, Just Faaland, a Norwegian development economist and friend, was actually in the building that week. Our Bangladeshi board member, Syeduzzaman, made a brilliant suggestion: why not hire Just as IFPRI's acting director for a year? I was quickly delegated, as the one who knew him best, to find him and make him the offer. He was obviously extremely surprised and, understandably, reluctant to make an immediate decision. Equally understandably, he wanted to know, before coming to a decision, who was to become the new board chairman. Obviously I could not tell him because we had not yet broached that topic. If I were to become the chairman, Just told me, the prospect could become quite attractive to him. The idea that I should become the new chairman had also been put to me by a group of professional staff in a private meeting on the edges of the "real" meeting on the day before. I had pooh-poohed the idea, saying that I could not possibly spare the time for such an undertaking. When I now returned to the board meeting to report on my conversation with Just, I was stunned to learn that they had, in my absence, agreed unanimously to elect me as the new board chairman. At first I refused. It was absolutely true that I simply did not have the time. But they insisted – they said there were no realistic alternatives. In the end I saw no alternative but to agree.

Very early the following morning I wrote a letter to the chairman of the CGIAR explaining all of the board's decisions and assuring him that everything at IFPRI was under control. About a week later – a week during which I agonized, back at our summer cottage, over what we might possibly do if Just said no and in which I called him more than once at his home in Norway – Just Faaland agreed to be our acting director. But matters at IFPRI were still far from "under control." And it would be hard to exaggerate my lack of preparedness for the task ahead. I returned home from the emergency board meeting deeply worried about my capacity to carry out these new responsibilities. At that time I didn't even yet know how onerous they were going to become.

In the last week in August I had already been invited in my professional capacity to attend an IFPRI conference in Washington, and I now saw this as a useful opportunity to learn more about my responsibilities as board chairman. John Mellor, the conference organizer, invited me to his home for dinner on the evening of my arrival. We had a long conversation about IFPRI, its problems, and its future. I assured him that the board had expressed confidence in his continued leadership, had no hidden agenda, and that the decision to grant him a year's leave was straightforward and well intentioned.

At IFPRI the following morning, however, Just Faaland, the acting director, told me that members of the senior staff wanted a private meeting with me as soon as possible. We met in a private corner office, next to that of the director, immediately after the conclusion of the conference sessions in the late afternoon. Every divisional head in the institution was there. Each spoke. Their message had been carefully prepared, and it was unanimous: in terms of personnel management and personal relations John Mellor had lost their confidence and had to leave IFPRI permanently. I pressed some of them, whom I knew to be John's previous allies, as to the reasons for the abandonment of their prior support. They claimed that staff morale had collapsed, and that the board's decision to grant John a one-year leave was viewed by all as mistaken. Needless to say, I was appalled by the situation. I went directly from this meeting, for which I thanked everyone, to a telephone. I called John Mellor and told him that I had to see him that very evening, and would be coming to his home. There I conveyed to John what had transpired. At first he had difficulty believing it, but he soon accepted the reality.

In the morning, I had Just's secretary prepare my announcement of John's resignation for immediate distribution to the board, all staff, and the CGIAR as soon as it could appropriately be done. John waited until the afternoon and then slipped the fact that he would not be returning casually into some comments about other issues in the conference. But my announcement, circulated immediately thereafter, was not stated in casual terms.

At the same conference I met with the (newly constituted) external review team and with a representative of the CGIAR secretariat. The former told me of the extreme nervousness of the IFPRI staff about the future of their institution and their employment; they urged me to conduct a meeting simply to introduce myself to them since, except for some of the professional staff, none had any idea who I was. I took their advice and held a short meeting with them in which I told them some important truths: that I had not sought the chairmanship, I was already more than fully employed, and I had little experience with such tasks. But I also promised that I would nevertheless attempt to learn quickly and do my best to reconstruct everyone's confidence in IFPRI. I was assured that it had been very helpful for them simply to see my face and my apparent honesty. In my meeting with the CGIAR representative, I discovered that there were going to be much heavier claims upon my time: CGIAR chairpersons were expected to attend all meetings of the overall group, and, in particular, the meetings of the Committee of Board Chairs. These CGIAR meetings took place at least once a year (in fact, it was usually twice) and related committee meetings could be more frequent.

In retrospect, it was extremely fortunate for IFPRI and for me that an external review happened to be taking place at the time of the management crisis (although it certainly did not seem that way at the time).

The report of the external reviewers was full of detailed advice as to what needed to be done at IFPRI, including the need for a complete review of the bylaws and administrative/management practices of the organization. IFPRI had grown from a relatively small institution with appropriately informal and relaxed procedures to a size and degree of complexity necessitating more formal arrangements. It was relatively easy to simply follow the reviewers' advice, beginning with the employment of an experienced consultant to guide us in the details. With this guidance and effective interim leadership from Just, the board instituted a top-to-bottom reform of the institution's rules, procedures, bylaws, and manuals. The new regime included tight conflict of interest rules and provision for regularized procedures for staff appointments, promotions, and salaries. These and other reforms made it easy for me to explain and conscientiously defend our (rapid and radical) progress before the entire CGIAR, as I was required to do when the external review was presented the following year. Staff morale seemed to improve enormously. I initiated the practice of speaking to a meeting of the entire IFPRI staff after the completion of each board meeting. The institution truly had been saved. According to some, so had the entire CGIAR system. The IFPRI example of board-initiated crisis management and reform was subsequently cited within CGIAR circles to demonstrate the efficacy of independent boards and external reviews.

But there were still some severe glitches in the rebuilding process. They began at the next regularly scheduled board meeting. Just Faaland declared that, given the depth and extent of IFPRI's problems, he could not possibly begin to address them seriously in the space of only one year. Nor was he very interested in a simple holding operation. He would require two years, he told the board; otherwise he would leave immediately. This ultimatum did not at first sit well with all board members, but after some debate, it was agreed that it was probably inherently a good idea and would provide greater opportunity to find the right director for the longer term.

The following year, an even more serious crisis arose. This time it followed Just's announcement to the board meeting in the fall (the beginning of his second year) of his intention to appoint his old friend, Nurul Islam, as IFPRI's deputy director. (The external review had recommended the appointment of a deputy director.) This was not well received by some board members, who questioned both Nurul's qualifications for the post and the procedures for such an appointment. I myself had some doubts, both on professional and procedural grounds, about his suitability. Nurul's initial senior appointment at IFPRI (by John Mellor) had been controversial among some staff because it had not gone through any regular recruitment channels. The senior staff did not seem to have been involved in this decision either. Moreover, it did not seem reasonable to make an appointment of this nature before the new long-term director, for whom we were initiating a search process, had assumed office. The board decided that appropriate procedures for such a senior appointment as a deputy director would have to be agreed with the board, and that the appointment would best be deferred until a new director had been appointed. At the same meeting, the board decided to ask Vernon Ruttan, a much-respected American agricultural economist with close connections in the CGIAR system, to chair the search committee for the new IFPRI director; I called him up and he agreed immediately.

Following the board meeting, Just and I met with the entire staff, as was now our custom. I was looking forward to announcing the newly decided search process for the new director, a matter which I knew was of very great staff interest. Just spoke first. To my complete and utter astonishment, he announced that he had encountered a fundamental disagreement with the board and would be unable to continue as acting director. He had provided no inkling of such an intention in his prior interactions with me. The staff meeting was thunderstruck. So was I. So hurt was I by this surprise that I was close to tears as I rose to speak. I stumbled my way through a few words, making it quite clear that I had been taken by surprise, and finally announced the new directorship search process. In the brief discussion that followed, a senior staff member declared that he had lost all confidence in the board's capacities and that the decision to appoint Ruttan was the first sign of hope he had seen.

Immediately following this perfectly dreadful meeting, I hastily summoned the board to return to a resumed emergency session (they were already planning their trips home) and related what had happened. Some, particularly those who had already been annoyed with Just, were very angry. Just was leaving virtually immediately for an assignment in Ethiopia, which would occupy him for another week or two; and he had not specified the timing of his intended departure from IFPRI. It would be difficult to engage him in conversation in the meantime. There was little the board could do but to delegate to the chairman the responsibility to try to sort things out with Just when he returned, while keeping the board informed. I waited a week or so to let everyone cool down. Then I wrote a long letter to Just, including what I hoped might be the basis for an agreement between Just (and all subsequent directors) and the board. I attributed our disagreement to misunderstandings between us as to the role of the board, and called for a clarification of our respective roles. There followed an exchange of letters that resulted in an agreed set of lists: matters on which the board required information, matters on which the board's advice would be sought, and matters which were for the board's decision. Our eventual agreement on these issues, ratified by the board, became part of the IFPRI manual. Just agreed to return. And the reform process continued.

As chairman of the board I participated in the search committee's activities and deliberations over the course of the next several months. With our agreement, Vern Ruttan hired an expert on search procedures who did most of the detailed work of correspondence, collecting references, and the like. It was an extremely thorough search. Applications came in from around the world. We made special efforts to elicit interest from candidates in developing countries. At its final stages, the five shortlisted candidates (embarrassingly, none were from developing countries) were each to address open sessions of the entire IFPRI staff, explaining their hopes and plans for the future of the institution. At this point, one of the candidates withdrew. Only four spoke to the staff, and they all did so eloquently. Committee members then interviewed each and every staff member, secretaries as well as senior professionals, to collect staff views of the candidates. It was far and away the most open search and competition process I have ever experienced. During the next few days, two more of the remaining candidates withdrew their names. The committee therefore submitted only two names to the full board, and it made no recommendation as to which its members preferred. The two candidates knew each other well. Both were invited to Washington to meet the board members prior to the session in which the board was to make its decision. It was a very exciting board meeting. As chairman I tried to discern a consensus, but initially there was none. Those who had opinions seemed to be about evenly split in their preferences between the two candidates. The meeting went on and on. (I later learned that the two candidates were telephoning one another to ask whether they had heard anything yet.) Eventually, after much further discussion, a unanimous decision was reached. I ran out to call the candidates. Per Pinstrup-Andersen, a Danish national, a former divisional director at IFPRI, and at this time a part-time member of a key CGIAR committee, who was now based at Cornell University, was appointed. That evening, as I accompanied him to dinner with Just Faa-land, he told me that it was the greatest day of his life. It proved to have been an excellent decision.

Per had enormous energy and he "hit the ground running." IFPRI thereafter seemed to go from strength to strength. Its position within the CGIAR significantly strengthened; its funding increased (even in a period of declining funds for others); its internal structures and consul-tative processes were improved and solidified; and overall staff morale soared. Per's style was, on the face of it, relaxed, but there was no miss-ing his determination and ambition for the organization. My anxieties for IFPRI soon dissipated, and I was able to enjoy the remaining years as chair, secure in the knowledge that the organization was now in safe hands.

One of the more memorable events, for which I have retained power-ful memories, was our board meeting in Cairo in November 1993. Egypt had been wracked by terrorist bombs earlier in the year and security was tight. Because I was apparently an important foreign visitor, I was assigned an armed security guard who at first followed me everywhere and sat outside my hotel room whenever I returned to it. I found this highly disconcerting and likely to endanger my security by calling atten-tion to how "important" I must be; and I was able finally to persuade the authorities to call him off. When we went to meet with President Hosni Mubarak – a courtesy call – the security was formidable: several rows of machine-gun emplacements surrounded his residence. I did not enjoy this meeting. There seemed to be altogether too much mutual congratulation, much of it in pursuit of a United States Aid Agency (USAID)–financed IFPRI research project in Egypt. Also memorable in Cairo was the enormous breakfast spread offered at the morning break of the high-profile conference on agricultural policies in Egypt, which we held immediately prior to our board meeting. I had never before seen such a magnificent feast, mainly of very sweet pastries, on the occasion of an academic conference. I had the distinct impression that many of the attendees were more interested in the break than they were in the content of the conference.

I got along well with both Just and Per. Both made a practice of din-ing with me in the evenings before board meetings to fill me in on any forthcoming problems, and these evenings were always productive and pleasurable occasions. Apart from the ructions with Just, described above, disagreements were few and relatively minor. I made it a point to stay out of management issues, even when others tried to draw me

in. When Just and Per, for instance, failed to renew any of John Mellor's part-time IFPRI contracts with senior research economists who
already had full-time academic appointments elsewhere, one of them
protested vigorously to me and sought my intervention; I refused on
the ground that I had promised a free hand to management in accord
with the terms of our newly created agreement. Inevitably there were
some disagreements. I was not pleased, and said so, when a new video
about IFPRI's important work for developing countries opened with
a shot of a tall white man (Per) walking around an African market (no
doubt doing research!). On substantive matters, I thought that Per did
not give sufficient emphasis to capacity building in Africa (he later did
somewhat more), and I at first thought that his (eventually very successful) "Vision 2020" initiative to try to galvanize world attention on
world food and poverty issues would unduly deflect IFPRI energies
away from fresh research. I was also less enthusiastic about purely market solutions to agricultural and development problems than Per (or
the World Bank). Nor did I think he should be seeking funding from
private corporations. I often found the publications and some of the
practices not only at IFPRI but also throughout the CGIAR system (and
its donors) rather too glossy for my tastes. (Earlier I had IFPRI down-
grade the Washington hotel in which the board was accommodated.)
But such disagreements or differences of emphasis did not, I think, seriously affect our mutual respect.

Generally, I tried to focus more upon ultimate objectives rather than
upon the building of IFPRI as an institution. (I did the same at IDRC.)
I argued that a very high priority should be assigned to the building of
African capacity for agricultural economic policy analysis and that, if
possible, the effort should be undertaken by an independent African
institution such as the AERC. I undertook to interest the IDRC and the
AERC in such efforts, with eventually some success (but a lag of about
ten years). IFPRI chose for many years to launch its own (very modest)
effort, confined principally to a college in Malawi and later in Ghana.

The CGIAR system began to experience serious budget difficulties
during my tenure. It also undertook a major restructuring of its activities, with a new emphasis upon environmental issues, bio technology,
and intellectual property, in all of which IFPRI was to play a prominent role. All of this necessitated many extra meetings and great volumes of paper to be read. These were extremely busy years – and I had
already been fully engaged in other research and research management
pursuits. Somehow or other everything got done. Suffice it to say that

things subsequently went relatively smoothly and well during my tenure as chair. In my final meeting with the staff, when one of the senior researchers described me as having been, Mao-style, "The Great Helmsman," I was able to respond that I thought my leadership was more in the spirit of Mahatma Gandhi – "There go my people. I must follow them, for I am their leader." And I thanked them for having made the board look so good. I had learned a lot and enjoyed working with a wide range of interesting people, including representatives of donor agencies and scientists with whom I would not otherwise have been in contact. Board members included both old friends and new ones, and, by and large, I enjoyed my interactions with them. When asked by CGIAR staff whether I would, in principle, consider serving on other CGIAR boards, however, I responded that I would do so only on condition that I did not ever have to serve as a chairman again. That seemed to do it. Somewhat to my surprise, and even slight disappointment, I was never approached thereafter. It might have been nice to have been asked.

16 Wilder with WIDER

The World Institute for Development Economics Research (WIDER) was established by the United Nations University (UNU) in 1984 and began its activities at its Helsinki headquarters in the following year. Its first director was Lal Jayawardena, a well-known Sri Lankan economist with interests and experience in international finance. I had known Lal for some time. I first met him at a conference on international finance in Dubrovnik in 1980, where we had a long lunch together. Subsequently, he had been a member of the Commonwealth group on the Bretton Woods system that I chaired in 1982–3.

Shortly after his appointment he began to "reach out," as he always expressed it, to old friends who could further the activities of the new institute. The prospect of luring established scholars to a new and untested development institute in Finland seemed to him, quite properly, remote. He therefore offered opportunities for scholars in other locations to organize interesting research projects, using WIDER funds and under WIDER auspices, employing the physical facilities in Helsinki only for conferences and occasional visits. Among those to whom he reached out in this way in his earliest days were Amartya Sen (who had been instrumental in WIDER's creation), Stephen Marglin, and me. Sen developed conferences on poverty, gender, and Western (as opposed to non-Western) approaches to development. Marglin organized conferences on more radical approaches to economic analysis and the postwar "golden age" of Western capitalism. My mandate was to develop programs and conferences on international economic issues – trade, finance, alternative stabilization programs, and, at one point, the potential for middle power diplomacy in development issues.

In the early spring of 1985, Lal came to Toronto for discussions with Carlos Diaz-Alejandro (who had flown in for the occasion) and me about his plans for the new institute and specific research activities in which we might ourselves become involved. Carlos and I agreed that, together with Lance Taylor, we would initiate a WIDER research program on alternative (non–IMF/World Bank) analyses of developing country stabilization and adjustment programs. At this time Carlos had also agreed to join the leadership, together with Max Corden and Ian Little, of a major World Bank–financed research effort on the record of their adjustment programs. Our proposed program at WIDER seemed like its perfect complement, and Carlos the perfect bridge between the two projects. I remember these meetings particularly well because, alas, it was the last time I was to see Carlos; he died only a few months later.

A few weeks thereafter I spent several days in Helsinki where I was able to see the new facilities, meet some of the local personalities, and write up a potential research program on international economic issues for WIDER. There followed a series of conferences in Helsinki over the next couple of years. In the fall of 1985 I helped to organize a high-level conference (attended by Robert McNamara, among others) on research priorities for WIDER (and others) in international trade and finance, for which my paper was one of the basic inputs. It was agreed that the participants would constitute an International Advisory Group for such WIDER activities, but they never actually met again. Immediately thereafter WIDER held the first conference of its research project on alternative stabilization programs. By this time we had, sadly, lost Carlos. Lance Taylor and I were formally co-directors of this research project, which involved papers on eighteen developing countries, thirteen of which were written by nationals of the countries on which they were conducting research. Lance, however, was its real intellectual leader. My principal contribution – apart from helping to organize it all – was my detailed critique of his draft summary volume in which I successfully persuaded him not to try to offer a single alternative analysis to that of the IMF (which he very much wanted to do – his original title was "Tropical Problem, Temperate Medicine") but, rather, to emphasize the great variety in the experiences that our authors had analysed. The result was his highly successful little book *Varieties of Stabilization Experience, Towards Sensible Macroeconomics in the Third World.*[93] We were told that its checklist for policy design[94] was later frequently used by developing country policymakers as they prepared for IMF negotiations. The most memorable part of this particular venture for me was the last session of our final Helsinki conference in August 1986, a session which I chaired. We had invited Morris Goldstein and Mohsin Khan, both of the IMF, to attend this final conference to offer their critiques of country papers. They made it clear that they thought our analyses peculiar. But this final session degenerated into an extremely bitter set of exchanges, centred in particular upon Argentine experiences with the IMF. The fiery arguments went on and on. The meeting was scheduled to close at 6 p.m., but the debates had not ended by then. With everyone's consent we went on for another hour and a half, while I did my best to retain some order. It would have been even longer had it not been necessary to close the building. It may have been from that meeting onward that WIDER began to be known, in some orthodox circles, as "WILDER."

Lance Taylor led further WIDER research with more or less the same group as that engaged in the stabilization studies for another two project "rounds": on medium-term adjustment, for which I did a paper on trade policy, and longer-term finance and structural issues associated with the role of the state. I chose to employ WIDER resources to go off in another direction.

I now launched a WIDER project on appropriate trade policies for developing countries. Lal permitted me extraordinary leeway. Because of my reluctance to take on further travel obligations, he permitted me to hold meetings in locations other than Helsinki. The first was in Toronto in the spring of 1987. I gathered a number of prominent trade policy analysts and theoreticians, whom I considered to be working on the frontiers, for a brainstorming meeting on research needs related to new trade theories and, in particular, what had become known as "strategic" trade policy, and what they might imply for developing countries. From that came a Helsinki state-of-the-art conference on new trade theories and developing countries in 1988. (In the summer of 1988 I also spent a couple of weeks, with Georgia, as a visiting fellow in Helsinki. Summers in Finland are climatically lovely, and WIDER headquarters was always lively then. Winter there was another matter.) This project resulted in an Oxford book, *Trade Policy, Industrialization and Development*,[95] which was quite well received.

I was very conscious, however, that this research undertaking was somewhat theoretical and had only limited developing country participation, and was anxious to launch a trade project that was "closer to the ground." In September 1990, again with Lal's indulgence as to the location, I assembled a number of developing country authors (some of whom had participated in the earlier WIDER project on stabilization), together with some empirically oriented trade/development analysts (including Dani Rodrik, Howard Pack, and Moshe Syrquin), at the IDRC in Ottawa to begin collaboratively to work out a research program on trade and industrialization policies. We aspired to improve upon and update the very influential OECD-sponsored work by Little, Scitovsky, and Scott of a decade earlier.[96] Enthusiasm for this project was high. Its authors met again twice to compare notes and comment on one another's papers – both times at the OECD Development Centre in Paris rather than in Helsinki. This project generated two books. The first was a very large volume (570 pages), so large that it proved difficult to find a publisher for it. Routledge finally took it on and in 1994 published *Trade Policy and Industrialization in Turbulent Times*.[97] It contained fourteen country case studies, all of them written by nationals of the countries concerned. The fairly extensive introduction, which I wrote, drew on comments from and discussions among all of the authors. It was truly a collaborative project. We all thought it to be an important contribution and a significant challenge to the existing literature in its attention to the roles of exchange rates, export subsidies, and non-trade instruments of industrial policy. But it received only limited attention. While it has quite a respectable citation record, to this day I do not think I have seen a single review of this book into which we poured so much. The second volume, which built upon the work of the first, was published in 1995.[98] It was much shorter, contained only five country studies, and focused upon manufacturing for export. Ironically, it got more (a few) reviews. I subsequently wrote a summary paper for WIDER's new Discussion Paper series in which I tried to distill for a wider audience the principal results of our trade policy research. But I soon learned that WIDER's distribution list was extremely weak, and this paper too received limited attention; I had to ask WIDER to send copies to a dozen or so key people when I first learned that no one had seen it. Never before had I quite realized how greatly marketing and influence really matter in the dissemination of ideas. Such experiences no longer shock me (I have seen many similar phenomena since, with G-24 papers, as already mentioned, among such instances), but whenever I think of this one it still churns me up.

There were other worthy WIDER enterprises during Lal Jayawardena's tenure as director. At one memorable meeting in Helsinki, which was basically my idea and which I helped to organize, we attempted to develop "middle power" strategies for influencing international economic decision making in a more progressive direction. The discussions

were lively, but the initiative went nowhere. Nor was there any publication. In 1988, urged on by Jeff Sachs, WIDER financed a meeting
of developing countries in Mexico City (which I attended) to discuss
approaches to the debt crisis. On another occasion, in which I was again
heavily involved, WIDER jointly sponsored, with the World Bank, a
conference in Washington on alternative analyses of economic reforms
in developing countries. Again, the discussions were lively, but there
was no publication or follow-up. (In the latter case, the World Bank
seemed to drag its feet about publishing the proceedings, though they
strenuously denied they were doing so.) At the latter Washington conference, Lal received a standing ovation for his work at WIDER, which
was now coming to a close.

Lal did not build a significant presence for his institution in Helsinki.
Nor was he particularly careful with his spending. If my own experience was indicative, he was fairly casual about approving projects. To
make matters worse, Lal came from a wealthy (business) family and
enjoyed living well. The Finnish press and elements of the government
of Finland eventually gave him quite a hard time. Ironically, at literally
the same time that he was being feted on his retirement in Washington,
he was being pilloried in the Finnish media for his "imprudent" policies. The atmosphere in Helsinki by the time of his retirement was so
difficult that his designated successor, Keith Griffin, changed his mind
about the job after he first encountered it in person. There followed
a two-year interregnum under Mihaly Simai, a Hungarian, formerly
chair of the UN University council and a CDP member with me.

In 1997, at the urging of the new WIDER director, Giovanni Andrea
Cornia, formerly of UNICEF, for whom I had written an enthusiastic
letter of reference for the job, I took on my last WIDER project. As part
of his (very successful) rebuilding of WIDER, he had asked me for both
my support and my ideas as to priority research. One of my (many)
early suggestions was to undertake a careful study of the potential and
problems for non-traditional exports from sub-Saharan Africa. In the
end, under his pressure, I agreed to take this on myself. As before, I
insisted upon local (in this case African) authors and total collaboration
in the development of the research program. This time I also worked in
parallel with another African project – on financial liberalization – led
from WIDER by Nguyuru Lipumba, a Tanzanian economist in temporary exile, later to become a prominent political opposition leader (of
the Civic United Front) in Tanzania. We conducted our authors' meetings together – one in Kampala in June 1997, the second in Addis Ababa

the following year. Although we began with nine African country cases, data and other quality problems reduced their number to only five by the time we finished. The resulting book, *Non-traditional Export Promotion in Africa: Experience and Issues*,[99] devoted about as much space to other countries' experiences, from which Africa might learn, as to African ones. Such were the exigencies of economic research projects in Africa at that time.

I also had a hand in the late 1990s' WIDER project on global governance directed by Deepak Nayyar, participating in its original planning meeting and eventually contributing a paper on developing country issues in the published volume, *Governing Globalization*.[100] After Andrea Cornia's departure, however, I had little further contact with WIDER for some time. I was very happy, however, to be invited by the latest director, Finn Tarp, whom I had long known and liked, to both the twenty-fifth and thirtieth anniversary conferences in 2010 and 2015. At the latter I did not even have to present a paper or appear on a panel. These were wonderful occasions to reconnect with colleagues and friends. It was very heartening to see both the relative youth and the high proportion of Africans among participants at the 2015 event.

My association with WIDER was highly fruitful for me in terms of research projects completed, professional links, and domestic support (notably in the form of secretarial assistance and released time); and it is now at last having significant global impact, not least in its support of research and capacity building in Africa. I do wish that our earlier output had been able to make more of an impact upon global thinking and practice.

PART IV

An International and Development Economist in Canada

17 IDRC: Again and Again

The International Development Research Centre (IDRC) is a Canadian institution working in international development that has unquestionably made a significant difference. Founded in 1970, it was mandated to support research on the reduction of global poverty and particularly research in (as well as for) developing countries. It was provided with a fixed proportion (about 4 per cent) of the Canadian aid (CIDA) budget and was to be governed by an independent international board, half of which was to be non-Canadian. The members of its board, its chair, and its president were to be appointed by the government of Canada. It has done a lot of excellent work in a variety of fields. My own varied associations with it go right back to its beginnings and are a matter of some satisfaction and pride for me.

The first president, David Hopper, was an energetic Canadian agricultural economist, graduate of the University of Guelph, who was first known for his work in Indian villages (although then unpublished, it was notably cited by Ted Schultz in his influential 1960s book *Transforming Traditional Agriculture*[101]). During the period of IDRC's creation I was invited to a lively international meeting at Chateau Montebello at which ideas were exchanged as to what exactly it should do, and I had an opportunity to meet him. As one of my international friends there put it: "You Canadians are very funny people. You set up a wonderful and innovative new Canadian institution. Then you appoint such an American sort of person to run it." Shortly after it got going, I attended another planning meeting at its Ottawa headquarters at which prominent British board member Barbara Ward exchanged ideas with us as to what IDRC might do in the sphere of development economics. It was at that meeting that I met an old high school friend again, George Brown, who had been appointed the first head of the organization's Health Sciences Division following his work as a doctor and public health analyst in Haiti and North Africa. There followed other consultations in which I offered my views on needs in African universities; once, at David Hopper's request, I even wrote a background briefing for his use in a wider meeting on African agriculture at the US National Academy of Sciences. Among other matters, I pushed (as I had done elsewhere before) for greatly intensified training and research on African agricultural problems, drawing on the model of the successful Rockefeller Foundation–sponsored Agricultural Development Council in Asia. At one point, David and his wife, Ruth Zagorin (an American with special interests in education who had been appointed head of the IDRC Social Sciences Division) sought to interest Cran Pratt and me in the establishment of some sort of Toronto office of the IDRC in which we would take on some responsibilities for social scientific research projects in Africa; but such a role in research management did not appeal to either of us.

I have written in earlier chapters of important IDRC support for the African Economic Research Consortium (AERC) and its predecessor macroeconomic network activities in the 1980s; of its backing for my work for the African National Congress in South Africa in the 1990s; for the new Museveni government in Uganda in 1986; and for the G-24 over the late 1980s and 1990s. I also mentioned the IDRC connection (through Ivan Head) that led to my appointment to the board of the International Food Policy Research Institute (IFPRI). But all of these did not begin to exhaust my list of IDRC associations.

Initially, the most significant personal link was the IDRC's provision of a year-long research fellowship in 1975–6, which supported, through freeing me from teaching obligations, my research on developing country manufacturing for export and the role of importers and multinational corporations therein. This support was enormously useful to me at the time, freeing me not only to delve more deeply into whole new areas of research but also to devote more time to the establishment of the North-South Institute (see chapter eighteen) and to attend many conferences I would otherwise have been unable to get to. In later years, the IDRC's employment of many of my former students in positions of considerable influence provided a further link and means for my staying in touch with events there. The most significant formal link with the IDRC and all of its activities, not just those in which I happened to be involved, however, came from my years as a member of its board of governors (and thereafter its executive committee).

It was late in 1984 that I received a telephone call, out of the blue, from someone in a government office, asking me whether I would accept if I were nominated to the IDRC board. Although the non-Canadian board members were typically quite distinguished, many (or even most) of the Canadian board appointments were sometimes seen as somewhat "political" and were not always characterized by expertise in development issues. Since the government of the time was a Progressive Conservative one (the prime minister was Brian Mulroney, the external affairs minister was Joe Clark), the call was more than a little surprising to me. The caller actually asked whether I would be comfortable being appointed "by the Conservatives" (as I recall, that is how he put it). I said that I wouldn't be too comfortable in the company of some Conservatives, such as then trade minister, an arch-conservative named Sinclair Stevens, but would have no trouble with Joe Clark. I was duly appointed and received a formal document and a letter, signed by Mulroney, announcing that I had been appointed by the Crown.

My years on the IDRC board were vastly educational and also pleasurable. I learned all manner of things about agronomy, aquifers, diseases, information technology, and the myriad of activities in which the IDRC was then (and continues to be) engaged. At that time, the board saw, and was required to approve, the documents for virtually all proposed projects, except for the very smallest. The project docket for each meeting was huge – usually about eight to ten inches thick – and very heavy reading. The board was sufficiently diverse in its makeup that there was usually someone who knew enough about each topic to ask intelligent questions. And many intelligent questions were asked, and always intelligently answered, for the IDRC staff were all first-rate in their professions. But our project approvals were, in the main, pro forma. By the time a proposal had survived the labyrinthine bureaucratic preparatory processes, it was usually in pretty good shape and, in fact, was often already almost launched. I can count the number of times we delayed projects (I do not recall ever stopping one) on the fingers of one hand. Nor did we really make policy, as boards are supposed to do, or elect our own members and chair (they were government appointed). Rather, we typically approved policies and decisions, or simply discussed them further, that had already been thoroughly debated and refined by the IDRC's professional staff. Some board members were sometimes inclined to ramble on about their own concerns of the moment. IDRC staff members told me informally that they were often hard put to figure out "what the board really wanted." In the early days (and when I first arrived) it was the custom to transcribe the tapes of what was said at board meetings so that the board's views could be studied more carefully, but this practice was wisely discontinued. Votes were never taken. Nor was there always a clear consensus. But we did carry the ultimate responsibility.

As a member of the executive committee of the board, I attended meetings four times per year: two board meetings and two executive meetings. During my term, the chair of the board was Janet Wardlaw, dean of the College of Consumer and Family Studies at the University of Guelph. The president was Ivan Head, previously Trudeau's foreign policy advisor and speechwriter. He seemed to act more in the manner of a constitutional monarch than an executive director, leaving all of the management details (and the discussion of them) to his senior managerial staff, most notably Jim Mullen, a consummate administrator with a background in science policy, not development. I generally got along well with both Ivan and Janet (and Jim). Janet was an extremely self-effacing and humble chair, not at all like her flamboyant successor, Flora MacDonald, former Conservative minister of external affairs. Despite her retiring manner, Janet ran an effective meeting, and her common sense could be relied upon. I liked her a lot. Ivan was more complex and difficult to know well. Our relations were cordial but there was, on his part, a certain distance. One of my former students in IDRC reported that there were rumours in the organization that I sought his job. Perhaps this totally inaccurate perception stemmed from his knowledge (Ottawa is a small town) that, before his own appointment in 1978, I had been approached by Maurice Strong, then chair of the IDRC Board of Governors, about my interest in the presidency (I had none). Perhaps the problem was that I was both younger and had more development expertise. As I will detail below, he was quite unhappy about a critical report I helped to do for the board, midway through my term there, and our relations thereafter were noticeably cooler. His successor, Keith Bezanson, later told me that Ivan had actually warned him that I wasn't "loyal" to the organization! (In a broader sense I wasn't: I did always try to put the interests of those we were ostensibly trying to help in developing countries above those of the IDRC as an institution or Ottawa's policy concerns.)

Board meetings were quite convivial affairs, with time for personal interaction both with each other and with IDRC staff over lunch and dinner. Among the board members I recall with particular fondness are (Sir) Kenneth Stuart (a medical doctor, originally from the Caribbean),

Sadako Ogata (later UN High Commissioner for Refugees), Walter Kamba (vice chancellor, University of Zimbabwe), Gelia Castillo (an energetic sociologist from the Philippines), and Jorge Hardoy (an urban sociologist from Argentina).

Another benefit of board membership was the fact that every other year a board meeting was held overseas. This policy generated trips to New Delhi, Bangkok, and Nairobi, and, particularly on the Bangkok trip (in which Georgia came along), fascinating visits to projects in Thailand and Malaysia. In northeastern Thailand we had the bonus of meeting and spending time with the daughter of a close Toronto friend who was living in a village there doing anthropological research for her doctoral thesis at Berkeley. The Bangkok trip, however, generated some critical Ottawa press comment (basically accurate) about the use of taxpayer money to finance IDRC governors' travels to luxury Asian hotels.

One of the most significant events of my tenure on the IDRC board, at least for me, was a controversial report to the board, of which I was the principal author. An IDRC custom at the time was to have small board committees (usually two or three people) conduct in-depth divisional reviews (IDDRs) of a division of the organization. These board reviews were to be undertaken at the same time that the division reviewed its own activities. Early in 1987 Jorge Hardoy, a specialist in Third World cities, and I were designated to review the Social Sciences Division, which was at that time in a state of considerable disarray after years of budget and hiring freezes and relative neglect of this division within the overall organization. Staff morale in the division was low and a new director, Anne Whyte, still finding her way. We took our responsibilities extremely seriously, hired Frances Stewart and Al Berry as part-time consultants on elements of the division's previous activities, met the staff, and read copiously in the internal documentation that described what had been going on. To our consternation, Anne kept introducing changes and postponing delivery of the division's overall plan during the period of our review, making it difficult for us (or her staff) to see where the division was ultimately supposed to be going. Jorge and I believed that the appropriate role of the social sciences was not at that time well understood within the organization, and that significant changes to utilize their full potential more effectively were long overdue. We set about explaining why and how.

We presented a long (eighty-four mimeographed pages), detailed, and quite critical, though (in our view) thoroughly constructive, report to the board in early 1988. We began with philosophical reflections upon the role of the social sciences and then moved on to very concrete issues facing the Social Sciences Division. We considered weaknesses in the division's new mission statement, found deficiencies in its proposed reorganization, disagreed with some of its proposed priorities, and lamented the composition of its staff, particularly its weakness in economics. We also took on what we saw as weaknesses in the overall IDRC programs in which the Social Sciences Division was involved: the need for greater effort at multidisciplinary and interdivisional approaches and supportive organizational and financing measures; the need for greater devolution of decision making authority to regional offices; the need to review experience with African projects before the proposed significant expansion of financing for them; the need to improve elements of staff hiring, morale building, and professional development policies, and the like. We also called attention to the fact that a remarkable proportion of this division's expenditures were approved solely by management, having been approved neither by the board nor by the division's own professional staff. (This last bit of analysis must have been especially upsetting to Anne, Ivan Head, and some of his senior managers.)

Our report was evidently unlike any previous IDDR in the extent of its coverage, its frankness, its criticisms, and its specific proposals for change. Some of the professional staff loved it. One comment made by a (supportive) professional in an IDRC African regional office, which was reported to me, stated: "Now we'll see who really runs this organization." But Anne and Ivan, who had appointed and was protective of her, initially took it all rather badly. We certainly had implicitly offered them quite a lot of critical comment on elements of their management. In a shared elevator, just before our formal presentation of the report to the Nairobi board meeting, a very nervous-looking Anne told me that, depending upon what happened next, she could be "out of a job." That outcome had never been our intent. Ivan made it clear that he thought we were way "out of line." His approaches to us were correct but distinctly cool. In the end, having presented our report and listened to a rather unfocused and inconclusive board discussion of some of its points, we chose not to press the issues but rather to express the hope that our views would be considered, and reiterated our confidence in the professionalism of the IDRC staff. It clearly was impossible to discuss such a wide variety of important policy issues in a short meeting of this kind. After this session, some of the board members, including the chair, thanked us for the way we had handled the matter. I don't recall

Ivan having done so. On one future occasion, he did at least acknowledge in a passing personal exchange that the work we had done on this
report must truly have been "a labour of love" (his words, not mine),
and it was. A few years later, a new IDRC president re-read our report – I
suspect many others did as well – and seemed to act on many of its
recommendations. I took particular pride (and credit) in the significant
strengthening of staff expertise and programs, particularly in economics, thereafter. Much of this report still makes pretty good reading.[102]

The transition to a new presidency raised problems. Very oddly for
an outgoing president, Ivan launched a full-scale review of IDRC activity in his final year. The board thought it inappropriately timed and
dragged its feet to the extent that it could, but was powerless to stop
it. No doubt, apart from the (not inconsiderable) waste of staff time
that it involved, the review did no harm. But the new president made
it clear, from the moment of his arrival, that he had his own agenda.
The board had practically no input into the appointment of this new
president. I believe one or two (Canadian) board members participated
in the formal search process, but if they did, they did not communicate
with the rest of us. When the new president, Keith Bezanson, a former
Canadian ambassador in Latin America, was announced by the government, none of us knew who he was or felt any sense of "ownership" of
his appointment. This is no way, in my view, to run any organization –
even the peculiar institution of a Crown corporation.

In the end, Keith, a much more hands-on leader than Ivan had been,
dealt effectively both with the severe cuts in the real IDRC budget that
he faced upon his arrival and with the threat to the very existence of
the organization that followed a few years later, when the Conservative government did a major "weeding" of Crown corporations (including the Economic Council of Canada, the Law Reform Commission,
the Science Council, and the Canadian Institute for International Peace
and Security). The IDRC, so Keith told me at the time (we continued
to interact frequently although I was no longer on the board), was on
the original list for axing. The fact that Prime Minister Mulroney was
soon to speak at the 1992 Earth Summit conference on the environment
in Rio de Janeiro made it possible for the IDRC leadership to seize the
initiative and, with some judicious Ottawa politicking, to have IDRC
emerge as the Canadian implementing agency for the Agenda 21 agreed
there, and thus the star of the prime minister's speech on what Canada
intended to do for the global environment. I think it fair to say that,
whatever else his regime did or did not achieve, Keith's lobbying at that

time saved the IDRC – and that was no mean achievement. Had Ivan, a known enemy of all things Conservative, still been president, the IDRC would almost certainly have been done for.

As noted in an earlier chapter I resigned from the board prematurely in 1991. My roles in the G-24 research program, IFPRI, AERC, the North-South Institute, a forthcoming IDRC-funded mission in South Africa, and a host of other activities made it clear to me that there were bound to be conflict of interest issues for me, now that an IDRC policy on such conflicts was finally to be instituted. When it came to a choice between my IDRC board position and my other research and advisory activities, there was absolutely no contest. But Keith kept me informed and involved in other ways. The South African venture was very much an IDRC one, and led to further presentations and writing under IDRC auspices. Shortly thereafter, he asked me to join him and his Peruvian friend, Francisco Sagasti (later a board member), on a committee searching for a new director for his Social Sciences Division; and I was happy to oblige.

In the late 1990s, as currency crises engulfed Mexico, East Asia, Russia, and elsewhere, there began to be greater discussion of reforms in the international financial architecture. One of the ideas to which I had long been attracted was that of resurrecting some version of what in the 1970s was known as "the Bellagio group," an informal gathering of informed academics and officials to discuss international monetary issues that were not being adequately addressed in purely official meetings. The group was highly effective in moving forward the discussions then taking place on international monetary reform. In the context of the late 1990s and the early years of the new century, there seemed to be an urgent need for something similar, with the critical difference that now, unlike then, the developing countries would have to be directly involved. At about this time, Lal Jayawardena, Sri Lankan former director of the World Institute for Development Economics Research (WIDER) in Helsinki, now back as economic advisor to the prime minister in Sri Lanka, wrote a short paper recommending the creation of some kind of informal group of this kind; this paper helped to legitimize the idea in circles, like those in the IDRC, already attuned to listening to Southern voices. With my help in the planning, a small group was convened at the IDRC in mid-1999 to consider the idea. It included Jose Antonio Ocampo (then head of the UN Economic Commission for Latin America and the Caribbean, UNECLAC, later UN under-secretary-general for Economic and Social Affairs), Jan Joost Teunissen (from the

Netherlands, who had been running a series of meetings of a somewhat similar kind for some time), Ngaire Woods (a New Zealander friend from Oxford, now running the program there in global economic governance), Roy Culpeper, Aziz Ali Mohammed (from the G-24), and some other developing country friends, including Kwesi Botchwey (former finance minister in Ghana). It was agreed that a way had to be found to have developing countries' views heard and discussed by Northern officials in a non-threatening and informal environment. From this sprang the IDRC decision to proceed with the Global Financial Governance Initiative. Having guided the idea to the originating meeting, I was aware that it was open to me to take responsibility for the whole thing; but I had just retired and, bedevilled by health problems, was cutting back on obligations so, when asked, I declined. Instead responsibility for the initiative was divided; three working groups were established to address, separately, short-term issues like financial crises, long-term development finance, and institutional governance. It resulted in some very good meetings and written output, but its success was hampered by the unwillingness or inability of the relevant Northern officials to participate. We had thought, at the outset, that we had the backing of the Canadian Department of Finance for this venture, but unfortunately they subsequently backed away.

In 2002 I drew on the IDRC once more for an initiative in support of the poorest and smallest countries' trade negotiators. In the Prebisch Lecture I had delivered at UNCTAD in December 2000, although it was not the main thrust of my address, I had noted:

> [T]he capacity of many, perhaps most, developing countries to participate effectively in the WTO system – to take advantage of their rights and to defend their interests, indeed even to meet their obligations in the WTO – is very much in doubt. The WTO is a member-driven organization in which delegates from member countries must be actively involved in its day-to-day activities if their interests are not to be ignored … The requirements for effective participation place an enormous burden on resource-constrained smaller and poorer countries. When they are represented at all, their staffing is inadequate for handling the ever-increasing complexity of issues and the rising number of meetings and obligations now characterizing WTO processes …
>
> Let us [therefore] have an organization of "Lawyers Without Borders" (with some economists, I hope, thrown in among them) – committed not to the earning of the highest fees from the wealthiest clients but to the

principled defence of the rights of the poorest and weakest in the global economy's legal system and the building of their capacity to defend themselves. Needless to say, it could also function usefully in a variety of non–WTO-related "cases" – helping to negotiate with foreign investors and creditors, draft domestic legislation, negotiate bilateral and regional agreements, and the like. Such principled lawyers (and economists) do exist; they already work without fanfare or much reward in many countries. Isn't it time for the launch (and, of course, funding) of such an international apolitical, and therefore necessarily non-governmental, organization – both to create fairer international outcomes and to provide hope and inspiration for otherwise jaded young students in schools of international law and economics around the world, particularly those in developing countries?[103]

I had also pitched this idea publicly at my own university and at a meeting on trade, development, and other issues at the IDRC in Ottawa, where it had received good immediate responses from senior staff and some board members there (including my old friend, Sir Alister McIntyre, now vice chancellor of the University of the West Indies). The University of Toronto Faculty of Law, led by an enthusiastic Dean Ron Daniels, a former student of mine, soon had a small grant from the IDRC to permit it to explore the idea further.

There followed a major IDRC-funded conference in Nairobi in the spring of 2002, hosted by the AERC, which launched a new nongovernmental organization that aspired to address these issues: International Lawyers and Economists Against Poverty (ILEAP). The conference program was jointly put together by Ademola Oyejide, a prominent Nigerian trade economist and me. Rather than addressing trade issues, we planned the sessions to address the different areas of need: technical advice in negotiation, background research, advocacy, and capacity building. Invitees and attendees (there were few refusals) were distinguished practitioners and academics in trade law and economics. They included representatives from the WTO, World Bank, UNECA, ACBF, UNDP, Third World Network, IDRC, bilateral donor agencies, foundations, African governments, and universities.

With a solid international board (including Alister McIntyre, Kwesi Botchwey, Ademola Oyejide, Ron Daniels, and me, who was persuaded to chair) and assured startup funding from a private (Comart) foundation, ILEAP was soon able to get to work. After an exhaustive search we were able to employ an experienced Camerounian economist as executive director, Dominique Njinkeu, who had previously worked

17.1. With Ambassador Ali Mchumo and Kwesi Botchwey at ILEAP Trade
Conference, Arusha, Tanzania, 2006

for AERC and had, in fact, carried administrative responsibility for
the Nairobi launch conference. Dominique had a great many contacts
both in Africa and in the donor community, and he put ILEAP very
quickly into operation with technical support, papers, workshops,
and advisory services for African governments. Additional financial
support was remarkably speedily raised from a great variety of other
donors, including IDRC, UNDP, the Ford Foundation, CIDA, and a
number of other countries' aid agencies. Within two years ILEAP had
a CAN $2 million dollar annual budget.

ILEAP always had a very small professional staff of its own. It
operated primarily by contracting with economists and lawyers from
around the world for the writing of briefs and background research
papers, the provision of advice, and contributions to its informational,
experience-sharing, and training workshops, all geared to the needs
of African trade policymakers and negotiators. It was particularly

focused on negotiations within the World Trade Organization (WTO), negotiations of economic partnership agreements (EPAs) between the European Union and African regional bodies, and African regional cooperation. Wherever possible, ILEAP drew on available African (or Caribbean) expertise. In some instances it not only participated in African intergovernmental strategy discussions, but it actually wrote parts of policy papers for the African Union and others. ILEAP was a leader in the development of a coordinated African response to the push for "aid for trade" in the WTO, and published what is still the best available source book with recipient perspectives on this subject.[104] In addition to its workshops, it also sought to build capacity through the professional mentoring of less-experienced trade negotiators and the provision of fellowships for them in relevant African ministries and Geneva embassies.

The first (board-commissioned) independent evaluation of its work in 2007, while identifying some serious organizational weaknesses (of which we were already painfully aware), concluded that it was doing good work and deserved expanded and reliable financial support. By late 2007 and early 2008, however, this kind of support had not arrived and ILEAP's future, always tenuous because of its dependence upon the relatively short-term support of a fickle donor community, remained highly uncertain. Others with deeper pockets and better organization were, in any case, by now addressing the gap that ILEAP had been created to fill. After a discouraged Dominique departed in 2009, ILEAP phased its activities down, focusing its expertise on trade in services and negotiations thereon, before finally leaving its work entirely to others in 2015. During its relatively short life, ILEAP performed an important and pioneering function and was recognized as a significant, if small, player in its area of expertise and activity. The money and effort invested in it was certainly not wasted.

Under the Harper Conservative government, the IDRC s work was hindered by reduced budgets and what can only be described as cabinet indifference or ignorance of its remarkable record or its importance, not least to Canada's image abroad. Non-Canadian board members were no longer appointed. Board appointees were now from the government itself or were those with Conservative credentials. Many concluded that it could only be a matter of time before the science-averse Harper government closed it down. And yet it survived – finding new funding sources and struggling on. With a new government, there is hope for renewal of its truly stellar record.

18 The North-South Institute:
Present at the Creation (and Demise)

For nearly forty years the North-South Institute (NSI) served as the primary independent Canadian research institution focusing upon international development and, in particular, Canada's role in it. It developed a considerable reputation for the quality of its analyses and the independence of its judgments. In its later years, its annual Canadian Development Reports presented, among their other contents, compendia of authoritative data on the major elements of Canadian relationships with the developing countries. Although always quite small and financially fragile, it became a significant Canadian institution, called upon regularly by the Canadian media and parliamentary committees, as well as internationally, for contributions to current debates in the areas of its expertise. I am proud to have played a major role in its creation.

In the early 1970s, and particularly following the first oil crisis in 1973 and the ensuing international discussion of the New International Economic Order (NIEO), there was intense debate in Canada as well as elsewhere about appropriate economic relationships between the industrial countries and the developing countries. This was a subject to which I had devoted quite a lot of my own research attention, having concluded, after my return to Canada from Tanzania, that a primary responsibility of the development economist, if not actually working on the front lines overseas, was to conduct research and educate upon the international economic constraints facing developing countries, matters about which "we" in the North could do something if we chose to. Not only did I attend many academic conferences and write on these matters at this time, but I also began to speak publicly in more popular fora.

Perhaps the most significant of my scholarly activities during this period was the organization and chairmanship of a conference, held under the auspices of the Dag Hammarskjold Foundation, in late August of 1974 in Uppsala, Sweden. It gathered "a number of experienced and sympathetic authors to consider, analytically and carefully, what unexploited possibilities might be open for the less developed countries, both jointly and individually, in international economic affairs: which measures were likely to work and which were not, and why." (This description is from the preface of the resulting book, *A World Divided, The Less Developed Countries in the International Economy*, which I edited and for which I wrote an introduction.[105] This volume was well reviewed, attracted widespread attention, and was even adopted as a text in some university courses.)

In this sphere I was greatly impressed by the research and public educational activities of the UK's Overseas Development Institute (ODI), then run by a friend from Tanzanian days, Rob Wood, and the American Overseas Development Council (ODC). It was striking to me, and unfortunate as I saw it, that Canada possessed no equivalent institution and that the quality of the Canadian debate was therefore significantly lower (and pressures to contribute upon people like me significantly higher!). I began to talk, among friends and acquaintances, about the possibility of establishing a fully Canadian "institute" to play a similar role to that of the ODI and ODC, and I spoke to my friends in the latter institutions about how one might best go about it.

The first formal record of these musings that I can find in my files is a letter to Clyde Sanger, a Canadian journalist friend with a significant African past, then working at the IDRC while stringing for *The Economist*. The letter is dated 16 August 1973 (as it happened, our fifteenth wedding anniversary), and it was written from our cottage. In it I described having been inspired by reading the latest ODI annual report and, in consequence, having decided that the time for Canadian action had surely arrived. I described the role I could see for such a Canadian institution, the fact that I had been advocating its creation for several years, the need for leadership in its creation (I suggested that Clyde's talents would be better employed there than in the IDRC), and called for a meeting of like-minded people to discuss it further. I copied it to my political scientist friend, Cran Pratt, whom I knew to be sympathetic.

In May of the following year – perhaps at Clyde's instigation – I held discussions with David Hopper, then president of the IDRC, about the need for increased research in Canada on international economic policies. In September Hopper called me with the elements of a specific proposal: the creation of a private, non-profit Overseas Development Council, with a board of trustees including representatives of the IDRC and CIDA, which would jointly finance it, quite liberally, on a fifty-fifty basis. Its function would be to screen (and support) research proposals from the academic community in the general field of development, in much the same manner as the Canada Council did in other fields. He suggested a January meeting of potential founding directors to get it going. Welcome as such an initiative certainly was (and still would be), it did not meet the need as I saw it – for public education, total independence, and, above all, policy relevance. My intention had never been simply to support more academic research on development. I therefore wrote a letter to Hopper asking a number of critical questions – a letter which evidently was widely circulated within his organization – and requested broader discussion and acceleration of the process for consideration of these ideas. Somehow his proposal bogged down in the Ottawa system. The meeting to consider it never happened.

Informal discussions and lobbying on my own proposal continued. Several allies kept discussions going in Ottawa, prominent among them Bernard Wood at the Parliamentary Centre, Richard Harmston at the Canadian Council for International Cooperation (CCIC), Kendal Rust at CIDA, and Clyde Sanger at IDRC. In Toronto I gained the interest of John O'Callaghan of Woods Gordon, Forrest Rogers of the Bank of Nova Scotia, and Don Taylor of the Steelworkers. By May 1975 Bernard Wood and I, with the encouragement of Gerald Wright, then employed at the Donner Canadian Foundation, had arranged a small exploratory startup grant ($6000) from the Donner Foundation; and the University of Toronto agreed to serve as the formal grantee. This grant enabled the "organizing group," as we now called ourselves, to hold a series of meetings over the next few months among potentially interested parties (in current terminology they would be called "stakeholders") in Toronto, Halifax, and Montreal. The Halifax meeting was conducted on the periphery of a major conference at St Mary's University on "Canada and the NIEO," a conference which I organized and chaired at relatively short notice because the original organizer had backed out. The Montreal meeting was organized by Pierre-Paul Proulx, then director of the Centre de recherches sur le développement économique (Centre for Economic Development Research, CRDE) at the University of Montreal. At the same time, Bernard and Clyde (together with Roy Matthews) put together a draft prospectus for an institute, which was shared with participants in the later meetings.

The most significant of these meetings was certainly the first one, held in Hart House at the University of Toronto, which all of the above (and several more) attended. John Sewell, then vice president of the Overseas Development Council in Washington, was invited to the meeting to share his experience of institutional innovation. From that meeting on, events moved quite quickly. The Montreal and Halifax meetings showed that we had widespread and enthusiastic support. By year-end we had an agreed prospectus and had made formal applications for much more significant funding to the Donner Canadian Foundation and to the IDRC. The Donner Foundation indicated their support very quickly, so quickly that we were able to organize a search committee (Harmston, Proulx, Taylor, O'Callaghan, and me) for our first executive director by February 1976. (Unfortunately the IDRC initially offered only a token contribution.) After much discussion, we agreed on the name for our new institution. As I recall, it was first suggested by Kendal Rust of CIDA, over coffee in one of Ottawa's darker and dingier hotel lounges. Government officials who had to approve the titles of new corporations initially believed, we were told, that the "North-South" in our proposed name referred to Canadian-American relations. Applications in response to our executive director advertisement poured in. By May we were legally incorporated and had appointed Bernard Wood, at that time only thirty-two years of age, as the first executive director to begin formally on 1 August. We also had agreement from many prospective directors, including former CIDA head Maurice Strong, former Commonwealth secretary-general Arnold Smith, York University President Ian McDonald (once my tutor in second-year economics), and Carleton University President Michael Oliver, to join our inaugural board. On the other hand, the Bank of Nova Scotia decreed that Forrest Rogers should dissociate himself from our venture, and he was unable to join us. Our first major cheque from the foundation arrived in July.

The inaugural board meeting took place in September 1976, at the invitation of President Michael Oliver, in Carleton University's Arts Faculty Lounge. Bernard had worked assiduously to build a stellar board, with representation from a variety of constituencies from all across the country. In addition to those already mentioned and, of course, the original group, the board now also included Jacques Hébert (president, Canada World Youth), Paul Martin (president, Canada Steamship Lines, later prime minister), James Peterson (later the Liberal minister

for International Trade), Hugh Winsor (the *Globe and Mail*), Maryon
Brechin (president, Consumers Association of Canada), Bill McNeill
(executive director, World University Service of Canada), Charles Per-
rault (president, Conseil du Patronat du Québec), and others. Everyone came to the inaugural meeting, and there was great enthusiasm for
the new venture. Equally distinguished board members were to join
shortly thereafter. By prior arrangement, we elected Arnold Smith as
chairman. Arnold had been a respected diplomat and the first secretary-
general of the Commonwealth Secretariat in London. His name would
gain us, we hoped, instant credibility. He remained in the chair for the
next fourteen years. I was elected deputy chairman. The executive committee was rounded out with Don Taylor (from Labour), Charles Per-
rault (business), Richard Harmston (NGOs), and Pierre-Paul Proulx. A
draft initial program was discussed, to be further refined at the next
meeting in January. It was agreed that the institute would begin with
an experimental three-year program, following which its future would
be reviewed. The North-South Institute was under way.

In our anxiety to get going there was one serious oversight. The
bylaws neglected to include provision for the rotation of directors.
This detail may seem like an obscure administrative matter, but as the
years rolled by and the NSI prospered, very few directors felt inclined
to resign. Particularly awkward was the situation with respect to the
esteemed board chairman. Arnold began as an excellent and energetic
chairperson. But he was aging. In his later years he frequently used
the occasion of board meetings to deliver himself of short lectures on
matters not on the formal agenda. Board members were fairly tolerant
of these lapses, but the executive committee finally decided that action
was required. We devised a system of board and executive committee
rotations, argued its merits on grounds of general principles, and persuaded the chairman to go along. The blow was softened by the creation
by the NSI of a development scholarship in Arnold's name at Carleton
University, a gesture which clearly moved him deeply. I was elected as
the new board chair – for a fairly short term; our newly devised rotation
rules required my own departure within two years. Our clever reforms
may have somewhat overshot our intentions. Rotations ever since may
have been a bit too rapid.

Although we did not experience many board resignations, one was
a bit of a cause célèbre. Sam Fox of the Amalgamated Clothing and
Textile Workers Union felt sufficiently strongly about a NSI study of
Canadian protectionism, particularly in the clothing and textile sector,

that he maintained he could not continue on the board – this despite the board's prior agreement that directors would take no responsibility for the contents of the NSI's independent studies that they had mandated. (If directors had been required to agree on the contents, the NSI could never have published anything of value.) To my knowledge this incident was the only such resignation in the NSI's history.

The board took an early decision that sitting members of Parliament should not be board members. But over the years many distinguished former MP's joined the North-South Institute board – among them, Andrew Brewin, Marc Lalonde, Robert Stanfield, Joe Clark, Barbara MacDougall, and Ed Broadbent. Gender balance and representativeness gradually improved, with special efforts made to incorporate First Nations people, Third World diaspora, and developing country representatives. The NSI was always very well served by its high-quality board.

The first "senior" (he was about thirty at the time) member of the full-time research staff was Randy Spence, a very able former doctoral student of mine at the University of Toronto. He produced, remarkably quickly, excellent papers on commodity issues, food aid, Third World debt, and, together with Bernard, an attention-catching "report card" on the overall Canadian record of economic relationships with the developing world in which various elements were assigned grades of A to F. After two years, he unfortunately felt it necessary to leave because of the enormous workload's impact upon his well-being. On his departure he also expressed to me his concern that the NSI's rapidly expanding agenda risked making the load upon the small staff even heavier and, worse still, risked declining quality. Indeed there were some glitches over quality in the next few years, but, by and large, high standards were retained. Junior staff, often recent master or doctoral graduates, were hired and carried heavy and responsible loads. The heavy workloads were compensated for them, I suspect, by the excitement of their responsibilities. Margaret Biggs, for instance, an inexperienced but enthusiastic and fast-learning young economist, and the NSI's first junior research employee, took responsibility for the NSI's work on trade and protectionism; it quickly earned widespread attention for its policy relevance and high quality. (Margaret later held senior rank in the Privy Council Office, then became CIDA's president, and now chairs the IDRC board.) The NSI hired a whole succession of former postgraduate students of mine – so many that at the institute's tenth anniversary celebration I was moved, in my brief remarks, to explain (only partially in jest) the motivation for the creation of the NSI as a device for providing employment for my former students. Staff turnover was fairly high in the early years. Much to our frustration, the NSI became, in effect, a training ground for employment in higher-paying jobs in the federal civil service. On the other hand, one of the later members of the research staff, Roy Culpeper, whose PhD thesis some years previously was the first I had ever supervised, was enticed by the NSI away from the Department of Finance (for whom he had most recently been working at the World Bank in the office of the Canadian executive director). Roy took responsibility for the NSI's work in international finance, for which the NSI now began to acquire a firm reputation, and subsequently became its president. Although he took something of a hit in terms of salary and security by moving to the NSI, he undoubtedly had much greater public influence and presence there than he ever would have had tucked away somewhere in the bowels of the civil service.

Needless to say, when the initial three-year experiment came to a close, the board unanimously agreed that it was essential to keep the NSI going. Finance was, of course, the principal problem. After some vigorous lobbying and what I gathered was intense debate within its board (the IDRC was intended to support research in developing countries, not in Canada), the IDRC finally came through with critically timed and significant core funding, albeit much less than (roughly half) that we had requested. Despite extreme board nervousness about the implications for the NSI's independence of significant reliance upon government funding, CIDA later became the most important single source of its finance. In 1980–1 another major issue of principle arose with respect to the NSI's relationship with government. Although I was not myself enthusiastic about the project, Bernard obtained significant CIDA funding for an independent evaluation of CIDA activities in four developing countries. There followed passionate board debate over the terms of the NSI's agreement with CIDA and, in particular, the terms under which NSI employees would be permitted access to CIDA documents. CIDA demanded Royal Canadian Mounted Police (RCMP) security clearance for all NSI employees who might see classified materials in connection with their research, and Bernard and his staff at first saw no problem with such a requirement. Michael Oliver and I led a determined resistance at the board level. It seemed to us that compliance with this requirement would, in effect, set a terrible precedent, giving the RCMP, through its (dubious) security clearance system, a degree of control over hiring at the NSI. The tone of the debate may be indicated by excerpts from a fairly "purple" letter I sent to Bernard on the subject:

> As an independent research Institute, we must neither do the government's own work for it nor be beholden to it. We are neither employed by government nor under contract to it. If we were either, the situation would be quite different and the issues would have been settled when the employment or the contract began. The Institute's employees are much more like academics than they are like government servants, at least in the principles that should govern their activities and their employment.
>
> I am among those who would regard security clearance for employment in our universities as an intolerable infringement upon our freedom both as individuals and as a nation ... I would believe this even if I had confidence in the capacity of the RCMP to assess "security risk," which I do not have. I believe it even if, at any moment in time, the clearance procedures are a mere formality, a farce.
>
> If an individual research worker, whether academic or other, learns that he can only gain access to governmental information on condition that he subject himself to clearance, he is free to choose whether to do so or not ... and the decision is entirely his own as to whether investigations are to be made concerning such matters as his political past, sexual preferences, mental illnesses and the like. When faced with this choice, some decide not to carry their search for these particular types of information – at least through these channels – any further.
>
> I do not believe that "security clearance," as understood by governmental protectors of our security(!) has any place in our Institute's conditions for employment ...
>
> Only if the individual(s) concerned are presented with the right NOT to subject themselves to governmental security clearance, without prejudice to their employment at the Institute, can we truly say that security clearance is no part of our employment requirements. It would appear that there is no particular nervousness on the part of the people concerned this time. But what about next time?[106]

Michael and I were delegated by the board to try to work out an acceptable way to proceed. Such a compromise was finally arrived at, in which only two of the team members would be security cleared, with the presumption that they would be able to press for the de-classification of (typically overclassified) materials and/or seek clearance for others if the need should arise. (Of course, it didn't.)

It was obviously inappropriate for a board member to do research and/or publish in the NSI's program. From time to time, however, I was persuaded to do so as a co-author. On one such occasion, my good friend from Yale Growth Center days, Carlos Diaz-Alejandro, agreed to co-author with me a critical think piece on the next set of GATT trade negotiations. It was jointly released by the ODI in the United Kingdom, the ODC in the United States, and the NSI. Playing on a recent academic analysis that had described trade as "a handmaiden of development," we entitled our piece "Handmaiden in Distress."[107] It generally went down quite well, as did the content of the paper (except in Washington, because we had been highly sceptical of the merit of recent US trade policy initiatives). (At the last minute Carlos had to back out of the Washington launch of our paper at the ODC, leaving me to face its policy "wolves" alone; I fear it was not one of my better performances.) But at the next board meeting, which (perhaps fortunately) I missed, the NSI was denounced by one of its members, Margaret Fulton, president of Mt St Vincent University, for the sexism of our title. This potential problem had never occurred to us. Perhaps today we would have given it more thought.

After twelve years at the head of the North-South Institute, Bernard announced his departure to head another new (but this time fully publicly funded) research institute, the Canadian Institute for International Peace and Security. We organized a surprise dinner in his honour in the evening after his final board meeting with us. With the connivance of his family and the organizational support of his administrative secretary, I was able, on the pretence of a quiet dinner with Arnold and me, to lead him, unsuspecting, into a completely reserved, somewhat rowdy, restaurant full of board members, staff, and friends. (To everyone's dismay, not least Bernard, who felt, quite properly, that he had been betrayed by those who appointed him, his new institute was subsequently closed by the Mulroney government as part of its ill-conceived orgy of purported Crown corporation "cleansing" and cost-cutting, the same orgy that carried off the Economic Council of Canada and very nearly also took the IDRC.)

I chaired the search committee (I was still board deputy chairman) to find Bernard's successor. Such was the high reputation of the NSI by this time that there was tremendous interest in his job. The quality of the applicants was quite remarkable. We finally settled on Maureen O'Neil, at that time a deputy minister in the government of Ontario. This appointment was a surprise to many because she had not at that time been prominent in development circles as much as those in women's rights, citizenship, and immigration. Energetic, personable, experienced in management, and fluently bilingual, she seemed to us exactly what the NSI most needed at that time. She did a creditable job in her term as president, which included the period during which I chaired the board, and she kept the NSI very much in the public eye. But her failure to do much developing country research of her own proved, in a small research institution, to be a significant issue, engendering staff concern which, in my then capacity as board chairman, I did my best to mollify. Her training in development affairs and the contacts she made at the North-South Institute undoubtedly prepared her well for her future role as president of the International Development Research Centre, for which she was by then eminently suited.

My retirement as NSI board chairman was marked by some very happy occasions. After my last executive committee meeting in the November afternoon preceding the full board meeting the next day, in the Lord Elgin Hotel in Ottawa, I was looking forward to dinner with some friends. I found myself, instead, at a large surprise dinner party in the hotel banquet hall downstairs, with all kinds of current and former NSI board members (including former chair, Arnold Smith, among others) and staff, and other friends in attendance. Speeches were made, together with the presentation of a lovely leather-bound collection of letters and poems for me. In his speech on this occasion, Roy Culpeper, now NSI president, announced that there was to be a Festschrift conference in my honour. The latter conference took place in June 1994 and gathered friends and colleagues from around the world. It too featured a wonderful dinner in my honour, held at the National Arts Centre. The resulting Festschrift volume, *Global Development Fifty Years after Bretton Woods*, came out a couple of years later and was well reviewed.[108] I was and still am greatly warmed by all of this friendly attention.

In the years since my formal departure from the North-South Institute, I remained very much in touch with it. Roy Culpeper and other staff consulted me regularly on research plans and drafts, on matters about which I still knew something, and I was happy to oblige when I thought I could.

Although still financially fragile and dependent upon the energy and dedication of a few key staff members, the North-South Institute continued to play an important role in Canadian foreign policy discussions up until mid-2014, when the Harper government pulled the final plug on its (still significant) share of funding, and it was forced to close its

doors. Joe Ingram, its last president, had been optimistic about governmental funding, but it was not to be. The board decision for closure took
many of its supporters by surprise. I was moved to write a short piece
in Ottawa's *Embassy* newspaper, as follows:

> After nearly 40 years of widely respected and objective evidence-based
> research and public reporting on issues of global poverty and develop-
> ment issues the North-South Institute, the leading Canadian institution
> of its kind, is closing its doors. Although it had no difficulty continuing to
> raise funds for a variety of significant international research projects and
> data reporting systems, in recent years it has now been starved, like so
> many others, of core support from the Government of Canada. The Insti-
> tute was not a creation of Government and could not be shut down by it.
> But its independent Board decided, in the face of its immediate financial
> pressures, not to attempt to continue.
>
> Why did the Harper Government do this? (In response to a parliamen-
> tary question it simply said that it doesn't do core funding anymore.)
>
> The Institute's stated mission was "Research for a Fairer World." Its
> research has always been evidence-based and policy relevant. Its work
> could not, by any stretch of the imagination, be described as radical or
> partisan. The Institute's founders were careful to include representatives
> of business, labour and nongovernmental organisations on its governing
> Board; and then, once general directions as to what areas needed further
> research, to give its research personnel full independence, subject only to
> quality control. That Board has had many distinguished Canadians serv-
> ing on it – including Paul Martin, Robert Stanfield, Joe Clark, Ed Broad-
> bent and a whole host of scholars, ex-public servants and politicians, and
> NGO, labour and business leaders, as well as distinguished personalities
> from abroad.
>
> The Institute was a primary source of expertise before countless par-
> liamentary committees and in the Canadian media. It carried an inde-
> pendent Canadian voice into international debates on global poverty. Its
> online "development platform" was a unique and valuable source of data
> on Canadian relationships with developing countries. The Institute was
> widely known and respected internationally, not least with research part-
> ners in the developing world.[109]

The NSI's externally funded projects (from foundations or other
governments) were absorbed by Carleton University, the University of
Ottawa, and the Conference Board of Canada. Carleton University's

Norman Patterson School of International Affairs (NPSIA), led by its director, Dane Rowlands, a longtime friend and supporter of the NSI (and former PhD student of mine), quickly offered a home for an appropriately restructured NSI but it had few resources beyond its goodwill to offer. It remains to be seen whether this new arrangement will be viable over the longer run. A group of previous board chairs, myself included, had sought to persuade the by now diminished and dispirited NSI board to stall the final agreement with Carleton until sometime after the 2015 federal election, but this effort was too little and too late. Canada still needs, and its citizenry and Parliament deserve, a high-quality independent institution conducting policy-relevant "research for a fairer world."

19 Trying to Influence Canadian Foreign Policy

Sifting through my files, decades later, I have been somewhat surprised to rediscover how involved I once was, especially in the 1970s, in attempts directly and personally to influence Canadian government policies. In the years immediately after our return from Tanzania, my records indicate that I worked a great deal to that end – sometimes dealing directly with CIDA, sometimes making presentations to parliamentary committees, writing to the media, or speaking to and strategizing with NGOs. In more recent times, my self-image has been more that of an international actor and academic, a little disengaged, primarily through lack of time, from direct involvement with Canadian government institutions (IDRC obviously apart) or NGOs. I recall my genuine shock when an old Canadian friend from Yale days told me, when we met again sometime in the late 1970s or 1980s, that he had heard through the grapevine that "I had become quite political." I didn't see myself that way. But, on the evidence, by the normal standards of the economics profession, I guess I was.

I certainly know that upon our return from Africa, aware that I was unlikely – because of the complexities of our youngest son Peter's health – to work there for extended periods again, I consciously resolved to do what I could to assist development efforts, both professionally and personally, from where I found myself, in Canada. This assistance involved developing expertise and making contributions with regard to Northern, and particularly Canadian, policies relating to developing countries. I tried to influence other Africanists and development specialists around me – graduate students and faculty – to do the same. This reorientation away from research on Africa drove me toward intensified research and advocacy in the sphere of international economics, and to the offering of my favourite graduate course, "International Aspects of Economic Development," or what I sometimes mischievously called "International Economics as if Developing Countries Mattered." This reorientation also appeared to offer me the opportunity more effectively to use the tools of economics. "Development" seemed, and still seems, a highly complex matter, involving far more than just economics, and its effective study requires the specific field-level experience and knowledge that I knew I would not be able to maintain or acquire anew. I recall at about this time telling my friend Carlos Diaz-Alejandro, who also worked in international economics and development (in Latin America), that if he ever saw me taking up development as my primary field, he would know that I had given up economics. I used to joke that my work to establish the North-South Institute was to relieve the speaking and advisory burden upon me (and to provide employment to my graduate students); but there was actually considerable truth to this story in that, once it got going, I did deflect a tremendous number of requests relating to Canadian foreign policy issues to the NSI, and I myself did seem to accept fewer grass-roots direct requests to speak, write, or advise on them. It also has to be said that CIDA was no longer in later years quite so active in seeking outside academic advice, at least not mine.

The first NGO activity in which I recall engaging, in 1969, was my active membership, by invitation (along with Cran Pratt and Peter Ruderman of the University of Toronto Faculty of Social Work, among others), in a newly created Oxfam committee on government aid. Henry Fletcher, then Oxfam's executive director, seemed quite nervous about his agency's becoming involved in "political" matters (this now seems remarkable, considering Oxfam's activities in later years), but he had an enthusiastic and energetic young assistant, Linda Freeman (later my student and colleague), who kept things moving. Together we drafted a letter to the prime minister (Pierre Trudeau) recommending the adoption by the government of Canada of the recommendations on aid and trade policies of the recently released international Pearson Commission report, together with some ideas on its implementation. The chairman of the Oxfam board was induced to sign it (dated 5 December 1969), and a number of other (later) prominent Canadians attached their names, including, in addition to ourselves, Gerry Caplan, Hugh Winsor, Mel Watkins, Dave Nowlan, and an MP from each of the major political parties (Ed Broadbent, Gordon Fairweather, and Ralph Stewart). Still a little naive about how these matters work, I considered it something of a triumph to have received a detailed and friendly reply from Trudeau.

Our group also organized a conference (entitled "Unequal Partners") on the theme of the Pearson report, which was quite well attended.

The Pearson report elicited a great deal of public discussion. Lester Pearson had been mandated by Robert McNamara, the newly appointed president of the World Bank, to chair an international group of eminent experts who were to assess the state of development (a "Grand Assize") after some twenty years of serious postwar effort. The Pearson Commission was supported by some excellent full-time staff, including my old Yale friends, Carlos Diaz-Alejandro and Dharam Ghai. The 1969 report, *Partners in Development*,[110] was balanced and fair, but unremarkable in its modest and mildly reformist recommendations. Barbara Ward, at that time holding a well-endowed chair at Columbia University, was determined not only to hold a solid conference on the report but also directly to involve the next generation of development economists in its proceedings. That goal meant that my age group was very much engaged in the conference, and I was privileged to participate. In addition to the "grandees" in attendance, the list of participants in the two parts of the conference in February 1970 – the first in Williamsburg, Virginia, the second in New York – included almost a who's who of the most prominent development economists of the next thirty years, most of whom were at that time still relatively unknown. Mahbub ul Haq's humorous note – on the willingness of India and Pakistan not to demand immediate payment on the United Kingdom's historical debt to them – was a sensation. I thought I.G. Patel's sober analysis of the realities of aid relationships was the best paper of the conference, and I have since quoted from it frequently. My own paper on Africa was prominent in the volume that subsequently summarized and reported on the findings of the conference.[111] Robert McNamara's speech was something of a bombshell in development policy circles in its emphasis on social objectives and its declaration of the inadequacy of GNP growth as a development target. No less arresting was the Columbia Declaration,[112] which was thrown together by a small group of us, organized by Richard Jolly on the next-to-last night of the New York meeting, and signed by virtually all non-official participants on the final day. (The other young draftsmen – there were no women – were Michael Bruno, Reginald Green, Mahbub ul Haq, Branko Horvat, Enrique Iglesias, and Bola Onitiri.) The declaration spoke of the fact that the report had leaned too far backward to appeal to Northern audiences and fell considerably short of what was likely to be required to address "the widening gap" between North and South. Particularly dramatic was

the moment when Goran Ohlin, the research director of the commission, rose and crossed the room to sign a declaration that severely criticized the commission's report.

In the next few years, I spoke or worked with numerous groups in the
NGO community, the churches, and the media. For a while I accepted
nearly every invitation to speak – in public or on radio or TV – on development issues and the need for enlightened Canadian policies toward
developing countries. In retrospect I am somewhat astonished at the
enormous volume of material in my files that relates to such activity. In earlier chapters I wrote of my interaction with relatively high-
profile governments and international organizations, and it would be
easy to believe that these were the only important ones. Particularly
in my younger years, however, they certainly were not. As I became
busier with higher-profile and international activities, and the North-
South Institute became active, I did find it best to step back from more
local NGO activities. In later years, overwhelmed by other obligations
including pressing family ones, I routinely turned down almost all
NGO requests to take on anything extra.

Periodically I did speak to international NGO meetings in New York,
Washington, Geneva, Amsterdam, Ottawa, and Toronto. These engagements included meetings of NGOs at the UN, the international YWCA,
Eurodad (European debt network), the (Jesuit) Centre of Concern, Bread
for the World Institute, Parliamentarians for Global Action, Commonwealth Youth, a couple of NGO-organized counter-conferences alongside IMF meetings, and the like.

On a few occasions I spoke to business groups – the Conference Board
of Canada, the Montreal Economics Association, and the Toronto Association of Business Economists. Once I spoke to a retreat of Ontario government economists. But these latter occasions were not really my métier. I
wasn't entirely comfortable in them. Nor were they probably comfortable
with me. In chapter twenty-two I describe a memorable day in which I
interacted both with bankers and with the L'Arche (NGO) community on
the same day. I was always more comfortable with NGOs.

At CIDA, Maurice Strong, then its (first) president, contacted me in
mid-1969 for discussion of a paper of mine on investment in Africa that
had come to his attention. We never did get together on this topic, but
shortly thereafter he engaged Cran Pratt and me for a study of the role
of Canadian universities in overseas development. Our report, based in
large part on our access to CIDA files, warned of the already apparent
dangers of tied aid and high overheads when Canadian universities

were deployed to undertake development overseas on CIDA's behalf. We called for a better model in which Canadian universities served as partners only as requested by the potential beneficiaries, who, we argued, should receive untied funds (and better information about possible Canadian suppliers). We failed to persuade.

The Pierre Trudeau government issued a hugely disappointing foreign policy white paper at about the same time. I and many of my colleagues had expected rather more from the proponent of a "Just Society," particularly coming so soon after the release of the Pearson Commission report. But it was clearly to be business as usual, complete with continued aid-tying, tariff preferences for apartheid South Africa (by now expelled from the Commonwealth), and high protection for Canadian textile, clothing, footwear, and other firms competing with developing countries' exports. Short-term Canadian economic interests were to continue to dominate foreign policy in development issues as in everything else. I did not spare my criticism – in *Behind the Headlines* (the outlet of the Canadian Institute of International Affairs, CIIA), *Canadian Forum* (where I wrote an editorial, at editor Abe Rotstein's suggestion, under the name of "Econoclast"), a letter to the prime minister, various "popular" speaking engagements, and testimony to a parliamentary committee. In the *Forum* piece, I concluded:

> The overall message is abundantly clear. The Third World cannot expect any leadership in the international development effort from Canada, Just Society or not. In this review, Canada is conspicuously opting out of the much-discussed possibility of its establishing an international role as one of the key initiators in the world development effort. This is a major tragedy both for Canada and for the still staggering international development community.[113]

In these and subsequent efforts, my continued refrain was that support for development was not merely, or even primarily, a matter of the aid budget. Trade, monetary, and financial policies had to be geared toward development objectives as well. In mid-1973 and again in the spring of 1975, I was invited to speak at day-long in-house strategy sessions organized by CIDA's Policy Analysis Division. For a while I placed particular emphasis upon the potential for the use of the IMF's special drawing rights (SDRs), then requiring the payment of only a nominal interest rate upon use, to expand resource flows to poor countries (and even got some official response on this in the form of an extensive exchange of letters with Canadian Finance Minister John Turner). In the spring of 1974, I was invited to a Department of External Affairs consultation with academics on "Canada's Interests in the Third World" (a revealing title for a meeting on development issues) and was actually financed by CIDA to attend an OECD Development Assistance Committee conference in Paris.

Shortly thereafter, probably through the good offices of Lewis Perinbam, a progressive vice president for special programs within CIDA, the office of then president of CIDA, Paul Gérin-Lajoie, approached me for a personal consultation concerning an address he was to make in a university setting. We had a good conversation in his office, during which I urged him strongly to speak out on "the big picture," the non-aid issues. At his request I followed it up with a letter detailing my views as to the changing state of the world and the place of the developing countries (and Canada) therein. I was told that it was circulated widely at least within CIDA, and many elements appeared in Gérin-Lajoie's address at Queen's University on a snowy night in December (a draft of which was provided to me for critical comment in advance). Apparently few attended, and it received little attention anywhere else. Nor did Gérin-Lajoie frequently return to this theme. I suspect that he might have been politically instructed to "knock it off" and stick to his (CIDA) task.

At least some people within the government were highly receptive to my messages and urged me to keep the pressure on. In April 1975, Lewis Perinbam invited me to still another CIDA advisory event. This time, however, the event was pretty much a "front" for an interview he had arranged for me with Ivan Head, principal foreign policy advisor and speechwriter to the prime minister, Pierre Trudeau. Lewis very much wanted my views to be heard at high levels. We (Ivan and I) spoke of Canadian imports from developing countries and Canadian protectionism (on which I was by now engaged in research), the potential for the use of SDRs to generate increased aid to developing countries, and the need for an independent Canadian research institution to analyse and monitor Canada's relations with the Third World (what later emerged as the North-South Institute). Ivan was polite but a little distant; I had the impression that he had been pressed into this interview and that he was humouring both Lewis and me. As usual, I followed it up with a letter and further supportive material. I also invited the prime minister or his external affairs minister, Allan McEachern, to speak to a conference in August at St Mary's University, Halifax, on "Canada and the New International Economic Order." I had been induced, via extreme arm-twisting and the provision of a limitless telephone card and carte blanche authority, to organize and chair this conference; and it was shaping up as a potentially significant occasion, for which the government might like to provide a policy announcement. (The government eventually declined. Evidently it had little new to announce.) Still hopeful at the time, little more than a week after my meeting with Ivan Head, I wrote a detailed letter to another contact in the prime minister's office, whom I had met on a domestic flight (to a conference in Moncton) and who urged me to do so, outlining what I saw as the key political decisions that Canada should take in its relations with the developing world, together with my assessment of their domestic political viability. I urged a "Trudeau Plan" incorporating its main elements. In the meantime I wrote the prime minister again about Canada's failure to implement an OECD memorandum of understanding concerning the opening of bilateral (tied) aid procurement to developing country suppliers (already implemented by the majority of other OECD members, including even the United States and Japan), and I received an unsatisfactory and off-putting reply from the Department of External Affairs (to which, of course, I had to respond). Toward year-end 1975 I appeared again, making the same pitches, before the House of Commons subcommittee (of its Standing Committee on External Affairs) on international development. Among the most supportive MPs at that time were Douglas Roche (PC), Andrew Brewin (New Democratic Party, NDP, for whom I had campaigned, together with my friend, his son John, when I was still in grade school), Bob Ogle (NDP), and Herb Breau (Liberal). By this time the plans for the launch of the North-South Institute were quite advanced.

Of some significance to some (and certainly to me, because of contacts made there) was a speech I made in Winnipeg at the annual Canadian Institute of International Affairs (CIIA) conference (this one focusing upon Canada and the UN, and attracting a stellar cast of prestigious speakers) in May 1977, in which I vigorously pooh-poohed the Canadian government's record on assistance for development. This point won great applause, at least from the committed, and the undying friendship of King Gordon (one of Ottawa's "grand old men" of social justice and foreign affairs, a founding member of the CCF), among others. It was also the first time I had interacted at all with Sonny Ramphal, secretary-general of the Commonwealth. I criticized the praise he had offered for Canadian policies in his address as inaccurate and evidently thereby caught his attention.

My links with the CIIA, which until then had been cordial and had involved periodic panel appearances and writings, were permanently severed in February 1980. Upon reading their announcement of a perfectly dreadful and hopelessly one-sided proposed study tour to South Africa (it would have been impossible for a Canadian black to participate), I wrote a two-sentence letter to its executive director:

> Please cancel my membership in the CIIA. Your proposed study tour to "Southern Africa" is a travesty.

Although never again a member, I still found myself periodically invited to CIIA events. But the CIIA remained, for me, although it was formally an independent body, rather too much of an establishment organization, and I felt little compunction ever to rejoin.

In the fall of 1979, at a time of great international financial stress (the second oil price crisis), when I was working actively on appropriate international responses, both with Sonny Ramphal and the Commonwealth Secretariat and with the G-24, I was greatly incensed at the narrowness of vision of the Canadian Department of Finance. A new Conservative government, with Joe Clark as prime minister, had just entered office. Finance Minister John Crosbie's smug and (so it seemed to me) ill-prepared address to the annual IMF meetings in Belgrade and the pre-IMF meeting of the Commonwealth finance ministers in Malta drove me, so to speak, "over the edge." When it was reported to me by my Commonwealth Secretariat friends, I reacted precipitately, writing a perhaps somewhat intemperate letter to Prime Minister Clark:

> I write to protest against the positions being taken and the sentiments being expressed by Mr. Crosbie on the subject of International Monetary Fund lending and official development assistance to the developing countries ... I refuse to believe that they [his views] can represent those of your government, and having just returned from a visit to London, I can assure you that their expression as such is already doing profound damage to our credibility abroad.
>
> The provision of expanded lending facilities for the developing countries at a time of precarious economic stability for the world is a matter of immediate global self-interest. Much of the private banking community, the International Monetary Fund, the OECD, and informed opinion is agreed on this ... Might I suggest that your Minister of Finance join those who are urgently debating means of overcoming the problems rather than delivering homilies appropriate only for a smalltown grocer and playing to the yahoo element of the gallery at home ...

I urge you to take leadership in these matters. It is not too late to put your government back on track.[114]

I was told that my letter, circulated widely in officialdom, created something of a stir. Crosbie's anodyne reply assigned me to the ranks of "advocates of radical change" who "do not appear to be in the majority." Within months, this government, in any case, was gone.

For the next few years – during both the renewed Trudeau government and that of Brian Mulroney – my relationships with the government were both less tense and less intense. I testified before parliamentary committees from time to time, for example, on financial issues before the House Task Force on North-South Relations in September 1980. Probably through the influence of Bernard Wood, head of the North-South Institute, who interacted with the Ottawa mandarinate, I was invited to several invitation-only foreign policy consultations. In November 1980 I attended a retreat at the beautiful Chateau Montebello on the Ottawa River to consider the plans for the 1981 G-7 Summit. Organized and chaired by Michael Pitfield, cabinet secretary, and Allan Gotlieb, at that time the top official in External Affairs, it summoned the top echelons of government, top business executives, a couple of labour representatives, the heads of some think tanks, and a couple of academics. I was very impressed, and even somewhat intimidated, by my company. At a time when there seemed an obvious need for increased official finance to meet some of the needs of developing countries facing increased oil import prices and a global recession, the bankers in attendance were dead against any governmental role in the recycling of the huge emerging oil-related surpluses. I certainly disagreed with the bankers. I spoke briefly of the need for the initiation of a further GATT round of trade negotiations to forestall growing protectionist pressures, and the need for a stronger and improved GATT or International Trade Organization. What most remains in my memory is a quite inconsequential event: a brief conversation with David Mulholland, the bluff and outspoken American then heading the Bank of Montreal. At the time I was writing a paper for the G-24 on emerging international currency arrangements, including the potential for expanded use of the IMF's special drawing right (SDR) as a unit of account in international contracts. I asked this top banker whether his bank might denominate customer deposits in SDRs. I have never forgotten his reply. "Sure we would. We'll do them in wampum if there is demand for them." An innovative banker ready for every opportunity!

A month after the Montebello meeting, Michael Pitfield circulated a minute of the meeting together with a request for further informal reflections on a series of questions regarding Canadian interests and possible positions. I took the trouble to send him a four-page reply, together with some of my mimeographed papers and offprints, emphasizing my usual major points on the need for expanded official development finance, the potential for the use of SDRs for this purpose, the desirability of GATT action and reform, aid untying, and the like, and the need for political leadership. Also recommended was a more serious and positive response to the forthcoming (fall) North-South summit in Cancun – a product of the Brandt report – which had hardly been mentioned at the retreat. I received polite replies from both Gotlieb and Pitfield. I was encouraged to send a copy of my new book, *International Economic Disorder*,[115] to the latter and again received a polite reply.

In later years I participated in two other events of this kind – policy seminars on international economic issues, at the Department of External Affairs in March 1985 and at Willson House (later better known as Meech Lake) in February 1987 – at the invitation of the external affairs minister, Joe Clark, and the finance minister, Michael Wilson.

In 1983 I was honoured to be invited to join a research advisory group on international trade issues, chaired by John Whalley of the University of Western Ontario, to assist the Royal Commission on the Economic Union and Development Prospects in Canada (more generally known as the Macdonald Commission). We met perhaps half a dozen times to commission and review papers, including those written by our own group's members. It was a pretty orthodox group. My paper on Canada's economic relations with the developing countries (entitled "Underutilised Potential") was the only one that could have ruffled any feathers. I was told (by my niece, Anne Martin, who then worked for the commission) that Donald Macdonald liked it because, unlike all the rest, it had some new ideas. Rick Harris was a member of the group. His new conclusions as to the potential benefits of free trade with the United States, much greater than previously estimated, a result achieved by making new assumptions about the role of scale economies, were highly influential in the group and ultimately in the commission. When, after one of our meetings, my University of Toronto departmental colleague and member of the commission, Albert Breton, asked whether any of us had reservations about the desirability of entering into a free trade agreement with the United States, I was the only one to express some. The Macdonald Commission's report[116] was extremely influential, in the end, in moving Canada into its dubious (in my view) free trade agreement with the United States and later all of North America (North America Free Trade Area, NAFTA). I was not proud of my association with it, however limited.

Sporadic testimony before parliamentary committees continued over the years that followed – to the House-Senate joint committee on Canada's international relations in late 1985, the Senate committee on foreign affairs in the spring of 1986, a House committee on international financial institutions (in which my former student and friend, Steven Langdon, NDP, was prominent), twice to the House standing committee on foreign affairs and international trade in early 2002, and thereafter; and I have probably missed some. I even testified to US Congressional subcommittees on African debt and adjustment issues. In one of them, on the World Bank in Africa, I was pitted directly against Elliot Berg, the author of the Berg Report, which had launched the World Bank upon its ill-fated African "adjustment" campaign. Once I spoke about African debt and adjustment problems to an informal all-party luncheon of British parliamentarians in London's House of Commons, an event most memorable in my mind for the grey beady-eyed fish that was served as its main course. (Like my father and grandfather before me, all my life I have had a profound and irrational aversion to products of the sea.)

In 1991, the Canadian Council of Churches prepared a long brief on CIDA's performance and its relationship to an excellent previous report by a parliamentary committee (the Winegard Report,[117] named for its Conservative, but progressive, chairman, previously president of the University of Guelph), which had advocated major changes and a prime emphasis in all its programs upon addressing poverty. At that time, the new head of CIDA, Marcel Masse, appeared to be driving the organization in new directions, but they were not those of the Winegard Report. Having come directly from the IMF, where he had been the Canadian executive director, Masse seemed to be enamoured, above all, by the need for macroeconomic stabilization and "structural adjustment" Washington-style. The draft report for the church group, written by Cranford Pratt, Robert Fugere, and Marjorie Ross, took him on, but did so at times in the distressingly oversimplified manner already (and still) typical of much NGO commentary. The IMF, in this common view, seemed to be responsible for just about everything that was going wrong. The draft was full of minor misstatements. Restraining myself with some effort, I wrote only six pages of detailed commentary. Only some of my comments were taken on board. Cran subsequently told me that when the church group was challenged as misinformed and unprofessional in their later meeting with CIDA officials, they had defended themselves by noting that they had received expert advice and, when pressed, they had used my name. He hoped I didn't mind. Association with overly crude argument – unfortunately this wasn't the only instance – has always been a source of embarrassment to me. The case against the IMF's own overly crude approach was a valid one – one which I was pressing through UNI-CEF and elsewhere. Equally crude critics were, to my mind, unhelpful.

During this time I still wrote occasional letters to finance ministers, for example, to Donald Mazankowski (in the Mulroney government) on the need to not cut foreign aid in 1993 and protesting the abolition of the Economic Council of Canada and a number of other worthy bodies, including the Canadian Institute for International Peace and Security, in 1992. The former elicited not only a reply from the minister but also a letter from Jean Chretien, leader of the opposition, in which he denounced the idea of sacrificing foreign aid in an attempt at deficit reduction. The government he was soon to lead, however, behaved even worse in this respect. During the period in which Paul Martin was finance minister (the late '90s and early years of the new century), I was periodically invited to consultations between him and NGOs (he always seemed to enjoy hearing different views), but, by that time believing such events unfruitful, I let Roy Culpeper of the North-South Institute and others present appropriate suggestions, and I never attended them.

I did try, mainly through IDRC and G-24 initiatives which I had myself helped to promote, to influence Martin's approach to international finance in his Group of Twenty Finance Ministers (G-20) and, more particularly, to influence the agenda of the Halifax G-7 Summit conference in 1995. My efforts were directed at achieving some representation from the poorest countries in the G-20 (they had none) and increasing the influence of the developing countries in international financial governance more generally. As described in an earlier chapter, I advocated the creation of a new intergovernmental task force, along the lines of the Committee of Twenty of the 1970s, to consider the need for improved international monetary and financial governance in the next century. I spoke briefly to Martin about this at the Madrid (fiftieth anniversary) IMF meetings in the fall of 1994, where the G-24 had begun to press for this. I then followed up with a letter to Martin in January 1995, pleading for Canadian leadership to this end at the Halifax summit. Again, I received a polite reply – and nothing relevant to my efforts occurred there. From then on, I worked to stimulate more informal discussion of these issues among influential policymakers and, again as described in a previous chapter, succeeded in having an IDRC initiative launched: the Global Financial Governance Initiative (GFGI). As it turned out, the GFGI did not succeed in attracting the senior Canadian governmental participation that we had initially believed we might expect.

My NGO activities eased off somewhat over the years, particularly at the grass-roots level. I did still get called upon quite often, however, for expert advice and for some high-level conferences organized by the Canadian Council for International Cooperation (CCIC), the umbrella organization for Canadian development NGOs, and the North-South Institute. At one CCIC conference on aid in the late 1990s, my presentation went down exceptionally well. In a ten-point effort I had stressed recipient country ownership, reduced conditionality, donor coordination, sectoral and generalized budget support, untying, and the like. These were matters being more actively addressed at that time than ever before in the OECD's Development Assistance Committee; but, as far as I knew, Canada had not been prominent in the discussions of reformed approaches. Len Good, then a relatively new CIDA president, who attended, made a point of telling me, as he left, that he completely agreed with my approach and would work toward its implementation. At the same time, the CCIC's Brian Tomlinson asked whether he could put together a paper for the international NGO project on "The Reality of Aid"[118] on my behalf (I had stated my inability to attend their conference in Costa Rica or to do a paper for it), basing it on my presentation and a couple of previous papers I had written on related themes.[119] I was happy to agree. That was one of the two easiest papers I ever did! (The other was put together a few years previously by Cran Pratt from my parliamentary testimony, speeches, and earlier papers, this one for a church-sponsored volume on *Christian Faith and Economic Justice*, edited by Cran and Roger Hutchinson.[120])

At another CCIC conference on Canada's policies in the WTO, a few years later, where I was the lead-off speaker, the representative of the government of Canada, who was to be its discussant, declared that he could not readily discuss the paper since he had not received it in advance. It made me realize, not for the first time, how fortunate I had been to practice my analysis and advocacy in an academic environment rather than in official institutions.

Internationally, I put in guest NGO appearances for, among others: Eurodad, Fondad, and Parliamentarians for Global Action, in Europe; and the Center of Concern and the Overseas Development Council in

Washington. But these were obviously not directed primarily at Canadian policy reform.

Probably my last effort to influence specific policies was an email message I sent early in 2005 to the (now Conservative) Canadian minister of finance at the time of the Paul Wolfowitz nomination by George Bush for the presidency of the World Bank. Like most other professionals I was shocked, even horrified, by the prospect of so unqualified and ideologically hard line a president for the world's most powerful multilateral development institution. Bad enough that the IMF and World Bank heads continued to be appointed in a manner so distant from professionally acceptable governance practice – with the United States still permitted to appoint the World Bank president, while the Europeans appointed the managing director of the IMF. But the appointment of Wolfowitz, one of the architects of the disastrous Iraq war and an ideological crony of the worst elements in the Bush administration: this was really too much to bear. I spoke in my message – one of hundreds of others that were sent on the same subject – of the damage that would be done to the World Bank's credibility and to serious multilateral development efforts. Needless to say we had no effect on the outcome. To put it very mildly, Wolfowitz was not a success at the World Bank.

In 2009, much to my surprise, I was invited to join a newly reconstituted evaluation committee within Canada's aid agency, the Canadian International Development Agency (CIDA). The new president of the agency, Margaret Biggs, had been one of the early research appointees in the North-South Institute in the 1970s and had since risen to significant appointments within the federal public service. She had evidently persuaded her minister, Bev Oda, that it would be good to have, for the first time, some independent input in this potentially important committee that she herself chaired. There were now to be three such members, representative of academia, non-governmental organizations, and business. This innovation seemed to me to be a constructive one, and when I learned that the NGO invitee was to be Tim Brodhead, whose work in the NGO world I greatly respected, though still more than a little doubtful, I agreed to join. The meetings were interesting, not least for the insight into the processes and costs through which evaluation of Canadian aid activities were undertaken – by private firms on consultancy contracts. But my involvement in these activities was to be short-lived.

During the following year (2010), the aid minister made a series of unfortunate funding decisions, contravening the advice of her own personnel; and it became clear that evaluations played little or no role in her decision making. Tim Brodhead and I saw no point in continuing and wanted no association with the policies now being pursued. Our joint resignation letter (only slightly amended when published under my name in Ottawa's *Embassy* and *The Toronto Star* in Toronto) read as follows:

We have been honoured by your invitation to membership of CIDA's Evaluation Committee and have endeavoured, over the period of our membership, to contribute our professional experience and expertise to its important deliberations. We continue to hold CIDA's mission, your Presidency and your Evaluation Committee in high regard. Recent decisions as to the disposition of CIDA funds by the current Government of Canada, however, are so detrimental to CIDA's mission and mandate, and public confidence therein, that we have lost confidence in your Minister and cannot in good conscience now continue our involvement in the Committee.

The most recent in the Government's series of unfortunate decisions relating to CIDA concerns the Canadian Council for International Cooperation (CCIC), the highly respected umbrella body for over 90 Canadian-based nongovernmental organisations (NGOs) working in the sphere of development at home and abroad. The CCIC provides the opportunity for Canada's highly diverse development NGOs to exchange experience and concerns; and, where appropriate, to speak with one voice. That collective voice, representing the enormous range of experienced NGO employees, volunteers and contributors has always been both well-informed and deeply supportive of the poor and marginalised of the world. It is a voice that must and will, in one way or another, continue to be heard. For decades the CCIC has received modest supportive funding from the Government of Canada through CIDA, just as equivalent bodies receive governmental support in most other developed countries. Speaking to its annual general meeting, the previous CIDA President spoke of the CCIC as a "first order" partner; and so it has been. There has been no objective change in any of these circumstances. The recent cessation of all CIDA funding for CCIC therefore makes absolutely no developmental sense and, to our knowledge, there has been no governmental attempt to explain it publicly. Nor has there been any prior consultation either with affected partners in Canada and overseas or with the Canadian public. The Minister's reference to on-going CIDA support for "knowledge partners" who contribute to aid effectiveness and policy development makes curtailment of CIDA's funding all the more perplexing, since such contributions have been precisely the mandate of CCIC.

Official support for NGOs has always been predicated on the need for understanding and active engagement by Canadian citizens in our international development work, without which public support to meet our ODA commitments is weakened. It has also rested on a belief that the network of relationships created between Canadian organizations and individuals and their counterparts in the developing world benefits Canada and contributes to the building of more democratic civil societies in other countries. The evidence from recent decisions would suggest that the present Government instead sees any organization receiving CIDA funding as simply an instrument for implementing government policy and priorities. Lengthy delays in approving funding agreements, all too frequent occurrences even with organizations that have enjoyed good relations with CIDA going back decades (some of which we know CIDA management has tried to rectify), cripple organizations' finances and damage relationships with their overseas partners. What we are witnessing is the dismantling of the infrastructure that has permitted a wide diversity of Canadians to contribute actively to poverty eradication in poor countries. This is bound to result in a deliberate shift by overseas partners away from working with Canadians to working with others who are perceived as more responsive to their needs and priorities.

The amounts involved are not large by governmental standards, but the implications of this decision are serious. The success of Canada's efforts to address global poverty and promote human rights and sustainable development depends upon informed input to decision making, vigorous public debate and, ultimately, broad support from the Canadian public. It is difficult to think of a more frontal assault on all three than the cessation of funding for the CCIC. This decision cannot have been a casual one or the product of inadvertent oversight. There has been plenty of time to consider the solid arguments publicly made against it. Moreover, it follows the cessation during the past year of all CIDA funding for MATCH International and KAIROS, NGOs working with women's organisations and Canadian churches respectively. We can only conclude that the Government has an agenda in this arena that does not accord with that of the Canadians who have worked most diligently and effectively in the development arena.

We trust that these policy missteps will eventually be reversed. In the meantime we hope that CIDA will be able to withstand the current Government's continuing assault on some of the closest and best informed Canadian partners and supporters of development. We wish you and CIDA every success in your efforts to fulfill the parliamentary mandate to address global poverty and respond to those you are supposed to be assisting.

For our part, we have lost all confidence that the current Government listens to, or indeed even welcomes, professional assessments such as the

Evaluation Committee is presumably intended to provide. While we have never carried any responsibility for Governmental or CIDA policies the time has come for us clearly to dissociate ourselves from them. We hereby tender our resignations from the Evaluation Committee effective immediately.[121]

Some external membership of the evaluation committee for Canada's development assistance continues, even though CIDA no longer exists, having been absorbed into the Department of Foreign Affairs and International Trade, now renamed Global Affairs Canada.

The dismantling of CIDA was a profound blow to those who sought a Canadian foreign aid policy that focused on the reduction of global poverty, the objective actually finally ratified, after much argument, in an Act of Parliament. The Harper government had different aspirations. Rationalized by the purported need for coherence in Canadian foreign policy, CIDA's demise, in fact, marked the final triumph of the more business-oriented in Ottawa's never-ending turf struggles. I subsequently wrote in the *Embassy* as follows:

There has always been significant tension within the Canadian body politic as to how best to respond both to the pressing needs of the people in developing countries and to the ever growing opportunities for Canadian commercial gain there. The tension has been most obvious in the long-standing struggle over the policies of the Canadian International Development Agency (CIDA). At its baldest, the question is: in the potential conflict between the interests of Canada's developing country partners and Canadian interests, whose are to be assigned priority? This is by no means a new issue. Nor is it a purely Canadian one.

There is a profound longer-term global (and Canadian) interest in the development of poor countries. Reduced poverty and improved institutions abroad will contribute to a more politically and economically stable, more sustainable and healthier planet. This has long been motivation enough for the post–Second World War international development project. This mutual interest argument for Northern assistance for Southern development has a long history, extending back at least to the Pearson Report of 1969 and, later, emphasised in the Brandt Commission Report of 1980. The issues it raises extend into policies in trade, investment and broader foreign policy. But what about the specifics of development assistance?

Political and commercial objectives have always played some role in Canadian aid practice; they have never completely dominated them. As the commercial opportunities for Canadian business overseas continue to expand so do the political pressures upon the Government of Canada to assist with their realisation. Canadian companies are particularly active in extractive industries, and the current Government has already clearly (and controversially) been responsive to their concerns. Under an act of parliament, however, CIDA has been required to seek the reduction of poverty as its primary goal. Is the mandate for Canadian aid now to be amended to include the pursuit of Canadian business interests? If so, Canada will be out of step with the rest of the OECD.

Aid relationships have changed. At a series of meetings over the past decade in Rome, Paris, Accra and Busan, commitments have been made by OECD members, including Canada, not only to recognise but also to promote local "ownership" of developing countries' own programs. Among other reforms, they also committed themselves more effectively to align their aid contributions with local priorities. These and other promises to reform aid practices, although not as yet very effectively delivered, were designed to make their inputs more supportive of developing countries' and peoples' own development objectives. Clearly, these commitments are inconsistent with the Government of Canada's new emphasis on commercial objectives in Canadian official development assistance. It is this commercial thrust to the aid program that most bothers aid analysts. The change in CIDA's status seems to confirm this new commercially motivated Canadian foreign policy "coherence."

The Canadian private sector can be an important contributor to the pursuit of development objectives, with or without cooperation from the Government of Canada (as recently recommended by a Conservative-majority House of Commons report). But it is unquestionably best for Canadian commercial objectives to be pursued via governmental institutions and policy instruments other than development assistance. Otherwise confusion and dispute over aid policy and declining public support for it is bound to ensue. When there are two policy objectives efficiency requires that there be two policy instruments to pursue them ...

The Government of Canada must ... clarify its primary intentions, and its approach to conflicts of interest, in its development assistance. Current Canadian aid policies are inconsistent and confused. Moving foreign assistance into Foreign Affairs does nothing about this, and, given the current Government's demonstrated proclivities, the policy coherence it promises looks to most like the triumph of Canadian commercial interests. If the primary objective of Canadian development policy has now changed, or even if an important secondary aim has been added, it is best to be perfectly clear about it ... and to expect a parliamentary fight.[122]

One hopes for better things from the new Trudeau government.

19.1. With Georgia, at Order of Canada induction, Ottawa, 2002

   I am flattered by that part of my Order of Canada citation that says
that I "enhanced Canada's reputation as a caring and compassionate nation." Since I have undoubtedly been known as a Canadian as I
went about my teaching, research, and advocacy in other parts of the
world, there may even be some truth in it. But the much more important
truth is that, despite considerable effort, I have been unable to do very
much positive about my own country's policies toward poverty and

development overseas. Canada could have been an influential leader in this sphere. At a minimum it might have joined the Scandinavian countries, the Dutch, and the UK Labour government in "like-minded" progressive approaches to foreign aid and other development (and environmental) issues. Its multiculturalism could have given it special advantages and provided a high degree of domestic political support for such more progressive approaches. It has chosen to hang back, and it remains, cautious, around the middle of the OECD "pack" as far as development performance is concerned. I continue to believe that Canada could play a much more progressive international role in the struggle against global poverty than it has done, and that there would be strong domestic political support for its efforts to do so.

20 Political Economy and Economics at the University of Toronto

It may seem strange to have left an account of my experience at the primary place of my employment for the bulk of my career until so late in this volume. There is a logic to this. By the usual standards, my academic career has been successful. I have had excellent teaching reviews, many doctoral students, been widely published, honoured by election as Fellow of the Royal Society of Canada, and so forth. But my academic path has not been entirely smooth. I believe that the positions I have taken in the academic controversies in which I became involved in the University of Toronto's Department of Economics, indeed the controversies themselves, described in this chapter, are best understood against the backdrop of the international events I have been outlining and my own international and highly development- and policy-oriented career. Hence the ordering I have chosen.

In chapter three I wrote of my coming to the Department of Political Economy, as it then was, at the University of Toronto from Yale in 1965, and our departure for Tanzania only a year later. Upon our return from Tanzania in 1968, I discovered that departmental chair Tom Easterbrook had acquired a grant from the Ford Foundation to establish a new diploma-level training program for East African civil servants and that I was to be its director. Its rationale was to provide flexible and tailored postgraduate programs for a small number of African students with relatively weak backgrounds in economics. It had been found that many students from Africa had been having difficulty in existing postgraduate Ford Foundation–supported programs at Williams College and elsewhere. I had considerable doubts as to our department's capacity to offer useful training at that time, but did my best for half a dozen African students each year for the next three years in the East

African Development and Training Program. I provided a compulsory seminar for them, with lots of eminent speakers (whom I also used for other classes and seminars) for which the program happily had generous funding, and slotted the students into the rest of our courses, notably my own, as best I could. Academic visitors financed by the program included Steve Hymer and Dudley Seers, among many others. In one year I was able to bring André Raynauld from the University of Montreal to give a weekly seminar to my African students. In another I brought Knud Erik Svendsen from the president's office in Tanzania for several weeks in residence. In the third year of the program I brought Peter McLoughlin, formerly chief economist at the East African Development Bank, as a visiting lecturer. I was painfully aware that most of the standard courses (other than my own) were of dubious relevance to these students' needs. It was also quite clear that the students appreciated the opportunity to study abroad, regardless of the relevance of their courses; so at least some purposes were certainly achieved. Each year I travelled, somewhat ambivalently, back to East Africa to meet and select prospective students. The program also had a modest research budget for the support of activities of a small number of Toronto faculty. At the same time, efforts were being made to establish MA programs in economics at the University of Dar es Salaam and elsewhere in East Africa, and I believed that such efforts deserved support rather than competition. When the three-year Ford grant came up for renewal, I could not, in good conscience, see how we could justify it. It seemed like a very good deal for the University of Toronto but not a very socially productive exercise. Both the Ford Foundation and Tom Easterbrook seemed surprised but acquiesced in my recommendation for the program's termination.

These early (post Tanzania) years of teaching at Toronto were happy ones. I was infused with enthusiasm about my recent African experience and no less enthusiastic about imparting some of what I had learned to eager young students. In my enthusiasm, I organized small local conferences, one on "Socialism in the Third World" and another on "The Tanzanian Socialist Experience." The University of Toronto awarded an honorary degree to Julius Nyerere during this period, and my best students were greatly inspired by his convocation address. It was a time of radical student activism and lots of campus excitement. Such were the times that at one point I seriously suspected that, because of my obvious radical sympathies (however insufficient they may have seemed to the real radicals), the RCMP had installed a bug in my office ceiling. Returning to my office earlier than expected one day, I had surprised two workmen doing some unrequested repairs to my ceiling. Just to be sure, in 2008 I inquired, under the terms of Canada's new Privacy Act, as to whether there existed an RCMP file on me. I was officially informed that they could not find one.

My undergraduate classes at that time were of reasonable size, usually numbering only about thirty-five students. (By the 1990s they were more than twice that size.) I was able to get to know quite a few of the students, some of whom remain good friends to this day.

I fondly recall one seminar that my visiting Marxist friend from Tanzania, Erik Svendsen, offered during this period. Consistent with the student spirit of the time, and therefore very appealing to my undergraduate development students, it was billed as "Marxist Approaches to Development" and was well attended. As always, Erik presented modestly and quietly, without a hint of revolutionary zeal. He spoke of the importance of institutions, history, and income distribution; and of the many constraints, economic and non-economic, upon development in very poor countries. During the question period at its conclusion, one of my students asked: "How exactly does your Marxist approach differ from Professor Helleiner's?" Without batting an eye (or enlisting my concurrence), he replied earnestly: "Well, you *could* say we are all Marxists now." Perhaps so. I knew what he meant – that multidisciplinary approaches taking full account of interests, politics, class, and institutions were essential to an understanding of development processes. But I had never really thought of myself as a Marxist before, and never did thereafter. My economics may have been somewhat more "structuralist" or even "institutionalist." My politics, as noted earlier, are probably best described as "social democrat."

Relationships within the faculty were at this time relaxed and happy. My office was in Sidney Smith Hall (100 St George St), where the bulk of the Department of Political Economy and its administrative offices were housed. A "rump" of economists, associated with a new institute (for quantitative research on economic policy), was soon to be located "up the street" at 150 St George, and the centre of gravity for economics was to shift in that direction; but that had not yet happened. My interactions with political scientists were as frequent and as close as those with economists. Almost every day I lunched at the nearby Faculty Club with a collection of both. I did not form relationships as close as those I had had at Yale with any of the Toronto economists (our interests did not, after all, coincide so closely); but relationships were cordial and collegial. The department was still of a small enough size to make it possible to know everyone at least a little. I saw my father from time to time, both in his office and in the corridors, and our relationship did not seem to create any problems for anyone. (After I presented my first departmental seminar to a packed room, during my first year in Toronto, he told me that my presentation seemed interesting but he hadn't really understood a word.) Within a few years both he and the chairman, Tom Easterbrook, had retired. Steve Dupré, the new chairman, a political scientist, took clear delight in underlining the continuity of the department's traditions by inviting me to be one of the speakers at the formal retirement dinner for them.

As the East African program came to its end, I took a sabbatical leave – with support from the John Simon Guggenheim Foundation – at the newly created Institute of Development Studies at the University of Sussex, headed by Dudley Seers, who had left the public service to take on this responsibility. This year (1971–2) was a wonderfully stimulating and productive one, about which more in chapter twenty-one.

Upon my return from the sabbatical, I found myself the director of the PhD program in economics, a post I held for two years (1972–4). There were not too many students so it was not, at that time, a very onerous undertaking. I handled admissions and advised students as to their options and ways to meet the requirements of the program. The most difficult task was holding the hands of students who were experiencing difficulties, and helping to persuade some of them that failure in doctoral programs was not the end of the world.

There were some serious problems, however, with the PhD program in economics at the University of Toronto; and I spent quite a lot of time trying to resolve some of them. The department was at that time trying to establish a new system, more comparable to those of other leading North American postgraduate programs in economics. There were now to be compulsory courses together with a number of optional courses in "fields"; and there were comprehensive examinations, and efforts toward a more systematic approach to the preparation and defence of theses. I strongly supported all of these initiatives. There was already considerable disaffection, however, among the PhD student body, generated by what they saw as overwork in the new system, together with personality problems, idiosyncrasy, and superficiality in some of the compulsory theory courses. Then, as repeatedly thereafter, the "core theory" faculty saw it as their responsibility, indeed their right, to sort out the problems with the theory courses on their own. It was always my position that the content of the core courses should be discussed by the entire graduate faculty. It was already becoming clear to me, as I began to supervise more theses, that students were not being well prepared for thesis research and were forced to endure excursions into pure theory that went far beyond reasonable needs for a productive career in economics. During my tenure as director, a vigorous discussion as to the problems and possible solutions for the program began. At one point, I suggested, in a memo early in 1973, that we establish two streams toward the PhD in economics: one with heavy emphasis upon theory, the other of a more applied nature, in which some of the advanced theory would be replaced by a greater orientation to "problem sessions," which had recently been initiated, and field courses. I also argued that the problem sessions should be integrated more effectively with the theory courses. Needless to say, my suggestions were not well received by all of the theory group, and they floundered. Opposition was ostensibly based upon the fear that the quality of the overall program might be diluted. Strenuous efforts, led by Doug Hartle, my earlier mentor, now a faculty colleague, were later made to develop a postgraduate program in "applied economics and public policy." In the end it too went nowhere. These struggles were to recur.

Shortly after I had "graduated" from my administrative responsibilities within the department, I was summoned to the office of the dean of the Faculty of Arts and Science, where I was invited to consider the possibility of an associate deanship. I was given to understand that this idea had been promoted by my colleague and friend Donald Forster, at that time the university's provost (later to become president of Guelph University and, still later, president-designate of the University of Toronto, before he tragically succumbed to a heart attack only months before assuming office). I declined immediately and without the slightest hesitation. I never had the tiniest aspiration for, or interest in, university administration. Don periodically prodded me to reconsider; but for me it was always completely out of the question.

A major departmental decision, from my own point of view, was the decision to hire another senior development economist, this time with specialization in Latin America, for appointment at Scarborough College of the University of Toronto (cross-appointed to the downtown Toronto campus). I had not expressed unhappiness with Toronto, let alone threatened to leave, but I certainly did nothing to discourage the chairman's musings as to whether professionally I might be a little lonely and in need of an area colleague. After an extensive search, in which I participated, we zeroed in on Albert Berry, at that time teaching at the University of Western Ontario. I had known Al at the Yale Economic Growth Center where he, like me, had been a country studier (of Colombia) and eventually assistant director, but our times at Yale had not overlapped for very long. To my delight he responded positively to our offer and joined the Toronto department in September 1975. His presence made an enormous difference, not only to Toronto's development studies programs but also to my own morale over the years. When we hired another, more junior, development economist, Sue Horton, in the early 1980s (later vice president at Wilfrid Laurier University), our core development economics team was complete. The three of us worked well together for more than twenty years. There were also others working in the field of economic development during these years, notably Richard Bird, who was super active in development-related public finance; relations with him were always cordial and mutually supportive.

For several years, the increasing number of economists up the street at 150 St George (at what was now known as the Institute for Policy Analysis, IPA), where they seemed to be considerably better supplied with administrative and other supports than those of us in Sidney Smith Hall, had been expressing their dissatisfaction with the Department of Political Economy as a vehicle for the furtherance of their own particular interests. As they saw it, the need to accommodate political science and political economy concerns in departmental decisions both inhibited their ambitions for programs in economics and damaged their image within the economics profession. There was also some dissatisfaction and separatist sentiment among some of the professors responsible for the popular undergraduate program in Commerce and Finance, which seemed to them to have greater affinities with the Faculty of Management Studies than with the Department of Political Economy to which it was, for historical reasons, attached. When Ian Drummond, the Canadian economic historian whom I had known at Yale (in fact even earlier at my summer job in Ottawa, where he had helped to persuade me to apply to Yale), assumed the chairmanship of the department in 1977, he immediately constituted a "committee on departmental structure" to report directly to the dean of the faculty (at that time another economist, Art Kruger). Its mandate was to consider the implications of alternative future structures for what had by then become quite a large and unwieldy department. He asked me to join this committee. Pleading that the academic year 1977–8 was already

the most overloaded with teaching, supervisory, and research obligations that I had ever experienced, I asked to be excused. The committee,
chaired by eminent political scientist C. Brough McPherson, solicited
views from the department. I wrote:

> I believe it would be unfortunate if the Department were to be split into
> its political science and economics wings. I do not believe that the possible
> advantages of such a split could possibly make up for the losses which
> would certainly ensue therefrom. I think that many of the problems with
> our present departmental arrangements flow from our unfortunate dis-
> persion of physical facilities, above all the distance between the Institute
> for Policy Analysis and Sidney Smith Hall; if there are to be reforms, let
> them be in the geography of our department rather than in our discipli-
> nary makeup ...
>
> I think it is ironic that we should be discussing the breakup of our
> department at the very time that many other universities and founda-
> tions are calling for increased interdisciplinary cooperation between
> economists and political scientists. In the fields of my own direct interest –
> international economics and development economics – the emerging con-
> ventional wisdom is quite clear: more political/economic research and
> teaching is necessary. This was the thrust of an enormous Ford Founda-
> tion–financed survey of the field of international economics ... about three
> years ago, and its findings have not, to my knowledge, been disputed. In
> development economics, the interrelationships between politics and eco-
> nomics have been recognized for much longer, and are reflected in the
> makeup of virtually all the existing centres for research on development
> studies. The course which I share with Cran Pratt explores – successfully,
> I think – the areas in which politics and economics overlap in this sphere.
> Personally, I have derived a great deal from my close proximity to politi-
> cal scientists with related interests in research and teaching in the field of
> development. I would welcome more interdisciplinary effort in the field
> of international economics as well as development; and, frankly, I think
> some of our other international economists – and their students – badly
> need it ...
>
> As far as economics is concerned, the international reputation which
> our department enjoys lies in the policy related areas in which the
> political economy approach is inescapable. I hesitate to name names;
> but the narrow emphasis on economic theory, to which a departmental
> split would lead us in economics, would force us into our weakest suit.
> Other universities envy us for what we possess – in opportunities for

collaborative effort and interdisciplinary contact, if not practice. I think it would be folly for us now to seek to transform our economics department into a pale (very pale) replica of the narrow US postgraduate economics departments, at the very time when increasing numbers are finding fault with them and calling for arrangements more similar to those we already have ... My views are fully consistent with the (recent external) review of our economics programme.[123]

About half of the economists in the department took a similar position. The other half, based at the IPA, strongly felt that separation was necessary for the restoration, as they saw it, of Toronto's place in the front rank of Canada's economics programs. The McPherson committee (only five of whose members were economists, out of ten) recommended in 1978 *against* the breakup of the department but came down strongly in favour of a significant devolution of responsibilities to the already existing "associate chairmen" who carried responsibility for the separate disciplines within the department. This recommendation was swiftly implemented and the de facto creation of three separate sub-departments (political science, economics, and commerce) helped to ease some of the dissatisfaction among economists. Tom Wilson effectively directed the economics wing of the Department of Political Economy under its new chair, Bennett Kovrig of political science. But agitation among the IPA economists for separation continued unabated. In the spring of 1981, following consultations between Wilson and Kovrig, Ian Drummond was appointed to chair a small (seven person) committee composed solely of economists to review the new administrative structure as it related to economics. (Political scientists had evidently shown little interest in such a review at that time.) According to Kovrig's memo announcing the committee's creation and mandate, the review by economists was to constitute only the first stage of a possible later department-wide consideration. The membership included some clear separatists (Jack Carr, Frank Mathewson), some middle-of-the-roaders (Richard Bird, David Stager), and some like Sam Hollander, our eminent historian of economic thought, and me, who were known to be disinclined to separate. Economists were given two weeks to express their views to the departmental committee in writing, which they did with great vigour, following which the committee held a series of meetings to review the responses. It produced a report by July.

Its results were probably a foregone conclusion. The overwhelming majority of economists had become convinced that the maintenance of a large department was costing its members both influence and resources at the university level and no longer made administrative sense. Its political scientist chairman, it was asserted, was unable to represent the interests of its economics component effectively. The Department of Political Economy was now so large (about 150 full-time professors of various ranks) and its concerns so diverse that departmental meetings were scarcely feasible any longer. It was noted that the devolution of powers had already created what amounted to three separate departments, and while they each seemed to be working well, the continued success of this arrangement depended upon future personalities and relationships that might not prove as harmonious. At the same time, the rigidities of bureaucratic practice tended to treat all university departments equally, regardless of their size or complexity, in such matters as the provision of support staff. Dividing the department, we were told, might therefore increase the resources provided to it. These practical administrative considerations in the end overcame doubts as to the intellectual merits of the case for separation. It was also noted that the geographic separation of economists, and of social scientists more generally, was a more significant problem for academic exchange than any particular administrative arrangement. The committee therefore made a strong pitch for a common location for (at least) all of the economists. The doubters on the committee (myself included) insisted on, and won, explicitly stated guarantees of the continuing diversity of any new economics department.

The committee made three recommendations: a separate department for economists; the reunification of all economists (except those few who did not want it) at a single site; and a commitment that the new department "continue to embrace the broad range of interests, emphases, methodologies, and ideologies that have been present among the economists in the Department of Political Economy for many decades." It called for a mail ballot among economists on this package of recommendations and, if it was approved, quick implementation. In the ballot that rapidly followed, there was overwhelming (80 per cent) support for it among the economists. The chairman of the now-disintegrating Department of Political Economy, while calling for comment from the surprised (and, in many cases, shocked) students and members of the rest of the department, had little option but to carry the recommendations forward to higher university authorities. It was as if a Quebec separatist referendum had attracted 80 per cent support. By September 1982, with what for the University of Toronto was absolutely breathtaking speed, the deed was done. The new Department of Economics had been created. The bulk of the staff was henceforth to be located at 150 St George Street, where I was fortunate to land the largest and most attractive of its offices. (Was this some kind of payoff for my apparent qualified defection, within the committee, to the separatist cause?) The first chairman of the new department, selected by a committee of which I was a member, was Tom Wilson.

The new Department of Economics got off to a good start. In November 1981, even before its formal launching, the new chair arranged an out-of-town retreat for its members – something which had never happened before – for collective consideration of the department's future. It was a hopeful and exciting event.

Early relationships in the new department were relaxed and collegial. I felt a valued member. During the department's first few years, under Tom Wilson, I certainly had little reason to regret the decision of the economists to separate. In fact, I frequently argued the advantages of separation and geographic concentration in discussions with non-economists, and actually at one point turned down an invitation, suggested by Mel Watkins, to relocate my office to University College where interdisciplinary contact could have been greater. In retrospect, I was probably naive to believe that the third element of the Drummond committee's recommendations – the one relating to the continuation of breadth within the new department – would be sustained. Any political scientist could have predicted (and some did) that once the distribution of power had permanently altered, earlier agreements would soon become irrelevant.

The economists who had most vociferously argued for separation now set about the creation of the kind of economics department that they presumably had always had in mind. It was not one that valued tolerance or diversity of approach. It valued "core" economic theory, the content of which was theirs alone to prescribe and which seemed to me to contain greater elements of certainty (and of the market-obsessed University of Chicago) than was healthy. In the old Department of Political Economy, fields like economic history, the history of thought, and economic development were central to the efforts to link economics with political science. For that reason they, and the more applied and/or radical practitioners of economics, carried a degree of respect. Indeed departmental chairs tended to be drawn from these fields rather than from economic theory. Economic theory was seen as an essential input, but certainly not the only or even necessarily the primary one, to the development of an understanding of the real world of politics and economics; it was not seen as an end in itself. In the new department, things were to be different. Economic history, history of thought, and economic development were pushed to the margins of influence, respect, and power. Particularly in the graduate program, which meant the most to me, economic theory – of a particularly narrow variety – was now king. At one point it was even argued by those who by then dominated the department that only those whose field was economic theory would carry sufficient professional respect to be eligible for the chairmanship. (Not that anyone really wanted the job.) Instead of seeking to build on the enormous potential created by a large and diverse stable of economists, the postgraduate economics program at the University of Toronto now sought to replicate, without the requisite intellectual or financial resources, the PhD programs of much stronger American institutions. Instead of imaginatively creating a uniquely diverse alternative program, Toronto struggled to attract students to a middle-level conventional one.

The traditional departmental strength in economic history was soon de-emphasized. The separate PhD program in economic history, which had previously had somewhat lighter requirements for compulsory courses in economic theory, was now "beefed up" because of the purported perception that it was a "second-class degree." Henceforth the historians were to do just as much compulsory economic theory as everyone else. The result was, predictably, that enrolment in the separate economic history doctoral program plunged to zero and remained there. Alternative, more radical and wide-ranging, perspectives were also now expunged from the department. Mel Watkins and Abe Rotstein, their principal exponents who had chosen not to move to the new departmental location, now did not interact much with their economist colleagues.

Soon after departmental independence, there were moves, without department-wide discussion, to "tighten" the undergraduate specialist program in economics by making it easier for students to increase their emphasis on theory and mathematics, and to narrow the concentration of their studies. Changes were introduced that made it possible, and even "recommended," for specialists to do fourteen courses in economics (or mathematics) out of the required total of twenty.

The beauty of a large department, indeed, of a large university, is that individual faculty members can be remarkably free to "do their own thing." I happily went about my own independent research and teaching on international economics and development over the next several years without worrying too much about whatever else might have been going on within the Department of Economics at the time. Much of the research and writing undertaken by my colleagues was of no great interest to me; and I assumed that mine was of no greater interest to them. I proceeded on the assumption that support or at least tolerance for diversity was broadly shared within the department. I continued to supervise far more than my share of doctoral dissertations – roughly half of all of those completed in economics during the 1980s.

The numbers of PhD students in development economics, already larger than in any other field in the department, steadily increased during the 1980s as did my thesis supervisory obligations (for which no teaching credit was at that time provided). Al Berry, Sue Horton, and I usually shared the graduate-level survey course in development economics, except when one of us was on leave; and every year I offered a half-year graduate course in "International Aspects of Development." The latter was the one I enjoyed the most, and for which I was probably best known. I continued to teach one section of the undergraduate course in international economics, for which I regularly received pretty good student reviews (no doubt at least in part because I truly enjoyed introducing undergraduates to some of the most interesting current policy issues rather than remaining in pure theory). Student reviews of my graduate courses were also always very good.

My graduate students, particularly at the doctoral level, complained a great deal about their compulsory courses in economic theory. I usually told them simply to "hold their noses," regard them as part of their apprenticeship or initiation rites, and keep going until they were free to do their theses with supervisors with whom they could work. I did, however, very much share my students' resentment at the diversion of so much of their time and talent away from reading and research on issues in which they were keenly interested toward intellectual gamesmanship of little, if any, practical consequence. Because of the intense pressures of the compulsory courses in theory and econometrics, my students frequently found themselves with little time left for the required reading, research, or essay-writing in mine. Students with an interest in development were typically highly motivated toward socially useful activity when they entered the postgraduate program in economics and were probably even more frustrated by the vapid abstractions of the compulsory courses than the others, at least some of whom aspired to academic careers in which they would carry on the traditions of the profession.

The situation worsened when, beginning in 1986–7, by decision of the departmental graduate committee, PhD students were required to complete their theory comprehensive examinations by the end of their first year in the doctoral program rather than at the conclusion of their second. This change was intended to speed their progress toward work on their theses. But its principal result was a first year spent entirely in feverish study of compulsory "core" theory and econometrics.

All of this was bound to generate some heat, and it did. Early in the second term of the academic year 1987–8, a group of disgruntled first-year doctoral students approached me about the possibility of a discussion about the doctoral program in which they were enrolled. Most, but not all, were interested in economic development. I invited them to come to my home on a Sunday afternoon. About eight or nine of them turned up – over half of the class. They really vented. What they told me was certainly not news to me, but the degree of disaffection within the graduate student body was. The compulsory courses in economic theory and econometrics, they complained, were extremely demanding and extremely abstract. Worse, the instructors were rigid, unbending, and unresponsive to suggestions. "Technique, technique, technique … all I hear is technique," proclaimed one of the best of the students. " I haven't heard an *idea* since I got here."

I took up their cause, and there followed a vigorous exchange of memos on these problems with the director of the PhD program, Mike Denny. Shortly thereafter, in April 1988, Denny, without prior consultation with any of the relevant colleagues, delivered a memo addressed to all doctoral students in the first two years who had expressed an interest in economic development as one of their fields of specialization (and to faculty members teaching it), warning of the "weak academic demand" for it and advising them to build their strength in other areas. It was not a bad letter. Al, Sue, and I agreed with much of its advice. But it was accompanied by a separate letter to me in which his anxieties were expressed in more ominous fashion. "I have not yet placed any 'quota' on students interested in development," he wrote. "However, I am seriously thinking of doing something. I do not want to find the Department in a position where we cannot properly supervise students because there is an unreasonable burden on a small number of faculty members." He also argued that such concentration of supervision would make it difficult to achieve the objective of speeding up completion of the program, another recently declared objective. His concerns and suggested "solution" did not seem completely consistent with his

views (and those of others in the department for whom he was presumably speaking) on consumer sovereignty and the need to respond to the
market's revealed preferences. None of us had complained about our
"unreasonable burden," and he had never discussed it with us.

Al Berry, Sue Horton, and I felt it necessary to respond in vigorous fashion with a joint letter, copied to the same development-oriented graduate
students, pointing out that our students had not had difficulty finding
employment (both academic and non-academic) and that exclusive specialization in non-development fields would prejudice their marketability
for academic development jobs if they wanted them, and taking strong
exception to the idea of a quota on development students. We wrote:

> To turn away good students interested in development in favour of infe-
> rior students who happen to take an undersubscribed area is a demonstra-
> bly poor use of resources. If supervisory capacity is a constraint, this can
> and should be alleviated by additional faculty, either two year visitors ...
> if the additional student demand is perceived as temporary, or full-time
> faculty if there has been a permanent increase in demand ...
>
> Although some smaller economics departments in Canada have fol-
> lowed recent fads in their exclusive concentration on middlebrow theory,
> this is not a position that Toronto need feel compelled to follow. Toronto
> can and should utilize the breadth and diversity of its Department to best
> advantage. It is evidently the strength of our offerings in development and
> certain other non- theory fields that has brought us many of our best PhD
> students. We are confident that it will continue to do so. We therefore feel
> that the advice given to students in your recent letter, although in many
> respects sound, is in others misleading. It has aroused unnecessary con-
> cern among some students.[124]

In response to the spring's flurry of memos, a review of the core PhD
courses was duly launched in the fall of 1988 by the graduate committee. Graduate faculty members were invited to express their views
in writing. A great many did so. In my own submission, I appealed
for a broader review of the purposes of the program and the place of
the Toronto PhD within the wider professional community, a review
based on much more information than any of us yet had. I concluded
by expressing my suspicions that

> the compulsory core occupies a disproportionate amount of PhD stu-
> dents' time; incorporates disproportionate inputs of sheer technique as

opposed to economic analysis, thought or history; has frequently failed to survey the relevant literature in a balanced fashion; and has prepared the majority of students poorly for the thesis research that they have actually undertaken. The theory core is, in part, too large a part, an "'initiation rite" imposed by a self-appointed priesthood, perhaps rarely doing great harm but not doing nearly enough that is helpful either.

By emphasizing the "idiosyncratic" core so heavily we have driven away some excellent students, and played to the department's comparative disadvantage. Our top PhD students never come to Toronto because of our theory reputation. We should be encouraging more diversity and eclecticism, and greater time spent in non-compulsory learning of economics.[125]

Many senior members of the faculty wrote in similar terms. My old mentor Doug Hartle was particularly eloquent and persuasive in his contribution to this debate (at least to me):

Economics ... seems to have gone from one extreme to the other: roughly 30 years ago it was possible for a PhD in economics to graduate without taking any courses in economic theory or quantitative methods. This was a serious dereliction of our duty to our students. The department has since moved strongly in the opposite direction to the point that we have to now ask ourselves if we are not overdoing the theory at the expense of applied economics. My plea is essentially for reducing our required courses in theory and econometrics to the minimum (consistent with international standards) and allow our students the widest possible latitude in selecting their other courses ... I would judge that a ... realistic strategy would be to differentiate our product and seek to excel in some fields where we have comparative advantage: among the possibilities that come to mind are public finance/public choice, economic development, economic history and labour economics. It seems to me we are in danger of being unrealistic. This will be to the detriment of most of our students and will not take advantage of the strengths we already have.[126]

Very few of the dominant players in the core courses expressed their views in writing. They were, I suppose, not motivated to do so since the review had not been their idea. Nor did they need to, since they continued to hold the reins. To his credit, Mike Denny did so thoughtfully and in considerable detail. Although he confessed he did not know the details of the content of the core courses, he believed that the content was in the "right neighbourhood," as he now wrote:

> For better or worse we are "trapped" by the current standards of the profession. Arguments based on the profession being wrong should not be considered. Students have to find jobs and we cannot inflict on them a training that does not reflect current professional expectations. Those who wish to change the profession will have to accomplish this first before changing our PhD program ... Complaints by students do not focus on the content of the courses. Complaints are often about individual faculty behaviour.[127]

I did not agree with all of his facts or his assessments; but they were at least honestly and clearly expressed.

Regrettably, very little changed. Indeed there followed a formal *reduction* in the time devoted to the specialized applied fields in the doctoral program, even though an external review of the department, which had recently been completed, had specifically warned *against* the crowding out by the core of the more specialized field courses and "overinvestment" in theory.

Probably the majority of the North American economics profession had by this time already recognized its problem over emerging standards. Successive presidents and committees of the American Economic Association had called attention to the unfortunate overmathematicization of training and research in the field. There had been active discussion of the growing irrelevance of much of mainstream postgraduate training. A variety of "alternative" journals and contrarian websites have since then been successfully launched. Yet it was quite impossible to turn mainstream training and research standards around. The University of Toronto was at this time simply falling firmly into line.

Despite its many frustrations, and its ultimate failure to stop the juggernaut of overly emphasized compulsory courses in economic theory, the effort to improve the doctoral program was probably worthwhile. It resulted in periodic useful statements of departmental intention and probably helped to improve the quality of the offerings in theory, which had sometimes been extraordinarily idiosyncratic and poorly taught. It certainly served notice on the theoreticians that they were accountable and could not have complete freedom to do as they chose.

During the next couple of years, to my delight, the graduate students in development launched a regular series of evening discussion sessions held in one another's homes. Individual students and sometimes faculty members were invited to present ideas or thesis plans or recent experiences likely to be of interest to the group. These sessions also served as social occasions and helped to build a certain esprit de corps and to maintain collective morale. Al, Sue, and I attended these gatherings faithfully. This period and this collection of students – in the late 1980s and early 1990s – probably marked the high point of postgraduate studies in economic development at Toronto.

I was not completely inactive in departmental or university affairs in these years. My continued heavy involvement in graduate courses and the supervision of doctoral theses would not permit complete detachment. (Although the number of thesis supervisions declined a little, as fewer development-oriented students entered, or were permitted to enter, the program, I still had more than any other faculty member.) I even served on some more committees. But I now faced enormous commitments outside the university – to the G-24, IFPRI, WIDER, the North-South Institute, and others (each discussed in earlier chapters). Had I not been fortunate enough to acquire a wonderful and hard-working administrative assistant, Barbara Tiede, financed by my agreements with the G-24 and WIDER, I could not have begun to carry the load I did in the 1990s. The departmental administrative secretary, for most of the period Margaret Abouhaidar, was also most supportive by managing my various accounts. It would be difficult to imagine a department that was more flexible and accommodating to the needs and vicissitudes of my peculiarly "mixed" (academic and non-academic) career; and I was and remain extremely grateful.

Another major crisis in departmental relationships arrived early in 1995, when another narrowly oriented PhD director, Arthur Hosios, soon to become department chair, circulated a number of proposals for the reform of a doctoral program, which, in his view (he was certainly not alone), was not working well. He proposed to institute a new compulsory two-semester "research seminar," to increase the required courses in individual fields, and to eliminate, because of its "too high" opportunity cost, the previous PhD program requirement for a course in economic history or history of economic thought. Predictably, Sam Hollander, holder of the high honour of a University Professorship for his scholarship in the history of economic thought, was very upset at this last proposal. He was not the only one. At a meeting of the graduate faculty called for the specific purpose of discussing these proposals (a very rare event), there was vigorous debate about the wisdom of dropping the history/history of thought requirement. The debate seemed to me to be about evenly balanced. Since attendance at the meeting was far from complete, it was difficult to know what the overall position of the faculty was. No vote was taken – either at the meeting or anywhere else. Shortly thereafter the proposed changes were nevertheless implemented. That about did it for what was left of the traditions of the old Department of Political Economy and the 1981 agreement to preserve them when it split. Sam Hollander now made plans to leave the University of Toronto.

It seemed to me – perhaps it was only my hope or my imagination, for I did not really get to know many of them – that there was greater diversity, openness, and collegiality among the young newcomers to the once again actively recruiting department in the mid-1990s and thereafter. Although the political and intellectual "gaps" between many of my long-standing colleagues and me was by this time much too wide to bridge, my last few years in the department seemed less stressful than many of the earlier ones. And it seemed to me that, with the retirement of much of "our" evidently rather fractious cohort, there might be hope for better days in the future University of Toronto Department of Economics. On the other hand, from my post-retirement (1998) office in the Munk School of Global Affairs, I could also sadly observe that while a few economists occasionally participated as individuals, the Economics Department per se played virtually no part in Munk's multifold internationally oriented activities. It was the only department failing to contribute resources of any kind to its many seminar series, which included one on development studies. This fact undoubtedly meant lost opportunities both for the Economics Department and for the rest of the university.

From some of this account one might gain the impression that I did not enjoy my years in the Department of Economics at the University of Toronto. But that would be quite incorrect. Despite the many disagreements and disappointments, I thoroughly enjoyed and learned from my students, most of my colleagues, and the overall university environment. I have been proud of the many accomplishments of my former students and was deeply moved when they held a conference in my honour at the time I formally retired. (All the presentations at it, including poems, were subsequently published in a special issue of the *Canadian Journal of Development Studies*.[128]) Above all, I appreciated both the total freedom that I was always granted for the pursuit of my academic interests and the implicit support for my many off-campus activities. It was a *great* place to spend over forty years as a teaching and practicing economist.

PART V

Reflections on a Life in International and Development Economics

21 Intellectual Currents

It is difficult, or even impossible, to try to summarize one's own over-all intellectual evolution without vast oversimplification. The written record can obviously stand for itself. But who has read it all, or is likely to read it all, other than myself? Besides, the thinking behind it – with all of its uncertainties, internal inconsistencies, passing impressions, and confusions – are another matter entirely. Still, it may be worth trying to reflect a little on it in hindsight.

I think it fair to say that there have been some recurrent themes in my overall professional thinking:

- continuing scepticism of all-encompassing systems of explanation (theory) for real-world phenomena and events, whether religious, Marxist, neoclassical economics, or whatever; and relative comfort with complexity and the inexplicable; this outlook implies humil-ity about one's conclusions (some might call all this intellectual laziness);
- need for reasonably reliable evidence, preferably in quantitative form, for such statements and views as one offers ("show me the numbers");
- deep concern for overcoming poverty, involuntary unemployment, and inequity; and for the rights and voice of the most marginalized; and continuing distrust of the powerful; and
- respect for economics as the social science without which pursuit of social objectives is bound to be practically lacking, while recog-nizing its serious limitations and the need for broader spheres of knowledge for more complete understanding.

A footnote I attached to an early paper on Africa, written for Barbara Ward's 1970 conference on the Pearson Commission report, read as follows:

> If, as many believe, it is presumptuous, if not harmful, for foreigners to dispense advice on economic policy to independent African governments, how much worse must it be for them to venture into the delicate arena of social and political change in Africa. I am only too conscious of my proper place in this respect and of the fact that, whether one wants to or not, one cannot easily shuck off one's upbringing, cultural conditioning, and implicit or explicit value judgments. Yet Africans who prescribe for Africa also have individual biases; moreover, if everyone frets too much about his own, nothing meaningful is ever said.[129]

Over forty years later, I think that's not a bad statement of how I came to do whatever I did in the field of development and my humility about it.

The specifics of my professional interests have covered quite a bit of ground within the field of economics.

While an undergraduate and in graduate school, I was much more concerned (and relatively knowledgeable) about Canadian or US economic and social problems than about any of the rest of the world. In my first few years at university, I was even prepared to consider employment in the Canadian business world; but thereafter I pretty much expected my future work to be in academia or government in Canada. At the time I wrote my PhD thesis, I was very much concerned with the macroeconomic problems of a small, open, and resource-dependent economy like that of Canada. Appropriate exchange rate policy for Canada fascinated me and was the topic of my research essay in James Tobin's graduate course on monetary theory. My thesis research was thoroughly empirical rather than theoretical and addressed capital flows and capital market connections between Canada and the United States, and their implications. These concerns anticipated the issues raised by financial liberalization and globalization in the 1990s and thereafter.

In graduate school, the only research essay I did on a development topic was one that argued – before Ted Schultz's paper[130] in the *American Economic Review* made it conventional – that education and health expenditures, particularly the former, could be considered as investment rather than consumption. I mainly relied upon Indian data and sources. And I worried in this paper (and another for our student study group on development) whether there might be such a thing as a "premature" welfare state that spent too much on health at the expense of future growth. It wasn't until I joined the Economic Growth Center in 1961 that I began to read voraciously and think more broadly and more seriously about development. At this time I was greatly enamoured of Dudley Seers's arguments on "the limitations of the special case," the limited applicability of traditional Western economics for the analysis of developing country economies. In Nigeria my doubts about usable data and theory in the development context intensified. But so did my interest in getting better data and better economic analysis in support of development efforts. By the early 1960s, then, I was already intellectually deeply committed to the search for some better form of development economics (and disenchanted with much of the mainstream material I had read). My experience in socialist-aspiring Tanzania moved me toward greater concern for equitable income distribution and the need to address the problems of the poorest peoples and countries, but not toward traditional socialist ideology or its key instruments of state ownership and planning, which manifestly didn't work too well. Later work for UNICEF, the ILO, and others strengthened these concerns for addressing poverty and income distribution as well as growth (and, later, "adjustment" to exogenous shocks) in developing countries. I should add that I worked in a context of quite limited data, long before today's world of vast data sets and computational wizardry.

My scepticism of the more mainstream "wisdom" of development economics drove me to attempts to put forward intellectually defensible critiques and/or the development of alternatives. The former was obviously a lot easier than the latter.

Over the course of the next three decades I joined others in analyses, and usually critiques, in a number of different spheres, among them:

- the role of multinational corporations in manufacturing, technology transfer, and commodity trade;
- the role of IMF and World Bank advice and programs in the poorest developing countries, particularly in Africa;
- the impact of Northern trade, aid, and financial policies upon developing countries;
- the appropriateness of the mainstream (liberalizing) trade policy advice being offered to developing countries; and
- the appropriateness of capital account liberalization in developing countries.

More practically, these critical approaches generated, among my other possible accomplishments, and I do not want to seem immodest:

- some "leading edge" thinking on "outsourcing," and data collection on "intra-firm" international trade;
- serious early attempts to develop specific "alternative" stabilization and adjustment programs in Tanzania, Uganda, South Africa, and elsewhere;
- an active role in the efforts (eventually successful) to ease the burden of external debt on poor African countries;
- a pursuit (partially successful) of more balanced donor-recipient aid relationships in Tanzania and elsewhere;
- reasonably successful efforts to build indigenous African capacities for economic analysis and policymaking;
- efforts (less evidently successful) to identify the prospects and policy requirements for the development of non-traditional exports from Africa; and
- effective assistance to developing countries in their resistance to Northern pressures in trade negotiations.

In the opening overview in this volume I wrote of the conclusion, early in my career, that external development economists like me could be most useful by helping to ease the significant international constraints imposed upon the economic development prospects of poor countries and to strengthen these countries' capacities to make policy decisions in the interest of their own independent and sustainable development. The efforts and modest accomplishments listed here were certainly reflective of such deeper and unchanging objectives.

As I look back at my professional career, I am struck by how few of my main activities were linked to the American university scene where I began it. I have had enduring links with institutions in the United Kingdom and some looser but continuing ones in Scandinavia. I have also, of course, maintained many ties in the global South. But my interactions in the United States have latterly been relatively few and far between. Objectively, it seems remarkable that in the Festschrift volume in my honour, published in 1997, there are only two American authors (Gus Ranis and Keith Griffin, and Keith spent much of his professional life in the United Kingdom) and, to my recollection, only two other American participants (Lance Taylor and Jim Boughton, and Jim, whom I had not previously met, was simply representing the IMF). The great majority (six) were from the United Kingdom. Why this relative weakness in the US connection? In part, it must have reflected a difference between American and British (at least IDS Sussex) and others' approaches both to economics and to development, and my greater comfort with the British. Increasingly, I had found the American graduate schools' fixation with technique and what has recently been described as "mathiness" unhelpful and unappealing. But, in part, it probably was also the product of my own conscious choice, buttressed in the Vietnam years, to attempt to build stronger ties to non-American institutions and people rather than simply to take the more convenient American route of the majority of my Canadian economist colleagues. This choice was itself the product of my own conviction that Canadians could best play their "middle power" role, in which I firmly believed, by avoiding too close an association with the United States. That is not to say that I am, or ever was, anti-American. I did, after all, have some strong US ties, for example, with Carlos Diaz-Alejandro (until his death), Lance Taylor, Don Mead, and, for a considerable period, with Washington's Overseas Development Council. And I was very frequently in Washington and New York for various international events.

My links with the United Kingdom were significant. As I noted elsewhere, Dudley Seers, whom I had met at Yale, was one of the first to offer me post-Yale employment – with the British Ministry of Overseas Development. I declined but, as already noted, I was soon to join him for an important year in my early professional formation in a somewhat different capacity. In the early and mid-1970s, the Institute of Development Studies at the University of Sussex was where much of the global academic action seemed to be for those interested in development, particularly those toward the left of the political spectrum. Created in the late 1960s by Harold Wilson's Labour government, it aspired to build a strong and independent research faculty, to assemble the best library of currently relevant development material, and to become a major source of rigorous policy analysis. Its first director, Dudley Seers, was widely known as a somewhat iconoclastic economist and development analyst, with considerable experience in Africa and Latin America. Among the economists he gathered around him at the new IDS Sussex were Hans Singer (after a distinguished career in the UN system), Paul Streeten, Michael Lipton, and my old graduate school friend, Richard Jolly. Marxism was certainly not dominant at the IDS Sussex; but neither was it totally absent, as at Yale and most other North American institutions taking an interest in the developing countries.

In 1971–2, when I qualified for a sabbatical leave from Toronto and won a John Simon Guggenheim fellowship, which could be held anywhere, the IDS Sussex, seemed to me the obvious place to spend it. My initial enquiries there generated a warm response, and I was awarded the official title of Visiting Fellow and, more important, an office at which to work. It proved to be a highly enjoyable, productive, and even formative year. It contributed toward the solidification of my intellectual approach to development economics as oriented, above all, to international issues, and, as far as domestic/national policies were concerned, increasingly to distributional issues and human development rather than to sheer GNP growth.

While the principal foci for my research, writing, and advisory work varied greatly over the years, my intellectual approaches – for better or worse – probably did not significantly alter in their basics from the early1970s onward.

Throughout my career I emphasized that which economists do *not* know and thus upon research requirements. But I do not want to be misunderstood. I quote from the introduction to my 1990 book, *The New Global Economy and the Developing Countries*:

> Lest my apparent agnosticism concerning many of the conventional Northern economic wisdoms of the day be mistaken for disapproval of the discipline of economics (or international economics) let me make my position quite clear. I believe that there will always be early limits to the usefulness of either international or domestic policy analysis that is conducted purely in terms of economics. I also believe that members of the economics profession have frequently claimed greater knowledge than they had ... But economic analysis, properly conducted and with the analyst's objectives clearly stated, remains a potentially powerful contributor to social progress ... At the very least, as Churchill said of parliamentary democracy, I believe it is better than the available alternatives.[131]

I continue to believe in the potentially key importance of the basic tools of economics, properly deployed, in pursuit of inclusive and sustainable development. But today it may be more difficult for young people to enter the field of development economics with the idealistic hope of "making a difference" than it was in the 1960s. In my view, the mainstream of the economics profession has rather lost its way over the course of the past few decades with its preoccupation with abstract modelling and sophisticated econometric methodology. A modest student-led rebellion about this has caught media attention, but so far has made little impact upon teaching or academic performance. Were I to be young again, I am not sure I would want to pursue a doctorate in economics in today's conventional postgraduate teaching environment. Even in development economics the technical requirements often seem designed to stifle deep thought.

My retrospective assessments of overall trends in the economics profession, some of their implications, and possible hopes, particularly in Africa, were set out in my address to the Nigerian Economics Society in 2007. Events have not altered since. Let me quote from it at some length:

It is critically important that the economics profession continues to attract not only the best and brightest of students, but – no less important – those with a deep social concern. I fear that in recent years the profession has not always done well in this regard. I do not know the scene here so well but let me tell you of my concerns about the economics profession in North America. I fear that we have lost and are continuing to lose many of those we most need in the profession ... those who care the most about poverty, equity, social justice – those concerned with such fundamental values and objectives ... and those who want to contribute to public policymaking and the common good. There are many reasons for this. In part, it is the product of the increased emphasis, especially in postgraduate teaching programmes but not only there, upon abstract theory, often couched in the language of mathematics, and econometric methodology. These do not carry an obvious appeal to those who enter economics with a view to trying to make the world a better place ... and many are intimidated or put off, and drop out in favour of law, business, public policy or other programmes ... often replaced by students who have backgrounds in mathematics, or such fields as theoretical physics or astronomy, who are typically more enthralled by intellectual puzzles than motivated by social concern. My advice to those disaffected students whom I most want to stay in economics has generally been to regard the less appealing parts of their programme as "initiation rites" and to keep going, "holding their noses" if necessary, until they are accredited and free to do their own thing. Many have done so ... and gone on to be credits to their profession. But I have not always succeeded in persuading them. We have lost and continue to lose too many. I fear that our initiation rites – our screening system – has become, in social terms, totally dysfunctional.

But the situation may be even worse than that. There is documented evidence that students who study economics at the university level experience attitudinal change that is of dubious social value. Although we all should recognise that the profession's basic assumption of the individual's constant pursuit of self-interest is no more than a convenient simplification, students seem often to see it as more than that ... confusing it with reality. This can breed cynicism and despair about human behaviour, and can even lead to the further position that the calculated pursuit of individual self-interest is a positive virtue and that too much concern for one's fellow human beings can be harmful to society. Studies have shown that students who enter the study of economics in North America are already, on average, more self-interested than the norm. But what is even more distressing is that they are found to become even more so after taking our courses ... they become less interested in cooperative activity or behaviour, and more prone to seeking "free rides" from society wherever possible ... Social dysfunction should not be characteristic of our discipline. Its origins were, after all, with Adam Smith, who ... whatever else his attributes or errors ... was a moral philosopher ...

In order to retain those with social concern and to prepare them to be useful, teaching – both at undergraduate and graduate levels – must be seen to be relevant to the solution of real social and economic problems. And most research should move on a parallel path. Undoubtedly there are certain core elements of theory and econometrics that must be internalised by all in the profession. Who could quarrel with that basic need? But these core elements should always be seen as instrumental rather than ends in themselves ... and that is where so many Northern postgraduate programmes, to my mind, have recently gone off the rails.

Our profession, and the vast majority of its journals, assigns highest prestige to theoretical and methodological virtuosity. Research and teaching on the applications of economic theory and econometrics, even if enormously important to social well-being, are now too frequently regarded as somehow less challenging, less difficult, less exciting. At the same time, economic history and the history of economic thought have been systematically downgraded relative to more abstract matters. In most North American postgraduate programmes the study of economic history and history of thought is now optional; in many, even if a student chooses them, good courses can be difficult to find. In consequence of these developments, the gap between academic economists and practicing policymakers has typically widened to a ridiculous degree. Academics and practitioners often speak different languages and have little to say to one another. I pray that you will not let this develop or, if already present, develop any further here. There is so much need and opportunity for increased public understanding and for valuable research on important matters of policy here in Africa that such socially dysfunctional professional evolution would, in this context, be almost criminal. While there must always be room, everywhere, for purely theoretical and methodological pursuits within the economics profession, I hope that the mainstream in teaching and research in economics in Africa will not allow the importance of real world applications of economics, or of history, to be so downgraded ...

There must be incentives enough to encourage economists to devote their time and energy to the kinds of socially productive research, teaching and advisory work that I have been describing. Although I speak as an economist, I do not really mean to speak in this connection of salaries; of course, they are not irrelevant. I speak of pride, identity, self-esteem, knowledge that what one is doing is worth doing ... and public respect ...

What is to be done? What incentives can we devise? I, for one, would like to see important awards, prestige, appropriate journal outlets, and more opportunities for public dialogue and involvement on economic policy issues. If the best and brightest young people are to be attracted to our field and kept in it; and their mentors are to offer them appropriate role models, more thought must be given to such issues.[132]

22 Some Reflections for Others

I concluded the previous chapter with generalizations about economists. At a personal level, each economist – like most people – must find his or her own way, his or her own particular work-life balance. I have often reflected upon, and told others about, a memorable day in the life of this particular international and development economist who has had, in addition to his work, another very important and meaningful side to his life. The experiences of this day seemed to epitomize the interaction between the macro and micro concerns in my professional and family life.

I had been asked by colleagues at the University of Toronto's Institute for Policy Analysis to participate in a panel they were preparing for one of their regular public conferences for practicing business and government economists in Toronto. These meetings, held in downtown hotels, were mainly occasions for the presentation of the latest analyses and projections from the IPA's model of the Canadian economy, and they were typically well attended. This particular meeting took place in the early 1980s when the Latin American debt crisis had burst upon commercial bankers, so one of the topics on the conference program, to be addressed by our panel, was developing country debt. A banker on the panel presented the many reasons why concessions should not be made to the debtors and said that, in any case, it was essential to pursue a case-by-case approach to them rather than employing "general" solutions. In my own presentation I pointed out that, although they posed few problems for the private banks and therefore were as yet receiving little professional attention, the debt problems of lower-income countries, notably those in Africa, were actually already far more serious than those of Latin America and likely to be more intractable. The ensuing discussion of the Third World's debt problems was absolutely a bankers' discussion. It was hardheaded, calculating, and concerned, above all, with ensuring repayment to banks. The atmosphere was tough and cold. The economic, social, and political ramifications of the tough and unyielding "solutions" they suggested (which, later, they, of course, had to abandon) were of no apparent concern. Nor were they the slightest bit interested in Africa's problems with non-bank official debt. I came away thoroughly depressed.

At that time I was serving on the board of the L'Arche Daybreak community in the Toronto suburb of Richmond Hill (where our intellectually challenged son, Peter, now lives). My eleven years on this board involved monthly meetings and, from time to time, serving on further subcommittees. One of these committees – composed of some L'Arche assistants and a couple of board members, to consider the possibility of opening a new home for *children*, rather than only adults, with disabilities – was meeting at Daybreak later on the very same day. I drove straight from the bankers' discussion to the L'Arche meeting. It was as if I had travelled to another planet. It began with a simple prayer in search of guidance for the little group. The mood was gentle and compassionate. The participants were demonstrably living out the commitments they had each made to live with others in community, building relationships, respecting one another, and ultimately working to try to "change the world one heart at a time." These were warm and decent people, and I revelled in their sheer company. The issues they were considering were fairly "micro," and, in fact, they did not get very far in moving them forward in this particular meeting. But my company in this "insignificant" little gathering restored some of my faith in humanity and brought balance back into my day. I never forgot it.

Upon reflection, I have often thought that most of the bankers at the downtown meeting were probably neither cold nor inhumane in their own homes and communities. Rather, they were caught, in their professional lives, within a system and an environment that placed certain expectations upon them. They could not easily break loose from them without risking their credibility and probably their careers. They had behaved and spoken quite sensibly and rationally within the context of the market-driven financial world in which they worked. Different norms and expectations would certainly govern their activities at home and in their faith-based or other communities. Perhaps the assistants at my L'Arche meeting were, at least in part, also just responding to their own very different work environment. Whatever their motivation, it was the latter with whom I felt a much deeper bond.

But professional expertise has also always mattered greatly to me. I have never had much patience with misinformed or muddleheaded pursuit of social objectives that I share. The economist with social concern seeks to straddle the two worlds I encountered on that day, attempting to bring what I believe to be universally accepted micro-level values to bear on the harsher macro scene. It has always been a challenge to retain professional credibility while doing so. But I have tried and have had many friends who have also struggled on in this pursuit.

I have enjoyed my life as an economist. I hope I have been able to make some contributions toward making the world a better place. Certainly, while huge poverty and sustainability problems remain, the world has seen enormous developmental progress during the roughly forty years of my career. I would not dare to suggest that I played any but a tiny bit part in any of this remarkable progress. I have done my best over these years to strengthen developing country capacities and voice in the realm of economics, particularly in Africa. With rather less evident result, I have also tried repeatedly to influence powerful global decision makers to ease some of the constraints faced by the poorest developing countries in the global economy. What I can say without any hesitation, however, is that over my years as a professor, writer, advocate, and advisor I have learned a lot. In my convocation address at the University of Guelph in February 2005, I tried to pass on some of the main elements in my thinking and learning over the course of my career. Although some of the references may seem a little dated, the message is not. It seems as good a way as any with which to conclude this collection of memories and reflections. Here is the gist of what I said:

> Much of my professional life has been concerned with the reduction of global poverty and inequality. The inequality of the distribution of the world's income and wealth impacts upon global political stability, the global environment, the very future of our planet. But it is, above all, a profoundly moral issue. What drives most of those working in this field and keeps them there over the years is not intellectual curiosity, or the result of economic or political or other scientific analysis. Rather, the prime motivation for those with concern for global poverty and income distribution – whether in NGOs, business, government, academia, or religious communities – is a matter of values, values that, I am confident, we all share.
>
> Yet how difficult it seems to be to translate these universal values into actual global practice.
>
> "Poverty" is not merely a matter of incomes and opportunities, of infant mortality and literacy rates, life expectancy and the incidence of disease,

important as all these certainly are. It is also a matter of insecurity and, even more, a sense of powerlessness. When asked in surveys around the world what they most wanted, materially poor people have replied consistently that, among other more obvious needs, they desperately wanted a voice, a sense of participation in the decisions that affect them, a greater sense of their own importance. Voice and genuine participation engender dignity and self-respect, and these are fundamentally important to us all.

Policies that impact harshly upon poor and voiceless people are often less malevolent than they are thoughtless. Sometimes they are undertaken for the greater social good, as the powerful see it, with the politically weakest, as always, unable to be heard or to protect themselves against baleful side-effects. But such policies are also sometimes quite well-intentioned, ostensibly directed at the problems of the poor, as they are perceived "from above." In these cases, for better outcomes, it would be sufficient for the decision makers simply to listen more.

Genuine listening, it turns out, is a rare phenomenon.

From all of this it follows that "process" is enormously important in the pursuit of so-called development. This is probably the most important professional lesson that, over the years, I have had to learn.

Existing processes unfortunately leave a lot to be desired. All of this is true both at the global level and at the national or community level. Countries, as well as individuals, need to have a voice, a sense of participation, in the institutions and decisions that impact upon their welfare. By and large, the poorer countries, like poorer people, do not today feel they have such participation, such a voice. They do not feel that the global economy is governed fairly or that its current "governors" take their interests seriously into account when they make their major decisions. Nor, even when they truly are trying to be helpful, do they always, or even usually, listen well. Top-down prescriptions and conditions upon assistance are more typical.

Powerlessness in the face of blows from nature (drought, flood, pests, tsunamis) is extremely difficult to endure. But natural disasters are, in an awful sense, understandable ("aweful" spelled as in "full of awe"). Powerlessness in the face of harmful human decision making is another matter entirely.

How can anyone, poor or rich, explain the size of global military expenditures ... relative to those on global poverty reduction ... It is not earthquakes or floods but human decisions – to withhold the necessary funding – that are responsible for unnecessary deaths in Africa alone – from AIDS, malaria, TB and unsafe water ... EVERY MONTH, twice the numbers who died in the recent (one-off) Asian tsunami. Month after month this monstrous experience continues. To those who know these facts, they are more difficult to endure than tsunamis and other natural disasters.

One day the voices of the poor may be better heard and human decision making may improve ... but such change seems to come only slowly.

What can we do in the meantime?

There is a universal cry: "Listen to me. Please listen to me." In my experience, simply listening and "walking with" those whose interests need support and protection (while continuing, of course, to advocate for them in the corridors of power) goes a very long way. Progress can and will be made. (I have seen quite a lot of it over the years – the product of sustained effort from many quarters.) But, perhaps especially when change is slow and successes are few, genuine support, friendship and accompaniment – some call it "solidarity" – matter profoundly.

My appeal, therefore ... Whatever your walk of life, whatever your politics or religion, work to assist, to walk with, and, above all, to listen to the weak and the vulnerable ... both at the global and at the local level. If you cannot assist directly yourselves, try to support those who do. A nation's or a community's greatness, it has properly been said, is best judged not by its wealth and power but by the way it treats its most vulnerable. "Progress" in the development of our global village will be judged by future historians – I am sure of it – on the basis of the degree to which it supported, and listened to, its poorest and most vulnerable.

Perhaps all that is novel to you about my appeal is that I do not make it from a pulpit. I make it as a practicing economist. Yes, I base my appeal on values. In my own view, economists who (in the popular conception) "know the price of everything and the value of nothing" should be kept well away from policy matters. (Adam Smith, the father of modern economics, was, after all, a moral philosopher.) But I am also able to say, unequivocally, that the "scientific" evidence on these matters is quite clear: when the weak and vulnerable acquire more voice, policies and outcomes more frequently are of benefit to them; and when programmes and projects reflect the views of the prospective beneficiaries they are much more likely both to "work" and to be sustainable.

It is easy to succumb, in the face of obstacles and disappointments in the struggle for a fairer world, to cynicism and despair. Please don't. Don't succumb. The world needs the knowledge and skills you have acquired ... It needs people, like you, with hard heads. But even more it needs people who combine them with soft hearts. It needs them to counter those – and their numbers are legion – who have their heads and their hearts the other way around.

As Tommy Douglas used to say: "Courage, my friends. 'tis not too late to build a better world."[133]

Notes

1 Declaration on the Establishment of a New International Economic Order, Resolution adopted by the United Nations General Assembly, 1 May 1974. The text of the resolution can be found at http://www.un-documents.net/s6r3201.htm.
2 For details on the Brandt Commission, see chapter eleven and notes 61, 62.
3 For the text of the Paris Declaration on Aid Effectiveness (2005), see OECD, *The Paris Declaration on Aid Effectiveness and the Accra Agenda for Action* (2005/2008), available at http://www.oecd.org/dac/effectiveness/34428351.pdf.
4 See David Simon, "To and Through the UK: Holocaust Refugee Ethnographies of Escape, Education, Internment and Careers in Development," *Contemporary Social Science: Journal of the Academy of Social Sciences* (UK) 7, no. 1 (2012): 21–38.
5 Julius Deutsch, *Ein Weiter Weg. Lebenserinnerungen* (Vienna, Zurich: Amalthea-Verlag, 1960).
6 My father died on 26 February 1984 at the age of 81; my mother died at the age of 89 thirteen and a half years later. For more details on this period, see my father's tape, done for the University of Toronto archives where his records may be found. There is a file on my father in the archives of the Society for the Preservation of Science and Learning, now known as the Council for Assisting Refugee Academics, in Oxford's Bodleian Library. There is also an article by Paul Stortz describing some of the background to the assistance my father received from Canada. See Paul Stortz, "'Rescue Our Family from a Living Death': Refugee Professors and the Canadian Society for the Protection of Science and Learning at the University of Toronto, 1935–1946," *Journal of the Canadian Historical Association* 14, no. 1 (2003): 231–61.

7 Archives of the Society for the Preservation of Science and Learning, Bodleian Library.

8 Tjalling C. Koopmans, *Three Essays on the State of Economic Science* (New York: McGraw-Hill Book Company, 1957).

9 Theodore W. Schultz, "Investment in Human Capital," *American Economic Review* 51, no.1 (March 1961): 1–17.

10 Paul Samuelson, *Economics: An Introductory Analysis* (New York: McGraw-Hill Book Company, 1948). *Economics* is now in its nineteenth edition, with revisions by William Nordhaus, beginning in 1985.

11 Wolfgang Stolper, *Planning without Facts: Lessons in Resource Allocation from Nigeria's Development* (Cambridge, MA: Harvard University Press, 1966).

12 Lalage J. Bown and Michael Crowder, eds., *The Proceedings of the First International Congress of Africanists, Accra, 11th–18th December 1962* (London: Longmans, 1964).

13 Gerald K. Helleiner, *Peasant Agriculture, Government and Economic Growth in Nigeria* (Homewood, IL: Richard D. Irwin, 1966).

14 Julius Nyerere, *The Arusha Declaration and TANU's Policy on Socialism and Self-Reliance* (Tanganyika African National Union [TANU], 5 February 1967). The revised English translation from the Swahili, transcribed by Ayanda Madyibi, can be found at https://www.marxists.org/subject/africa/nyerere/1967/arusha-declaration.htm.

15 The lecture was soon published, not only in the party newspaper but also in the *East African Journal* in Nairobi, in a local journal, *Mbioni*, and then translated for publication in Sweden. See Gerald K. Helleiner, "Trade and Aid in Tanzania," *East Africa Journal* 4, no. 1 (April 1967): 7–17; Gerald K. Helleiner, "Trade, Aid and Nation Building in Tanzania," *Mbioni* 3, nos. 8–9 (1967): 12–38.

16 Walter Rodney, *How Europe Underdeveloped Africa* (London: Bogle-L'Ouverture Publications; Dar es Salaam: Tanzanian Publishing House, 1972).

17 G.K. Helleiner, ed., *Agricultural Planning in East Africa* (Nairobi: East African Publishing House, 1968).

18 Gerry Helleiner, "An Economist's Reflections on the Legacies of Julius Nyerere," in *The Legacies of Julius Nyerere, Influences on Development Discourse and Practice in Africa*, ed. David A. McDonald and Eunice Njeri Sahle (Trenton, NJ and Asmara, Eritrea: Africa World Press, 2002), 53–61.

19 Ibid., 58–9.

20 *Report of the Group of Independent Advisors on Development Cooperation Issues between Tanzania and Its Aid Donors* (Copenhagen: Royal Danish Ministry of Foreign Affairs, June 1995); reprinted in *NEPAD at Country Level: Changing Aid Relationships in Tanzania*, ed. Samuel Wangwe (Nkuki na Nyota, Dar es Salaam, 2002), chapter 1.

21 See also the account of this meeting in Wangwe, *NEPAD at Country Level*.

22 See note 3 on the Paris Declaration on Aid Effectiveness (2005).

23 Cited in a personal letter to the author from Ole Moelgaard Andersen.

24 Gerry Helleiner, "Local Ownership and Donor Performance Monitoring: New Aid Relationships in Tanzania?" *Journal of Human Development* 3, no. 2 (2002): 251–61.

25 Gerald K. Helleiner, "Framework for Holding Donors to Account," presented in a panel on Donor Coordination, IDRC, Ottawa, 9 March 2005.

26 Commonwealth Secretariat, *The Rehabilitation of the Economy of Uganda: A Report by a Commonwealth Team of Experts*, 2 vol. (London: Commonwealth Secretariat, 1979). Both volumes of this report are available on the Commonwealth iLibrary website: http://www.thecommonwealth -ilibrary.org.

27 Although some people in Uganda and elsewhere still attribute this phrase to Winston Churchill, coining of the description "the pearl of Africa" in reference to Uganda is now generally credited to Henry Morton Stanley. In "The Uganda Railway," *Saturday Review of Politics, Literature, Science and Art* 70 (1895): 719–20, Stanley says, "It is the 'Pearl of Africa' that is our object. I applied that somewhat grandiloquent term to Uganda because ... the truth is that the term aptly illustrates the superior value of Uganda because of its people, its strategic position for commerce, and for spreading Christianity – all of which make it pre-eminently a desirable colony for a trading and civilizing nation like ours." Echoing Stanley, Winston Churchill later referred to Uganda as "the pearl" in his book *My African Journey* (London: Hodder and Stoughton, 1908), 197–8, calling it "a fertile and inspiring region ... of docile peoples, of gorgeous birds and butterflies and flowers."

28 Gerald Helleiner et al., *Report of an Independent Working Group on the Ugandan Economy* (Kampala: Government of Uganda, September 1993).

29 Garth Legge, Cranford Pratt, Richard Williams, and Hugh Winsor, *The Black Paper: An Alternative Canadian Policy towards Southern Africa* (Ottawa: Canadian Council for International Cooperation, 1970). See also Garth Legge, Cranford Pratt, Richard Williams, and Hugh Winsor, "The Black Paper: An Alternative Canadian Policy towards Southern Africa," *Behind the Headlines* 30, no. 1–2 (1970): 1–18.

30 Linda Freeman, Gerald Helleiner, and Robert Matthews, "The Commonwealth at Stake," *Canadian Journal of African Studies* 5, no. 1 (1971): 93–112.

31 International Development Research Centre (IDRC), *Economic Analysis and Policy Formulation for Post-Apartheid South Africa* (Ottawa: IDRC, 1991).

32 Letter of 27 May 1981 from the author to David Steedman, director of the Social Sciences Division in the IDRC.

33 Ibrahim A. Elbadawi and Gerry Helleiner, "African Development in the Context of New World Trade and Financial Regimes: The Role of the WTO and Its Relationship to the World Bank and the IMF," in *Africa and the World Trading System*, vol. 1, *Selected Issues of the Doha Agenda*, ed. Ademola Oyejide and William Lyakurwa (Trenton and Asmara: Africa World Press, 2005), 289–324.

34 Ademola Oyejide et al., eds., *Regional Integration and Trade Liberalization in SubSaharan Africa*, 4 vols. (London and New York: Macmillan and St. Martin's, 1997–9). The dedication appears in volume 1.

35 Personal letter from the author to Alfred Maizels, principal economic adviser to the secretary-general of UNCTAD, 5 December 1979.

36 G.K. Helleiner, ed., *For Good or Evil: Economic Theory and North-South Negotiations* (Oslo: Universitetsforlaget; Toronto: University of Toronto Press, 1982).

37 Gerald K. Helleiner, "The Refsnes Seminar: Economic Theory and North-South Negotiations," *World Development* 9, no. 6 (1981): 539–55.

38 This material was presented in a letter to Jan Pronk, dated 18 July 1984, in response to his request to contribute to a special issue of the *UNCTAD Bulletin* celebrating UNCTAD's twentieth anniversary, which was to appear in September 1984 during the meeting of the Trade and Development Board at that time. I do not know whether that issue materialized.

39 The text of the Prebisch Lecture, "Markets, Politics and Globalization: Can the Global Economy be Civilized?" given by Gerald Karl Helleiner on 11 December 2000 is available at http://unctad.org/en/Docs/prebisch10th.en.pdf. It has also been published in *Journal of Human Development* 2, no.1 (January 2001): 27–46 and in *Global Governance* 7 (2001): 243–63.

40 UNICEF's annual *The State of the World's Children* reports are all available on the UNICEF website at https://www.unicef.org/sowc.

41 Giovanni Andrea Cornia, Richard Jolly, and Frances Stewart, eds., *Adjustment with a Human Face: Protecting the Vulnerable and Promoting Growth – A Study by UNICEF*, 2 vols. (Oxford: Clarendon Press, 1987).

42 G.K. Helleiner, G.A. Cornia, R. Jolly, "IMF Adjustment Policies and Approaches and the Needs of Children," *World Development* 19, no. 12 (1991): 1823–34.

43 Gerald Helleiner and Frances Stewart, "The International System and the Protection of the Vulnerable," in *Adjustment with a Human Face*, 1:273–86.

44 Gerald K. Helleiner, "Sub-Saharan African External Debt and Financing: Necessary Reforms for Development," in *Debt Relief for Africa: A Call for*

Urgent Action on Human Development, UNICEF Staff Working Paper no. 11 (New York: UNICEF, 1993).

45 Giovanni Andrea Cornia and Gerald K. Helleiner, eds., *From Adjustment to Development in Africa: Conflict, Controversy, Convergence, Consensus?* (New York: St Martin's Press; London: Palgrave MacMillan, 1994).

46 Gerald K. Helleiner, "Stabilization, Adjustment and the Poor," *World Development* 15, no. 12 (1987):1499–1513.

47 Advisory Group on Financial Flows for Africa, *Financing Africa's Recovery: Report and Recommendations of the Secretary-General's Advisory Group on Financial Flows for Africa* (New York: United Nations, 1988).

48 Ibid.

49 UN Expert Group on Africa's Commodity Problems, *Africa's Commodity Problems: Towards a Solution, a Report by United Nations Secretary General's Expert Group on Africa's Commodity Problems* (UNCTAD/EDM/ATF/1) (Geneva: United Nations, 1990).

50 *Financial Times*, 10 July 1990.

51 *Financial Times*, 24 July 1990.

52 Personal letter from the author to Hans Singer, 20 March 1991.

53 Personal letter from Hans Singer to the author, 11 April 1991.

54 United Nations Committee for Development Planning, *Crisis in Sub-Saharan Africa, Proposals for Action of the United Nations Committee for Development Planning* (New York: United Nations, Department of Public Information, November 1984).

55 Personal letter from the author to Sonny Ramphal, 23 November 1984.

56 G.K. Helleiner, "Multinational Corporations, Manufactured Exports and Employment in the Less Developed Countries," in *Tripartite World Conference on Employment, Income Distribution and Social Progress and the International Division of Labour*, Background Papers, vol. II, *International Strategies for Employment* (Geneva: International Labour Office, 1976).

57 Personal letter from the author to Francois Blanchard, ILO director-general, January 1976.

58 G.K. Helleiner, "Multinationals, Technology and Employment," *ILO Information* 4, no. 2 (1976).

59 International Labour Office, *Employment Growth and Basic Needs: A One-World Problem*. Report of the Director-General of the International Labour Office (Geneva: ILO, 1976).

60 Alister McIntyre et al.; Commonwealth Experts Group, *Towards a New International Economic Order: A Final Report* (London: Commonwealth Secretariat, 1977).

61 Willy Brandt et al.; Independent Commission on International Development Issues, *North-South: A Program for Survival: Report of the Independent Commission on International Development Issues* (New York: Pan Books, 1980).

62 Willy Brandt et al.; Independent Commission on International Development Issues, *Common Crisis: North-South Co-operation for World Recover* (London: Pan Books, 1983).

63 Commonwealth Expert Group, *Protectionism: Threat to International Order; The Impact on Developing Countries* (London, Commonwealth Secretariat, 1982).

64 Gerald K. Helleiner et al., *Towards a New Bretton Woods, Challenges for the World Financial and Trading System: Report by a Commonwealth Study Group* (London: Commonwealth Secretariat, 1983).

65 Alister McIntyre et al., *Guyana, the Economic Recovery Programme and Beyond: Report of a Commonwealth Advisory Group* (London: Commonwealth Secretariat, 1990).

66 G.K. Helleiner, "Lender of Early Resort: The IMF and the Poorest," *American Economic Review* 73, no. 2, Papers and Proceedings of the Ninety-Fifth Meeting of the American Economic Association (May 1983): 349–53.

67 G.K. Helleiner, "The IMF and Africa in the 1980s," *Canadian Journal of African Studies* 17, no. 1 (1983): 17–33; G.K. Helleiner, "The IMF and Africa in the 1980s," *Essays in International Finance* (Princeton University) 152 (July 1983): 1–24.

68 Gerald K. Helleiner, "The Question of Conditionality," in *African Debt and Financing*, ed. Carol Lancaster and John Williamson, Special Report 5, Institute for International Economics (Washington, DC: IIE, May 1986), 63–91.

69 John Loxley, "Alternative Approaches to Stabilization in Africa," in *Africa and the International Monetary Fund*, ed. Gerald K. Helleiner (Washington, DC: IMF, 1986), 117–49.

70 Gerald K. Helleiner, ed., *Africa and the International Monetary Fund: Papers Presented at a Symposium Held in Nairobi, Kenya, May13–15, 1985* (Washington, DC: IMF, 1986).

71 Ibid., 1–11.

72 For the published article, including the quoted paragraph, see Gerald K. Helleiner, "The IMF, the World Bank and Africa's Adjustment and External Debt Problems: An Unofficial View," *World Development* 20, no. 6 (1992): 779–92.

73 Vittorio Corbo, Morris Goldstein, and Mohsin Khan, *Growth-Oriented Adjustment Programs: Proceedings of a Symposium Held in Washington, DC,*

February 25–27, 1987 (Washington, DC: IMF and World Bank, 1987). Gerald
   K. Helleiner's discussion comments can be found on pages 107–114.

74 Jo Marie Griesgraber and Bernhard G. Gunter, eds., *Rethinking Bretton
   Woods*, vol. 4, *The World's Monetary System: Toward Stability in the Twenty-
   First Century* (London and Chicago: Pluto Press with the Center of
   Concern, Washington, DC, 1996), vii.

75 Elliot Berg et al.; African Strategy Review Group, *Accelerated Development
   in Sub-Saharan Africa: An Agenda for Action* (Washington, DC: World Bank,
   1981).

76 Gerald K. Helleiner, "Policy-Based Program Lending: A Look at the
   Bank's New Role," in *Between Two Worlds: The World Bank's Next Decade*,
   ed. Richard Feinberg (New Brunswick, NJ: Transaction Books for
   Overseas Development Council, 1986), 47–66.

77 World Bank, *Sub-Saharan Africa: From Crisis to Sustainable Growth – A Long-
   Term Perspective Study* (Washington, DC: World Bank, 1989).

78 Letter from the author, 24 September 1997.

79 Personal letter from the author to Joseph Stiglitz, December 1999.

80 Edward S. Mason and Robert E. Asher, *The World Bank Since Bretton Woods*
   (Washington DC: Brookings Institution Press, 1973).

81 Devesh Kapur, John P. Lewis, and Richard Webb, *The World Bank: Its First
   Half Century*, 2 vols. (Washington, DC: Brookings Institution Press, 1997).

82 "The World Bank's Hidden History," *The Economist* (2 April, 1998),
   http://www.economist.com/node/361460.

83 The paper and discussants' comments are published in François
   Bourguignon and Boris Pleskovic, eds., *Lessons of Experience* (Oxford:
   Oxford University Press and World Bank, 2005), 195–233.

84 Gerald K. Helleiner, "The Impact of the Exchange Rate System on the
   Developing Countries," in *The International Monetary System and Its
   Reform. Part II: Papers Prepared for the Group of Twenty Four by a United
   Nations Project 1979–1986*, ed. Sidney Dell (Amsterdam: North Holland,
   1987), 407–510; Gerald K. Helleiner, "Balance-of-Payments Experience
   and Growth Prospects of Developing Countries: A Synthesis," *World
   Development* 14, no. 8 (1986): 877–908.

85 Shahen Abrahamian, Edmar L. Bacha, Gerry Helleiner, Roger Lawrence,
   and Pedro Malan, eds., *Poverty, Prosperity and the World Economy: Essays in
   Memory of Sidney Dell* (London: Palgrave-Macmillan, 1995).

86 G.K. Helleiner, "A Conference on Finance and Development?" Presentation
   to the UN General Assembly's Second Committee, 15 October 1997. A
   version of this address is available on the Third World Network website at
   https://www.twn.my/title/helle-cn.htm.

87 Randall Henning, "The Group of 24: Two Decades of Monetary and Financial Co-operation among Developing Countries," in *International Monetary and Financial Issues for the 1990s: Research Papers for the Group of Twenty-Four*, vol. 1 (Geneva: UNCTAD, 1992), 137–54.

88 These papers were published in UNCTAD, *International Monetary and Financial Issues for the 1990s: Research Papers for the Group of Twenty-Four*, vol. 1 (1992). José María Fanelli, Lance Taylor, and Roberto Frenkel, "World Development Report 1991: A Critical Assessment," 1–30; Jose Antonio Ocampo, "Developing Countries and the GATT Uruguay Round: A (Preliminary) Balance," 31–53; Peter Pauly, "Transfers, Real Interest Rates and Regional Development: International Economic Implications of Financial Support for the Economies in Transition," 55–78; C. Nurul Islam, "Bank and Fund Approaches to Environmental Issues: The Concerns of Developing Countries," 117–136.

89 UNCTAD, *International Monetary and Financial Issues for the 1990s: Research Papers for the Group of Twenty-Four*, 11 vols. (Geneva: UNCTAD, 1992–9).

90 Gerald K. Helleiner, ed., *The International Monetary and Financial System: Developing Country Perspectives* (London: Palgrave-Macmillan, 1996).

91 Ibid.,10.

92 Charles Abugre and Nancy Alexander, "Non-Governmental Organizations and the International Monetary and Financial System," in *International Monetary and Financial Issues for the 1990s: Research Papers for the Group of Twenty-Four*, vol. 9 (Geneva: UNCTAD, 1998), 107–25.

93 Lance Taylor, *Varieties of Stabilization Experience, Towards Sensible Macroeconomics in the Third World* (Oxford: Clarendon Press, 1988).

94 Ibid., 69–74.

95 Gerald K. Helleiner, ed., *Trade Policy, Industrialization and Development: New Perspectives* (Oxford: Clarendon Press, 1992).

96 Owen Little, Tibor Scitovsky, and Maurice Scott, *Industry and Trade in Some Developing Countries: A Comparative Study* (London: Oxford University Press for OECD, 1970).

97 Gerald K. Helleiner, ed., *Trade Policy and Industrialization in Turbulent Times* (London: Routledge, 1994).

98 Gerald K. Helleiner, ed., *Manufacturing for Export in the Developing World: Problems and Possibilities* (London: Routledge, 1995).

99 Gerald K. Helleiner, ed., *Non-traditional Export Promotion in Africa: Experience and Issues* (London: Palgrave-Macmillan, 2002).

100 Gerald K. Helleiner, "Developing Countries in Global Economic Governance and Negotiation," in *Governing Globalization: Issues and Institutions*, ed. Deepak Nayyar (Oxford: Oxford University Press, 2002), 308–33.

101 Theodore W. Schultz, *Transforming Traditional Agriculture* (New Haven, CT: Yale University Press, 1964).

102 IDRC, "Report of the IDDR Board Review Panel, Social Science Division" (January 1988).

103 See note 39 on the Prebisch Lecture given by Gerald Helleiner.

104 Dominique Njinkeu and Hugo Cameron, eds., *Aid for Trade and Development* (Cambridge: Cambridge University Press, 2008).

105 Gerald K. Helleiner, "Preface," in *A World Divided: The Less Developed Countries in the International Economy*, ed. Gerald K. Helleiner (Cambridge: University of Cambridge Press, 1996), ix.

106 Personal letter from the author to Bernard Wood, executive director of the North-South Institute, 22 January 1981.

107 Carlos Frederico Diaz-Alejandro and Gerald K. Helleiner, *Handmaiden in Distress: World Trade in the 1980s* (Ottawa, Washington, London: North-South Institute, ODC, ODI, 1982).

108 Roy Culpeper, Albert Berry, and Frances Stewart, eds., *Global Development Fifty Years after Bretton Woods: Essays in Honour of Gerald K. Helleiner* (London: Palgrave-Macmillan, 1997).

109 Gerry Helleiner, "North-South Institute's Demise: A Blow to Independent Policy Research," *Embassy*, 24 September 2014.

110 Lester B. Pearson et al., *Partners in Development: Report of the Commission on International Development* (London, New York: Pall Mall Press, Praeger, 1969).

111 Barbara Ward, J.D. Runnalls, and Lenore d'Anjou, eds., *The Widening Gap: Development in the 1970s* (New York: Columbia University Press, 1971).

112 Ibid., 10–13.

113 Editorial, *Canadian Forum* (July–August, 1970): 156.

114 Personal letter from the author to Prime Minister Clark, 4 October 1979.

115 Gerald K. Helleiner, *International Economic Disorder: Essays in North-South Relations* (London: Palgrave-Macmillan, 1980).

116 Donald S. Macdonald et al., *Report of the Royal Commission on the Economic Union and Development Prospects for Canada*, 3 vols. (Ottawa: Ministry of Supply and Services, 1985).

117 William Winegard et al.; Standing Committee of the House of Commons on External Affairs and International Trade (SCEAIT), *For Whose Benefit? Report on Canada's Official Development Assistance Policies and Programs* (Ottawa: Queens Printer for Canada, 1987).

118 See the Reality of Aid project website at http://www.realityofaid.org.

119 Gerald K. Helleiner, "Towards Balance in Aid Relationships: External Conditionality, Local Ownership and Development," produced by Brian Tomlinson, with permission, from two earlier Helleiner papers

and a CCIC-sponsored roundtable presentation for the Reality of Aid International Advisory Committee meeting held in Costa Rica, September 2000. Available online at http://ibrarian.net/navon/paper/Towards_Balance_in_Aid_Relationships__External_Co.pdf?paperid=350059.

120 Gerald K. Helleiner, "Canada's Economic Relations with Developing Countries," in *Christian Faith and Economic Justice: Towards a Canadian Perspective*, ed. Cranford Pratt and Roger Hutchinson (Burlington, ON: Ecumenical Forum, Trinity Press, 1988), 91–112.

121 Gerry Helleiner, "More Government Folly at CIDA," *Embassy*, 11 August, 2010; Gerry Helleiner, "More Government Folly at CIDA," *Toronto Star*, 20 August, 2010.

122 Gerry Helleiner, "Policy Coherence? More Like Triumph of Commercial Interests," *Embassy*, 27 March 2013.

123 Letter from the author to Brough McPherson, chairman of the committee on departmental structure, Department of Political Economy, University of Toronto, 22 November 1977.

124 Joint letter from Gerry Helleiner, Albert Berry, and Sue Horton to Michael Denny, director of the PhD program in the Department of Economics, University of Toronto, 4 May 1988.

125 Submission by the author to the graduate committee to review core PhD courses, 15 November 1988.

126 Personal letter from Douglas Hartle to Yehuda Kotowitz, director of Graduate Studies, Department of Economics, University of Toronto, on the "Structure of Our Graduate Programme," 26 February 1989.

127 Submission by Michael Denny, director of the PhD program in the Department of Economics, University of Toronto, to the graduate committee to review core PhD courses, 11 March 1988.

128 The presentations in honour of Gerry Helleiner can be found in *Canadian Journal of Development Studies* 20, no. 3 (1999).

129 Ward et al., *The Widening Gap*, 361–2.

130 Schultz, "Investment in Human Capital." See note 9.

131 Gerald K. Helleiner, *The New Global Economy and the Developing Countries: Essays in International Economics and Development* (London: Edward Elgar, 1990), 5.

132 Gerald K. Helleiner, "Development and the Economics Profession: Some Fiftieth Anniversary Reflections," Address to Nigerian Economic Society Fiftieth Anniversary Conference, Abuja, 24 October 2007.

133 Gerald K. Helleiner, Convocation Address, University of Guelph, 24 February 2005.

Index

Page numbers in italics refer to illustrations

UN Development Program (UNDP), 70, 104
UN Economic and Social Council (ECOSOC), 131
UN Economic Commission for Africa (UNECA), 10, 48, 129
UN Educational, Scientific and Cultural Organization (UNESCO (Stone Town)), 73
UN Intellectual History Project, 117
United Kingdom (arms trade), 87
United Nations (UN), 4, 125–31
United Nations Centre on Transnational Corporations, 180
United Nations Children's Fund (UNICEF), 10, 121–5
United Nations Second Committee, 184
United Nations University (UNU), 212
United States: Canadian economic connections, 286; economics academic institutions, 288–9; free trade agreements, 254–5; invasions, 37
United States Aid Agency (USAID), 209
universities: in overseas development, 248–9; and role and socialism, 56
University Naval Training Division (UNTD), 24–5
University of Dar es Salaam, 53–4, 55–9, 100, 266
University of Ibadan (University College Ibadan (UCI)), 46–7
University of the West Indies, *145*
University of Toronto: grants, 235; honorary degrees, 266
University of Toronto (Department of Economics): doctoral program

reform, 281–2; economic history, 281–2; economic theory and econometrics courses, 276–80; postgraduate students, 276–8, 280–1; quotas, 277–8; undergraduate program, 275, 276
University of Toronto (Department of Political Economy): about, 39–40; African students postgraduate program, 265–6; departmental restructure, 270–4; development economists recruitment, 269–70; doctoral program restructure, 268–9; graduate course, 246; Marxism, 267; as overseas university support, 58–9
University of Toronto (Victoria College), 22–8

van Ameringen, Marc, 89
Van Arkadie, Brian, 37, 63
van der Hoeven, Rolph, 123
Van der Merwe, Mr., 93–4
Varieties of Stabilization Experience, Towards Sensible Macroeconomics in the Third World, 213
Venezuela, 196–7
"Vision 2020" initiative, 210
Volcker, Paul, 172

Wai, Dunstan, 105
Waide, Bevan, 63
Wangwe, Sam, 68, 100
Warburg bank, 126
Ward, Barbara, 221, 247
Wardlaw, Janet, 224
"Washington consensus," 166
Wass, Sir Douglas, 104, 125–7
Watkins, Mel, 246, 274, 275